A Book of

SERVICES MARKETING

For
MBA Semester - IV
As Per Revised Syllabus
Effective from June 2014

Mrs. Samita Kher
Professor
M.A. (Economics), MBS (HR)
Sinhgad Institute of Management
Pune

N2152

SERVICES MARKETING - MBA (SEM. IV) ISBN 978-93-5164-258-9

Second Edition : January 2016
© : Author

The text of this publication, or any part thereof, should not be reproduced or transmitted in any form or stored in any computer storage system or device for distribution including photocopy, recording, taping or information retrieval system or reproduced on any disc, tape, perforated media or other information storage device etc., without the written permission of Author with whom the rights are reserved. Breach of this condition is liable for legal action.

Every effort has been made to avoid errors or omissions in this publication. In spite of this, errors may have crept in. Any mistake, error or discrepancy so noted and shall be brought to our notice shall be taken care of in the next edition. It is notified that neither the publisher nor the author or seller shall be responsible for any damage or loss of action to any one, of any kind, in any manner, therefrom.

Published By :
NIRALI PRAKASHAN
Abhyudaya Pragati, 1312, Shivaji Nagar
Off J.M. Road, Pune – 411005
Tel - (020) 25512336/37/39, Fax - (020) 25511379
Email : niralipune@pragationline.com

Printed By :
Repro Knowledgecast Limited,
Thane

✦ DISTRIBUTION CENTRES

PUNE
Nirali Prakashan : 119, Budhwar Peth, Jogeshwari Mandir Lane, Pune 411002, Maharashtra
Tel : (020) 2445 2044, 66022708, Fax : (020) 2445 1538
Email : bookorder@pragationline.com, niralilocal@pragationline.com

Nirali Prakashan : S. No. 28/27, Dhyari, Near Pari Company, Pune 411041
Tel : (020) 24690204 Fax : (020) 24690316
Email : dhyari@pragationline.com, bookorder@pragationline.com

MUMBAI
Nirali Prakashan : 385, S.V.P. Road, Rasdhara Co-op. Hsg. Society Ltd.,
Girgaum, Mumbai 400004, Maharashtra
Tel : (022) 2385 6339 / 2386 9976, Fax : (022) 2386 9976
Email : niralimumbai@pragationline.com

✦ DISTRIBUTION BRANCHES

JALGAON
Nirali Prakashan : 34, V. V. Golani Market, Navi Peth, Jalgaon 425001,
Maharashtra, Tel : (0257) 222 0395, Mob : 94234 91860

KOLHAPUR
Nirali Prakashan : New Mahadvar Road, Kedar Plaza, 1st Floor Opp. IDBI Bank
Kolhapur 416 012, Maharashtra. Mob : 9850046155

NAGPUR
Pratibha Book Distributors : Above Maratha Mandir, Shop No. 3, First Floor,
Rani Jhanshi Square, Sitabuldi, Nagpur 440012, Maharashtra
Tel : (0712) 254 7129

DELHI
Nirali Prakashan : 4593/21, Basement, Aggarwal Lane 15, Ansari Road, Daryaganj
Near Times of India Building, New Delhi 110002
Mob : 08505972553

BENGALURU
Pragati Book House : House No. 1, Sanjeevappa Lane, Avenue Road Cross,
Opp. Rice Church, Bengaluru – 560002.
Tel : (080) 64513344, 64513355,Mob : 9880582331, 9845021552
Email:bharatsavla@yahoo.com

CHENNAI
Pragati Books : 9/1, Montieth Road, Behind Taas Mahal, Egmore,
Chennai 600008 Tamil Nadu, Tel : (044) 6518 3535,
Mob : 94440 01782 / 98450 21552 / 98805 82331,
Email : bharatsavla@yahoo.com

niralipune@pragationline.com | www.pragationline.com
Also find us on   www.facebook.com/niralibooks

Preface ...

Today, people in the western world as well as the majority in India, earn a living from producing services rather than making manufactured goods or farming. For consumers, the increase in wealth has resulted in opportunities to consume services which were previously not possible or had to be produced at home by themselves. For businesses, services are essential as companies are concentrating on their core business activities and buy specialist services from outside for better quality and reliability.

The growth of the services sector in India contributing more than 50% of GDP, has lot of opportunities for budding managers to build their career in India as well as across the globe. With development of world economies, there is a growing need for services.

This book develops frameworks for understanding services and the effective marketing of them. The characteristics of intangibility, inseparability, inventory, inconsistency and ownership, have major implications for the marketing managers in the services sector to develop their service offer, promote it and then deliver it. Traditional marketing mix frameworks, which apply to manufactured goods, are inadequate for services. Services are about processes as much as outcomes and these processes often involve considerable interaction between customers and operations people. Hence, marketing cannot be seen as an isolated function. Successful service companies make sure that their front-line people can competently deliver the promises which marketing people make to customers.

The book has been streamlined and restructured to sharpen the students and reader's focus on the essentials of services marketing and coverage of new concepts and ideals especially the use of technology.

Although it's impossible to mention everyone who has helped in the publishing of the book, we would start with Dinesh Furia and Jignesh Furia our Publishers who gave us the opportunity to write. Special thanks are owed to Nirja Sharma, Supriya Singh, Kumkum Tripathi for their research, valuable insights and editing of the text. We are also appreciative of all the hardwork put in by the editing and production staff in helping to transform our manuscript into a well finished published text. They include Akbar Shaikh and Prasad Chintakindi. It is hoped that the book will be of great help to the students. We welcome any suggestions for the improvement of book.

Author

Syllabus ...

1. **Introduction to Services Marketing:**

   Definition, Significance, Characteristics of Services: Intangibility, Inconsistency, Inseparability and Inventory. Classification of Services.

   Consumer Behavior in Services: Search, experience and credence attributes, Pre and post experience evaluation, factors influencing customer expectation of service, Moment of truth

   Extended Marketing Mix for Services: Need for additional three marketing mix elements in Services

   Financial and economic impact of service

2. **Traditional Marketing Mix Elements in Services:**

   Service Product: Customer perception, Customer satisfaction, Tolerance zone, Service quality - ServQual, GAP model and Critical incident model, Concept of loyalty and creation of a loyalty programme, Service recovery, Impact of service failures versus product failures, Nature of complaining behavior-Complaint Resolution, Service Recovery Process.

   Service Pricing: Costs of service delivery, Customer Profitability Measurement, Revenue management Techniques, Price Discrimination and Segmented Pricing.

   Service Place: Delivering services through intermediaries and electronic channels.

   Service Promotion: Integrated service marketing communication, Visual merchandising, Referrals, Challenge of Service communication

3. **Service Process:**

   Service design and standards – Process, Service blueprint, Demand and capacity management, Quality function deployment (QFD), Standardization (hard / soft measures), Service delivery, self-service technologies

4. **People and Physical Evidence:**

   Employees' Role in Service Delivery, Service Culture: Internal Marketing, Service-Profit Chain, Emotional labor, Customers' role in service delivery, Customer as a co-producer

   Physical Evidence: Experience Servicescape elements (to include architectural design), Virtual Servicescape

5. **Applications of Service Marketing:** Marketing in Tourism, Hospitality, Airlines, Telecom, IT and ITES, Sports and Entertainment, Logistics, Healthcare sectors (Examples/Case studies on these applications are expected)

Contents ...

1. **Introduction to Services Marketing**   1.1 – 1.48

2. **Traditional Marketing Mix Elements in Services**   2.1 – 2.68

3. **Service Process**   3.1 – 3.32

4. **Service People and Physical Evidence**   4.1 – 4.38

5. **Applications of Service Marketing**   5.1 – 5.46

    Case Studies   C.1 – C.4

Chapter 1...

Introduction to Services Marketing

Contents ...

1.1 Introduction
1.2 Services
    1.2.1 Introduction
    1.2.2 Meaning and Definitions of Services
    1.2.3 Difference between Marketability of Services and Goods
    1.2.4 Significance of Services
    1.2.5 Characteristics of Services
    1.2.6 Classification of Services
    1.2.7 Important Services
    1.2.8 Financial and Economic Impact of Service
1.3 Consumer Behaviour in Services
    1.3.1 Introduction
    1.3.2 Search, Experience and Credence Attributes
    1.3.3 Consumer Decision Making Process
1.4 Consumer Expectation of Service
    1.4.1 Introduction
    1.4.2 Expected Service: Levels of Expectations
    1.4.3 Zone of Tolerance
    1.4.4 Factors Influencing Consumer Expectations of Service
1.5 Moment of Truth: Service Encounters
    1.5.1 Introduction
    1.5.2 Types of Service Encounter
    1.5.3 Factors Leading to Satisfaction or Dissatisfaction in Service Encounters
1.6 Services Marketing
    1.6.1 Importance of Services Marketing
    1.6.2 Service Marketing Mix
- Points to Remember
- Questions for Discussion
- Multiple Choice Questions
- Project Questions

Learning Objectives ...

- To understand the concept of services and its classification
- To identify the unique characteristics of services which make them different from goods
- To discuss the stages of consumer decision-making process and pre and post evaluation experience
- To describe the factors influencing consumer expectations and perceptions
- To understand the extended marketing mix and reasons for additional three marketing mix elements in services
- To explain the financial and economic impact of service

1.1 Introduction

We as consumers use services every day. Getting a haircut, getting clothes cleaned from the dry cleaners, eating at a restaurant, taking a bus are all examples of service utilisation at the personal and individual level. The colleges and institutions at which students study, are themselves complex service organisations. These service organisations in addition to educational services provide services such as library, cafeteria, counselling, telephone services and many more. Businesses and other organisations are also dependent on an extensive range of services albeit on a much larger scale.

Services marketing concepts and strategies have developed in response to the tremendous growth of service industries. The economic importance of services can be seen by the fact that trade in services is growing worldwide. There is a growing market for services and an increasing dominance of services in economies worldwide. The tremendous growth and economic contributions of the service sector have drawn increasing attention to the issues and challenges of service sector industries all over the world.

Services have started to play an increasingly important role in the economy and in individual organisations. Services are particularly relevant in industries where competitive pressures are forcing companies to find ways to create competitive differentiation. However, there are significant differences between the marketing of services and the marketing of tangible products.

Although services marketing have been practiced by some enlightened professionals for decades, the concept of services marketing is still new to many marketing professionals. Many current marketing concepts and tools have simply been transferred from the manufacturing sector. There are common elements between services and products, yet there is a need for marketing methods, tools and concepts that are specific to services.

1.2 SERVICES

1.2.1 Introduction

The service sector now accounts for more than half of India's GDP. This sector has been governed at the expense of both the agricultural and industrial sectors through the 1990s. The rise in the services sector's share in GDP marks a structural shift in the Indian economy and takes it closer to the fundamental of a developed economy (in the developed economies, the industrial and service sectors contribute a major share in GDP while agriculture accounts for a relatively lower share).

The service sector has grown at a higher rate than the manufacturing industry which too has grown more or less in tandem. The fact that the service sector now accounts for more than half the GDP probably marks a watershed in the evolution of the Indian economy. India's large service industry accounts for 54% of the country's GDP while the industrial and agricultural sector contributes 29% and 17% respectively.

1.2.2 Meaning and Definitions of Services

The term services is not limited to personal services like auto servicing, beauty parlours, medical services, consultancy services etc. On the contrary, it has under-connotations according to management gurus. Services have been defined in several ways; however there is not any single universal definition for the same. Some definitions of services have been mentioned below:

- *"Establishments primarily engaged to provide various services to individuals, business and government establishments, other organisations, hotels and other lodging places, establishments providing personal services as per individual requirement, and entertainment services, educational institutions, membership organisations and other miscellaneous services are included.*

  - Sasser, Olsen and Wyckoff

- *"Services refer to social efforts which include government to fight five giant evils, which are wants, disease, ignorance, squalor and illness in the society."*

  - Sir William Beveridge

- *"Services can be defined as action(s) of organisation(s) which maintain and improve the well-being and functioning of people."* **- Hasenfeld**

This definition, though brief, covers services in a substantial way. The well-being and functioning of people are important and we can't ignore it while clarifying the perception and the very essence of services.

- "Services can also be defined as human efforts, which provide succour to the needy. It may be food to a hungry person, water to a thirsty person, medical services to an ailing person, education to a student, loan to a farmer, transport to a consumer, communication aid to two persons who want to share a thought, pleasure or pain."

  — A. V. S. Rao 'Services Sector Management'

- "Services are activities, benefits or satisfactions which are offered for sale or are provided in connection with the sale of goods." — American Marketing Association

1.2.3 Difference between Marketability of Services and Goods

Table 1.1: Difference between Marketability of Services and Marketability of Goods

Points of Difference	Marketability of Services	Marketability of Goods
(a) Tangibility:	'Tangibility' refers to anything that can be viewed. The marketability of services is found intangible because it is not possible to view the services. We can just realise the services used by us.	Marketability of goods is found tangible as one can view the goods that are bought by him.
(b) Transferability:	It is possible to transfer the services from the point of sale to the point of use.	On the basis of transferability, the goods can be transferred from one place to another.
(c) Heterogeneity:	On the basis of heterogeneity, the services can hardly be standardised.	On the basis of heterogeneity, the goods can be standardised.
(d) Reselling:	The services cannot be resold. For example, if we book a room in the hotel, we have no option but to use it or surrender it. We don't bear the right of reselling the same.	The goods bought by us can be resold. After limited use, the owner of the goods is in a position and also possesses the legal right to resell the same.

1.2.4 Significance of Services

The significance of the services may be discussed under the following headings:

1. **Support to Primary and Secondary Sector:** Primary sectors and secondary sectors are always in need of various services in order to function smoothly on a regular basis. Thus, services form an important part for the efficient functioning of these sectors.

2. **Creates Employment Avenues:** Service sectors create a lot of employment opportunities in various sectors like BPOs, hospitality, retail, tourism, entertainment, brokerages, software, aviation and more. This in turn promotes and develops the overall growth of the nation.
3. **Contribution to National Income:** Due to the growth and development of the service sector, the other sectors in the market are also witnessing an equal growth and development. Moreover, because of this rapid growth and development of all the sectors in the market, it automatically contributes to the overall national income of the country.
4. **Provision for Basic Services:** Service sectors provide the country with the basic services like hospitality, transport, educational institutions, courts, telecommunications, insurance companies, banks, post offices and a lot more. This facilitates the daily living of a common man like us.
5. **Adds to Comforts and Leisure:** Service sectors provide ample comforts and leisure to the life of a common man. By providing various services, it definitely makes our lives easy and smooth.
6. **Improvement in India's Image:** Various services in the Indian market like telecommunications, BPOs, software development, Information Technology Enabled Services (ITES) has helped in improving the image of our country in the eyes of the entire globe. Other nations have started considering India at par with them when it comes to its service sectors.
7. **Increase in Exports:** Due to the increase in the service sectors and the quality of the same, there has been a tremendous increase in the exports of the country. This in turn is adding rapid growth and development to the country in the form of earnings and ranking.
8. **Increase in Number of Working Woman:** Due to the increase in the service sectors and the employment opportunities in the same, it has given ample work opportunities to women too. This has marked the increasing number of working women in the country which helps in the overall upliftment of the entire economy.

1.2.5 Characteristics of Services

The services literature highlights differences in the nature of services versus products which are believed to create special challenges for services marketers and for consumers buying services. To help understand these differences a number of characteristics that describe the unique nature of services have been proposed. These characteristics were first discussed in the early services marketing literature and are generally summarised as intangibility, inseparability, heterogeneity and perishability (Regan, 1963; Rathmell, 1966; Shostack, 1977; and Zeithaml et al 1985).

Although, there has been a debate on the effectiveness of the four characteristics in distinguishing between products and services (e.g. Regan, 1963; Shostack, 1977; Onkvisit and Shaw, 1991) these are nevertheless widely accepted by scholars and marketers (e.g. Zeithaml, 1981, 1985; Levitt, 1981) and used both as the basis for examining services buyer behaviour and developing services marketing strategies. It is, therefore, important to establish the extent to which these characteristics reflect the perspective of the consumer. A US-based study by Hartman and Lindgren (1993) found that consumers did not use the four characteristics in distinguishing between products and services.

Bitner, Fisk and Brown (1993) suggest that the major output from the services marketing literature up to 1980 was the delineation of four services characteristics: intangibility, inseparability, heterogeneity and perishability. These characteristics underpinned the case for services marketing and made services a field of marketing that was distinct from the marketing of products.

4 Is of services backed by an O

Services have four distinct characteristics that need to be internalised by service professionals to create opportunities in the market place, to enhance both top and bottom line growth for the firm. Leading researchers have zeroed on Intangibility, Inseparability, Inconsistency, and Inventory while others mention Ownership as well. All these characteristics are providing opportunity as well as challenges to the service marketer.

The distinct characteristics of services need individual focus while taking decisions regarding their organisational set-up. They are mentioned below:

1.2.5.1 Intangibility

It is one of the most important characteristics of service products. It has no physical dimension and attributes. Service is a deed, a performance, and an effort. The customers buy performance as they cannot see, touch, hear, taste or smell a service before they decide to buy the product. This makes the perception of service quite subjective. For e.g. a buyer of health club package, for weight loss cannot see what the outcome will be till the programme is over. Therefore, the customers for many services have to buy them on trust as they cannot be inspected before use. In case of goods, a consumer can touch, taste and sample the product. The intangible nature of services makes consumers concerned about their providers.

For e.g. in case of Global Trust Bank, a few years back, the investments made were not as per Regulatory norms, and when it was released in the press, it left many customers uneasy about the financial instability of GTB and there was a withdrawal of deposits as investors' trust were shaken. Some customers lost total faith and stopped banking.

In fact some service providers like life insurance agents as per IRDA have to undergo 100 hours training to get a license to practice so that they are trained in their profession.

Service products are mostly intangible but are marketed with tangible evidence. This is referred to as **tangibilising the intangibles**. While services often are accompanied with physical evidence that enables the consumer to make the product less abstract and more tangible, there will always be an intangible element to the service product.

The level of tangibility in the service offer is based on three criteria:
1. Tangible goods which are included in the service offer and consumed by the user.
2. The physical environment in which the service production/consumption process takes place, and
3. Tangible evidence of service performance.

Where goods form an important component of a service offer, many of the practices in goods marketing can be applied to this part of the service offer. A firm's promotional efforts must state the benefits to be derived from a service rather than stressing on the service itself. It is used to communicate the nature and quality of service.

Take for instance an experience on a flight, the total service experience is an aggregate of many components such as experience at the airport, the nature of services on board, the in-flight entertainment. Here, there are some tangible elements but most are intangible elements.

Intangibility of services leads customers to have difficulty in evaluating competing services, perceiving and assessing high levels of risk placing more emphasis on personal information sources and often using price as the basis for assessing quality. Hence management responds by reducing service complexity, stressing more on tangible clues, focusing on service quality and facilitating word of mouth recommendation.

While some services are rich in such tangible cues like retail outlets, restaurants, other services provide relatively little tangible evidence like life insurance.

In case of restaurants, it represents a mix of tangibles and intangibles and in respect of the food element, few of the particular characteristics of services marketing are encountered. Therefore, production of the food can be separated from its consumption and the perishability of food is less significant than the perishability of an empty table which results in loss of business. The presence of a tangible component gives customers a visible basis to judge quality.

The tangible elements of the service offered comprise not just those goods which are exchanged but also the physical environment in which a service encounter takes place. Within this environment, the design of buildings, their cleanliness and the appearance of staff present important tangible evidence which may be the only basis on which a buyer is able to differentiate one service provider from another.

Tangibility is further provided by evidence of service production methods. Some services provide many opportunities for customers to see the process of production, indeed the whole purpose of the service may be to see the production process like dramas or skits.

Often this tangible evidence can be seen before a decision to purchase a service is made, either by direct observation of a service being performed on somebody else like watching the sculptor work on a statue or indirectly, through a description of the service production process by brochures which illustrate and detail the service process like education. On the other hand, some services provide very few tangible clues about the nature of the service production process.

The lack of physical evidence, which intangibility implies, increases the level of uncertainty which a consumer faces when choosing between competing services. The service marketer's programme consists of reducing consumer uncertainty by adding physical evidence and the development of strong service brands; in contrast goods marketers augment their products by adding intangible elements such as after sales service and improved distribution.

1.2.5.2 Inconsistency (Heterogeneity or Variability)

This characteristic of service also referred to as heterogeneity, is a function of human involvement in the delivery and consumption process. The inseparability of the production and consumption aspects of the service transaction refers to the fact that service is a performance, in real time, in which the customer cooperates with the service provider. Inseparability is a characteristic of a service indicating that it cannot be separated from the service provider of the product. Therefore a great deal of effort has to go into standardisation of delivery. Since buyers' and service providers' interpersonal exchange is involved, there is opportunity for customisation, which can be the Unique Selling Proposition.

Inconsistency occurs largely because different service providers perform a given service on different occasions. The service performed by an individual provider may differ over a period of time because interaction between customer and provider may vary. Every time a service is performed, the process and the customer experience are different. Services that are provided by individuals rather than equipment will vary, depending upon which individual performs the service, and these will even vary with the same service provider from one job to the next. The service will also vary according to the degree to which clients involved in the production of the service agree. The degree to which the service firm designs the service delivery system to control variability will influence the quality of the service experienced by the customer.

Customer uncertainty can be reduced by a combination of automation, standardisation and rationalisation. However, inseparability may be desired by those customers who want customised service, rather than standard approaches that are not appropriate for individual situation as in case of interiors for bungalows in exclusive schemes for high net worth individuals.

But it is not possible to standardise service industry output. In case of trips by the Shatabdi Express between Delhi and Agra, the consumer does not get the same quality of service day after day due to different service personnel, snacks, music etc.

The performance of a faculty in a lecture, is not of same standard in each performance, as it will depend on a host of factors like preparation, mood, participation of the students, ambience etc. In case of an income tax consultant, he may provide a different service experience to a high net worth individual and a salaried class clerk because of varying needs and depends on his moods and pressures at the time of the day when the interaction is taking place.

In order to provide consistent services, the firms should standardise staff performance through careful planning, control and automation. Firms which are automated have less people and hence they have lower inconsistency in services. A garage which has installed auto car wash facilities with mounting of the vehicle on the ramp can provide consistent services. Banks have installed Automated Teller Machines to provide consistent services due to automation. Fountain, Cola and Pepsi vending machines are some other examples.

While these firms achieve high homogeneity in service delivery, they increase the risk of being inflexible and the staff reacts poorly to the unforeseen problem. Inconsistency is an opportunity and firms can strengthen their brands by customisation with greater empowerment to the staff.

For services, variability impacts upon customers not just in terms of outcomes but also in terms of processes of production. It is the latter point that causes variability to pose a much greater problem for services, compared to goods. Because the customer is usually involved in the production process for a service at the same time as they consume it, it can be difficult to carry out monitoring and control to ensure consistent standards. The opportunity for pre-delivery inspection and rejection which is open to the goods manufacturer is not normally possible with services. The service must normally be produced in the presence of the customer without the possibility of intervening quality control. Particular problems can occur where personnel are involved in providing services on a one-to-one basis, such as hairdressing, where no easy method of monitoring and control is possible.

There are two types of inconsistency:

1. The extent to which production standards vary from a norm, both in terms of outcomes and of production processes.
2. The extent to which a service can be deliberately varied to meet the specific needs of individual customers.

Variability in production standards is of greatest concern to services organisations where customers are highly involved in the production process, especially where production methods make it impractical to monitor service production. This is true of many labour intensive personal services provided in a one-to-one situation, such as personal healthcare.

Factors leading to the inconsistency of services because they are being produced live often left to chance with no time to correct mistakes before consumption. It is sometimes difficult to blueprint the service process. This results in difficulty of presenting an image of consistent quality, high level of perceived risk by the buyers and building a strong brand.

1. Service firms have tried to reduce inconsistency and build strong brands by automation. Replacing telephone operators with computerised voice systems and the automation of many banking services are typical of this trend. Sometimes reduced personnel inconsistency has been achieved by involving customers in the production process like self-service petrol filling stations.

2. The inconsistency is the extent to which a service can be strategically customised to meet the specific needs of individual customers. Because services are created as they are consumed and because consumers are often a part of the production process, the potential for customisation of services is generally greater than for manufactured goods. The extent to which a service can be customised is dependent upon production methods employed. Services which are produced for large numbers of customers simultaneously may offer little scope for individual customisation like in case of mass transportation.

The extent to which services can be customised is dependent on management decisions on the level of authority to be delegated to front-line service personnel. While some service operations seek to give more authority to front-line staff, the tendency is for service firms to standardise their encounter with customers to minimise inconsistency. While industrialisation often reduces the flexibility of producers to meet customers' needs, it also has the effect of reducing inconsistency of processes and outcomes. The variability of service output can pose problems for brand building in services compared to goods. The service sector's attempts to reduce variability, concentrates on methods used to select, train, motivate and control personnel or simplify service offers with reduced skill content of jobs, backed by automation.

1.2.5.3 Inseparability

Many services are created, delivered and consumed simultaneously through interaction between customers and service producers, whereas goods generally, are produced first and consumed later on. As the customers are involved in the production process, the service quality becomes difficult to measure and control.

For e.g. a doctor creates, delivers all his services simultaneously but the consumer presence is required during the performance of the service. This means that in many cases, people are involved concurrently in the production and marketing efforts of the service organisations. In most of the cases, the customer receives and consumes the services at the service provider's premises. Since inseparability characteristic generally means the direct interaction between the service provider and client, it is direct selling.

Inseparability leads customers to being co-producers of the service either alone or with other co-consumers and often they have to travel to the point of production service. The management has to respond to this by separating production and consumption. It has to monitor consumer producer interaction and focus on continuous improvement in the service delivery system.

Production and consumption are separable for goods. On the other hand, the consumption of a service is said to be inseparable from its means of production. Producer and consumer must interact with each other in order to realise the benefits of the service; both must normally meet at a time and a place which is mutually convenient in such a way that the producer can directly pass on service benefits.

For services, marketing becomes a means of facilitating complex producer-consumer interaction, rather than being merely an exchange medium.

Moreover, the service cannot be stocked by the distribution partners, as in case of goods. This poses a major limitation for the service provider. For e.g. a car mechanic can only repair, say, four vehicles per day. Thus individual service seller's services cannot be sold in many markets or multi locations. This characteristic limits the scale and reach of operation of a service firm.

There are other services which can be sold by a representative of the main service provider e.g. insurance agent, travel agent, but at the final point of service delivery the service provider's presence is a must. Such services are generally sold by the institutions producing them.

The degree of involvement between transacting parties is dependent upon the extent to which the service is 'equipment based' or 'people based'.

Three Types of Service Production
1. **Self Services:** Customer uses the equipment and services provided and maintained by the service provider, for e.g. ATM (Automatic Vending Machines) for tea, coffee, cold drinks, etc. In the case of ATM, machine service can only be realised if the producer and consumer interact.
2. **Co-production:** The service provider and customer work together to create the service and to maximise the benefit for the customer. In a health club, the trainer guides his customer to gain maximum benefit from a weight loss programme. Health care services, coaching classes and dental services are some other examples.
3. **Isolated Production:** It has been possible to separate service production and consumption, especially where there is a low level of personal contact. The part of the service is performed outside the service provider's premises. For e.g. entertainment like cable viewing at homes, tele-banking from home or office, video conferencing are some other examples.

Inseparability has a number of important marketing implications for services. Firstly, whereas goods are generally first produced, then offered for sale and finally sold and consumed, inseparability causes the process to be different for services. They are generally sold first, then produced and consumed simultaneously. Secondly, while the method of goods production is to a large extent of little importance to the consumer, production processes are critical to the enjoyment of services.

1.2.5.4 Inventory (Perishability)

The perishability of services describes the real time nature of the product. Unlike goods, the consumer cannot store the service and the absence of the ability to build and maintain stocks of the product means that sudden demands cannot be accommodated as it can be done in case of goods. The buyer may decide to delay the consumption but may not consume more in advance than the requirements. For the buyer of services, the time at which they choose to use the service may be critical to its performance and therefore to the consumer's experience, for e.g., in a Pune Municipal Transport bus the experience in the rush hour is very different than in lean hours. Consumption of services is directly linked to the experience. In case of services, inventory costs are related to capacity utilisation. In idle service production environment, the inventory cost relates to reimbursing staff along with any needed equipment. E.g. If a lawyer is available but there is no customer during that period, the fixed cost of the idle lawyer's opportunity is the inventory carrying cost.

Some services have characteristics, where demand for them fluctuates, considerably by season and by day of the week and even hour of the day. An airline which offers seats on a 6.00 am flight from Mumbai to Delhi cannot sell any empty seats once the aircraft has left at 6.00 am. The service offer disappears and spare seats cannot be stored to meet a surge in demand which may occur at 8.00 am.

Few services have a constant pattern of demand over a period of time. Many show considerable variation like daily variation in cyber cafes towards the evening/night , weekends for travel by railways between Pune-Mumbai, seasonal for hotels, cyclical for mortgages or an unpredictable pattern of demand like emergency repair services like electricity after trees falling on electricity lines. For a travel agent, the demand fluctuates according to time and period and is linked to holidays in school and colleges, in summer and winter coupled to festivals like Diwali, Durga Puja, and Christmas etc., wherein the demand peaks.

The combination of perishability and fluctuating demand present challenges for marketers engaged in planning, pricing, promotion and distribution of services. The cellular companies try to spread out demand for their services by pricing off peak hours to make them more attractive to callers. They offer "happy hour" rates to increase traffic in lean periods of the day. The services providers focus on strategies for effective capacity management to reduce the inventory costs. Hence, even if volumes can be enhanced with a little margin over variable cost, the firm should push for it. An appointment with a dentist at a given time, on a given day, cannot be stored and if patient cancels the appointment last minute, the revenue is lost. The firms must monitor their capacity and review it periodically to ensure customers get better service as well as resources of the firm are optimally utilised.

Many services are bought even before they are experienced as in case of pension. Here the service firms have to tackle two issues: first, they have to develop image and reputation to attract customers; secondly, they must retain customers, as competitors try to attract them away, even though they have yet to experience the service.

Perishability occurs because of the inability to store services, inelasticity of short-term supply. This results in demand patterns being irregular with just in time production of services and if managed effectively congestion occurs at peak periods and loss of capacity at off-peak periods. Pricing and promotion are used extensively to encourage customers to utilise services at a time when it is convenient to the service operator in order to have better capacity utilisation.

To manage these characteristics efficiently the service provider has to use the optimum strategies. "The Problems and Strategies in Services Marketing" adapted from Parasuraman, Berry and Zeithmal, "Problems and Strategies in Services Marketing", and "Journal of Marketing" are tabulated for ready reference.

Table 1.2

Characteristics	Problem	Marketing Strategy
Intangibility:	Cannot be easily displayed Cannot be patented	Provide tangible clues Stimulate word of mouth Use personnel sources Use post purchase communication
Inconsistency:	Standardisation hard to achieve Hard to set up quality control Can only predict quality or determine it after the service is performed	Stress on standardisation and performance Focus on employee training Programs, performance evaluation Licensing and other forms of credential requirement
Inseparability:	Harder to mass produce Less efficient than production goods	Need strong training programmes, incentives Focus on personal attention
Inventory:	Customers must be present	Focus on convenience, saving time, faster service Extended hours Focus on competence and expertise Predict fluctuating demand Manage capacity to balance supply and demand

In addition to the 4 Is of services, ownership has been identified as a distinguishing feature of services by some researchers including Kotler.

Ownership is another distinguishing feature of service. The inability to own a service is related to the characteristics of intangibility and perishability. In case of service, when it is performed, no ownership is transferred from buyer to seller. The buyer is merely buying the right to a service process such as the use of a car park or a solicitor's time. A distinction should be drawn between the inability to own the service act, and the rights which a buyer may acquire to have a service carried out at some time in the future. In case of service, the buyer has temporary access to or use of it. What is owned is the benefit of service, not the service itself, e.g. for a holiday tour package to picturesque Manali in Himachal, the buyer has access to hotel, mountains, snow, waterfalls, rivers etc. but doesn't own any of them.

The inability to own a service has implications for the design of distribution channels, so a wholesaler or retailer cannot take title, as is the case with goods. Instead, direct distribution methods are more common and where intermediaries are used, who generally act as a co-producer with the service provider.

1.2.6 Classification of Services

We shall now distinguish between the various types or classes of services. Different types of services need different marketing strategies.

(A) On the Basis of Degree of Involvement of the Customer

This category is based on the degree of involvement of the customer.

  (a) **People Processing:** The customer has to be present at the place of delivery to experience or consume the service, like a training workshop, a dance class, health care, etc.

  (b) **Possession Processing:** Even if the customer's presence is not required, his possession or property needs to be deposited for service, like car servicing/repair, TV/VCD repair, laundry, courier service, etc.

  (c) **Mental Stimulus Processing:** In this case the customer's mental attention is required, if not physical presence, in order to experience services like career counselling, advertising, consultation and education services, etc.

  (d) **Information Processing:** In this case, data, information, knowledge are gathered and analysed for clients, like research studies, market surveys, data processing, accounting, legal services, programming, etc.

(B) On the Basis of Service Tangibility

Here the degree of tangibility (the tangibility spectrum) has been taken into consideration with the same number of classes.

  (a) **Highly Tangible:** The service includes physical products (highly tangible) for use during the contract period, like a cell phone or a house on rent.

- (b) **Services Linked to Tangible Goods:** These are the guarantee or warranty periods, during which the sellers provide free or subsidised services to the customer, like machines, vehicles, gadgets, etc.
- (c) **Tangible Goods Linked to Services:** Here some physical goods are given to the customer as part of a service, like food with a train/air ticket, hotel accommodation which includes morning breakfast, etc.
- (d) **Highly Intangible:** Here, no products are offered as part of the services, like haircuts, body massage, movie, etc.

(C) On the Basis of Skills and Expertise Required

The basis of the level of skills required to render a set of services, as:

- (a) **Professional (High Skill) Services:** These services require a higher level of qualification and training to provide services, like doctors, lawyers, pilots, IT professionals, etc.
- (b) **Non-Professional (Low Skill) Services:** These services don't require any special prerequisites in skills, and can be performed by anybody with some practice, like office security guards, babysitters, courier delivery boys, etc.

(D) On the Basis of the Business Orientation of the Service Provider

This kind of service depends on the business style or orientation (objective, purpose, aim) of the organisation, as:

- (a) **Commercial Organisations (Profit Oriented):** The main objective here is to make a profit by providing service. They strive to do all that is required to earn profits by keeping the customers satisfied.
- (b) **Non-profit Organisations (Service Oriented):** The main objective here is to serve the target clientele, without any motive to earn any profit. Of course money is needed for running such an organisation, and that is obtained from public donations, trust funds, or government aid. This category includes government bodies and also no-profit-no-loss (cost to cost) organisations. Schools, NGOs, welfare societies, disaster relief organisations, etc. are examples.

(E) On the Basis of the Types of End Users:

Services can be classified by the type of consumers who consume them.

- (a) **Consumer Services (B2C):** This is between the service provider (the company) and the individual customer for his personal consumption like medical treatment, fitness services.
- (b) **Business to Business (B2B):** This is between two companies, like one company hiring another, to do market research for it.
- (c) **Industrial Services:** This is the case where a manufacturing company buys services from a service provider like supply, erection, commissioning, and maintenance of the plant and machinery.

1.2.7 Important Services

(a) **Food Services:** Restaurants, cafeterias and hotels are offering food services to numerous individuals and families who have firmly developed the habit of eating out. These eating places are ever-growing as the service they sell is definitely wanted by the public. Small eating places offer simple and cheaper meals. Five-star hotels offer elegant and costly food with superb services and royal comforts. Increasing tourism has also boosted the development of the hotel industry. We also have caterers who specialise in supplying food and service for dinners and parties at our residences on ceremonial and special occasions.

(b) **Hotels and Motels:** Lakhs of people, every day, use lodging and boarding services all over the country. Tourism, hotels and motels are growing in numbers every year. Modern hotels provide a luxurious life to travellers and tourists. Tourism is now considered as a major source of foreign exchange in all countries. Modern hotels provide numerous amenities, comforts, refined and elegant services.

(c) **Personal Care Services:** Rising standards of living brought about the development in the personal care services (helping a customer to be well groomed). These services are offered by health and fitness centres, beauty parlours, barber shops, laundries, drycleaners, garment repair shops, shoe repair shops and so on. Health and fitness organisations are growing in importance and their popularity in all countries due to an ever increasing demand for improving individual personality and efficiency. In the anti-fat modern culture and lifestyle, figure consciousness and weight reduction (due to obesity) have assumed unique importance. People have money and they do not mind spending on themselves.

(d) **Car Service Firms (Garages):** Lakhs of car owners are dependent on car service centres. Petrol pumps sell both goods and services because of which they are now called service stations. There are also numerous garages and repair shops specialising in repairs and maintenance of cars, trucks, motorcycles and scooters.

(e) **Entertainment Services:** Increasing purchasing power and more leisure time are responsible for the steady growth of entertainment services. Movies, sports, amusement parks, circuses, car racing, cricket, billiards, music, dancing and drama are such popular forms of organised entertainment today.

(f) **Transport Services:** Railways, buses, ships and aeroplanes provide transport services for moving people and goods from one place to another. The fastest growth has taken place in air transport. A person can have a round-the-world trip in just one fortnight. Air transport has become very popular in international tourism.

(g) **Communication Services:** Nowadays, we have the latest means of communication such as the internet, mobile, telephone, telegraph, telex and postal services at our disposal. We also have television, mobile and satellite communications all over the world. The current technology has contributed tremendously to the rapid growth of all types of communication services.

(h) **Insurance Services:** Insurance gives protection against risk, e.g. accident, fire, death, theft, sickness, unemployment and so on. People can save for their children's education, daughter's marriage or for their retirement. Security of life and property provided by insurance gives us freedom from anxiety and peace of mind.

(i) **Financial Services:** Many consumers require the service of banks for financing their purchases of durable goods usually through installment sales. In foreign countries, they even have easy house financing through bank loans. Home owning is made easy with the help of mortgage loans. The modern high standard of living has become a reality for masses due to a customer-oriented marketing approach adopted by banks recently.

1.2.8 Financial and Economic Impact of Service

Services are a growing sector in almost all the countries of the world. This sector is majorly responsible for the overall growth and development of the country's economy. Any other fields like trade, tourism, hospitality and many more, even services have been a justified reason of pride for maximum countries including India. It not only increases the GDP of a nation but it also offers many advantages on a long-term basis. Following are a couple of booming benefits due to the growing service industry:

(a) **Generation of Employment Opportunities:** Service industry has definitely given a lot of employment opportunities in the country. Service is needed in almost every sector like tourism, communications, trade, marketing, manufacturing, international technology and more. Many organisations are considering quality service to be their mission and vision and they are really working hard to render quality services to their customers and thus retain them. Companies are open to employing adequate employees in this sector which will in turn be earning benefits for the company itself.

Thus, with the growth and development of service sectors, the employment opportunities have seen a remarkable growth. Most of the people have been employed in the service sectors of the country and have successfully added to the overall development of the economy as a whole.

(b) **Increasing the Standard of Living:** Due to the increase in service sectors, there has been an increase in the employment opportunities as well. Moreover, due to the increase in the employment opportunities amongst people, there has been increase in the earnings and incomes of every household. This in turn has automatically upgraded the standard of living of people as they can earn good incomes and spend the same to satisfy their growing needs and wants.

Standard of living also increases because the country is in a decent position to offer quality goods and services to its citizens. Thus, usage of quality products and an ability to spend for fulfilling one's desires is a big sign that highlights the increased standard of living in a particular country.

(c) **Optimum Utilisation of Resources**: India is bestowed with an ample variety of rich resources. Due to the increase in technology, the human resources have seen a slow fall in technology dominated fields like IT and manufacturing. On the other hand, it is the service sector that has given innumerable employment opportunities to all types of people.

Various services firms like tourism, entertainment, export, personal care services, hospitality and more have been booming rapidly. In fact, these areas do not utilise any of the country's natural resources and are based only on the human resources. Thus, service sector also helps in conserving the natural resources of the country for future generations.

(d) **Capital Formation**: Service sectors have been a major player in providing ample employment opportunities, increase in income and increase in the standard of living of people. With this, it has also expanded the capital formation of the country.

Various areas of the economy are highly dependent on the service sectors. They have seen immense growth and development just because of the growing service sectors in the country. Moreover, it is estimated that these specialised sectors will see further growth and expansion which will actually help the country in capital formation. This whole process of capital formation is also known as a nation-building process. Economic, political and social factors majorly signal further expansion of the service sectors. Performance of profitable services can absorb higher investments from various sources which in turn will automatically accelerate the rate of capital formation in the country.

(e) **Use of Environment-Friendly Technology**: Service industry is one of the fields which do not pollute or harm the environment in any way. Thus it is known as an environment friendly technology. Service sectors work closely only with the human resources and thus are harmless to the surroundings, unlike the manufacturing process which releases harmful gases, chemicals and wastes that harm the environment in various ways. Service sector has been indeed laudable in this regard.

(f) **Economic Liberalisation:** The process of economic liberalisation started in India in the year 1991. Since then there have has been visible changes in the overall business scenario of the country. Even the multinational players were allowed to enter the Indian markets thus giving further growth and development to the country's economy and trade. It also created ample policies and opportunities to the Indians to establish their own businesses and expand further.

(g) **Migration:** There has been a remarkable increase in the migration rate of the people from the rural and semi-urban areas to the urban areas. Desire for better jobs and better livelihood resulted in immense rate of migration. This in turn led to further expansion of businesses, trades, transport and other service sectors. Actually both the factors worked hand-in-hand to witness increasing demand in placement and personal services of the country.

(h) **Export Potential:** India is considered one of the major exporters in the world. There are various services that India offers to different countries like insurance, banking, transport, tourism, data services, communications, construction labour, accounting services, maintenance services, design engineering, education, entertainment, software services, healthcare and commercial services. Thus, the service sector has expanded the export potential of India.

(i) **Growth in Population of DINKS:** Due to increasing opportunities in the employment sector, both the spouses prefer to work and earn a decent livelihood. They prefer to choose their dream profession and dedicate themselves completely due to which they cannot or prefer not to have children. This situation has actually given a lot of growth in the DINKS population which is an acronym for Dual Income No Kids.

1.3 Consumer Behaviour in Services

1.3.1 Introduction

Service sectors are not actually a new thing. It has always been there in the market and has its own history. The importance of the growing service sector which is immensely adding to the development of the country is new. Service sectors were always there since the earlier times, either in the form of unorganised, small and localised activity. However, these small activities were never recognised as service sectors because history has its own disadvantages. The problem was that practices, customs and styles of functioning were accepted as the only way to operate and perform. This created a problem in people's perception which stopped the growth of new approaches trying to emerge in the market.

For marketing professionals, it is very important to understand the customer's behaviour. If employees fail to understand this, then they never create and deliver quality services that result in happy and loyal customers. Dealing with customers is never an easy task. Customer is always the king in the market. Moreover, employees need to know the right nerve of the customer so that they can deliver desired services to them. Thus, dealing with customers is not a new thing but customer interaction is new and many organisations have considered this element important for successful growth.

There have been many approaches in designing effective marketing strategies. However, the importance and success of it is actually based on quality customer services. It is very important to understand why a customer chooses a particular service provider amongst the various competitors available in the market? It is also important to know what type of service encounter the customer faces with service delivery and consumption. Certain other factors must also be studied like how customers interact with service employees, service facilities, and over other customers? What are the customer's expectations from the service provider and how they are benefiting from the rendered services? These points are to be closely watched to gain a complete background about a customer's expectations.

Service sectors face a lot of challenges on a daily basis. Since it directly deals with the end user, it has to work on multiple elements in order to convince the customer and retain him back each time. While buying a product or a service, customers look for various tangible and intangible characteristics and only after gaining a positive feedback on the same they plan to go ahead with it. Thus, customers are actually involved in the complete manufacturing and servicing process by giving frequent suggestions and feedbacks. This, self-involvement behaviour of customers actually influences the efficient working of the entire service operations.

1.3.2 Search, Experience and Credence Attributes

It is said that in order to judge customer behaviour in regards to services, it is important to build a cause-effect relationship between the characteristics of the services and their effect on customer's search. This is also known as an evaluation behaviour wherein a customer evaluates a product based on various factors. Nelson justified by saying that goods basically involve two types of qualities, that is search quality and experience quality.

Search quality is something that a customer searches for before buying the product. He may have certain things in mind about the product which he wishes to buy like the colour, fit, quality, style, price, design and hardness. These qualities can be looked for while buying products like furniture or jewellery. On the other hand, experience quality is that a customer understands by his own experience after the purchase and consumption of the service. Various attributes like wearability or taste falls in this category wherein the customer will be able to judge the quality only after using it. For example, airlines or vacations can be judged only after using the services. Thus, nothing can be said before the purchase and it is evident only after gaining a personal experience of the same.

Darby and Karni successfully added a third quality to the existing classification by the name of credence. Credence attributes or qualities are such that cannot be judged even after purchasing and consumption of services. Customers do not have that expertise knowledge or ability to judge certain services. For example, after visiting a particular doctor, patient will still not be able to judge his services as he does not have proper knowledge in the medical field. He will simply follow what the doctor says and has to accept his decisions blindly. In such cases, customers have to depend heavily on the marketer's reputation and assurances.

1.3.3 Consumer Decision Making Process

While purchasing any goods or services, customers actually go through a complex purchase process. This process has three major stages known as the pre-experience evaluation, consumer experience and post-evaluation experience. These separate stages are further divided into sub-stages as below:

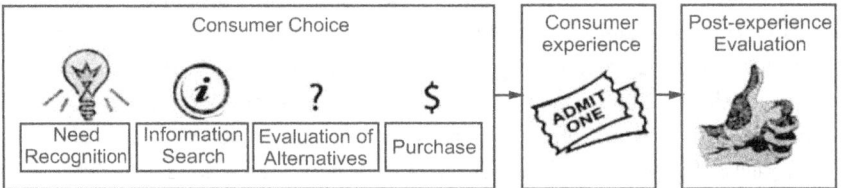

Fig. 1.1: Stages in Consumer Decision Making and Evaluation of Services

1.3.3.1 Pre-experience Evaluation: Consumer Choice

Marketers are usually concerned over the thought how customers choose a certain product over others and what is their decision-making process which leads to the final purchase of the product. Customers go through various stages of this phase like need recognition, information search, evaluation of alternatives, and purchase. Following is the explanation for each of the above mentioned sections:

(A) Need Recognition: The buying process actually begins with recognising the needs of the customers. There are various ways of recognising a customer's needs. However, Maslow's hierarchy specifies in the best possible manner the five need categories which are arranged in a sequential order right from basic-lower level needs to the higher-level needs. There are various services which can fulfil all the types of needs and these become increasingly important for higher-level, self-actualisation and ego needs.

- **Psychological Needs:** They are known as the basic or the survival needs like food, clothing and shelter.
- **Safety and Security Needs:** This includes shelter, security and protection from any dangers.
- **Social Needs:** These needs are for friendship, affection and acceptance amongst others.

- **Ego Needs:** After fulfilling the basic needs, people look for more satisfaction by fulfilling their ego needs. They would like to get easily accepted in the society and hence purchase products which will add to their image and status.
- **Self-actualisation Needs**: This involves enriching and self-fulfillment experiences wherein a customer believes in living their life to the fullest.

(B) Information Search: Once the customer recognises his needs, he then tries to gain information of the same. They start looking for other people's feedback and opinions which they can study and decide whether they can buy the product which they desire or can look for alternatives. Information may be quick and relatively automatic for small purchases and may extend to a formalised one in case of costly and big purchases.

People make use of both personal sources and non-personal sources for collecting information. Personal sources can be experts and immediate friends and non-personal sources can be websites, selective media and mass public. Seeking information actually invokes confidence in buyers and also reduces the risk of wrong purchases.

(C) Evaluation of Search Alternatives: In today's cut throat competition, there are a lot of options available in the market to choose from. Customers have a wide variety of alternatives and they have their own preferences of selecting one product over the above. Many a times, customers do not want to go through a daunting process of searching and evaluating the products hence they usually go in for the first option that is easily available to them.

If need be, they might look in for other alternatives which are available locally so that they do not have much trouble evaluating the alternative search. In order to purchase goods, customers visit retail stores where they keep various alternatives of the same type of products. In order to purchase services, customers visit establishments like banks or salons where they just render one type of service and do keep other options available.

Customers are heavily depending on the internet for their wide evaluation of search alternatives.

(D) Service Purchase: After following the above stages in a sequential manner, customers finally make the decision of purchasing the goods or services. The major difference between purchasing goods and purchasing services is that goods can be felt before buying. For example, people will try the product personally before buying a similar one for actual consumption. This gives them a fair idea of what they will be buying. Whereas in services, due to its intangible characteristics people may not know their exact product till they actually pay for it and consume it; or make part payments to know better. For example, eating a meal in a restaurant, a person has to consume the service to know it. In case like vacation planning, customer will have to make part payments to proceed with the plan and make full payment before finally leaving for the same.

1.3.3.2 Consumer Experience

Due to the various choices available in the market and the credence qualities of goods, it is difficult to make out what decision-making process does a customer go through. It is actually a customer's experience that influences his future purchasing needs and choices. Experience plays an important role in defining the decision-making process of the customers.

Experiences are of various types like funny, good, short, exciting, memorable and less exciting. Depending upon these experiences, people make their future purchase decisions. Thus organisations have realised the importance of customer behaviour and making all efforts to make their experiences happy and memorable.

(A) Services as Processes: Services are actions also known as performances that are done for the customers. Service is a process which involves various steps, activities and actions. For example, in medical services, the first step is a patient interacts with the physician. The second step is to follow the doctor's prescriptions and take the medications. Other steps may involve third parties like going to a lab for blood testing etc. Thus, this is known as a series of steps for one work which actually form an experience to the patient. When a person interacts with multiple people for one task and when this whole process takes a long time then it becomes a memory for him related to that particular task. This memory can be a good one, bad one or simply remain as an experience!

(B) Service Provision as Drama: Theatre works and dramas actually aim at giving a desirable experience through performances. A lot of hard work is put in this type by carefully managing the actors and physical setting of their behaviour at the backstage so that they can perform their best on the stage and leave a lasting impression on the viewer's mind.

(C) Service Roles and Scripts: Roles are actually a guiding list which orders a person to behave in a particular manner. Like stage plays and dramas have roles, even service delivery includes the same. For example, an air hostess or a waiter is expected to behave in a certain way which their job demands for. It is the work of a hostess in a restaurant to greet the customers warmly, help and guide them in selecting the food items from the menu, reserve place for the bookings, see that everyone is comfortably accommodated and that they are enjoying their dining experience. Service employees need to behave according to the customer's expectations otherwise they get frustrated and dissatisfied.

(D) The Compatibility of Service Customers: It is a human tendency of a person to follow others. Thus the crowd present at a location influences a customer's expectations immensely. The way others behave or react about a service affects other people's mentality too. Customers can get incompatible due to many reasons like differences in age, values, beliefs, experiences, appearance, health and ability to pay. Companies can concentrate on such incompatible customers and promote their individual decision-making process. However, they should also put in efforts to bring together the other lot by fulfilling their needs as desired.

(E) Customer Coproduction: In many services, customer participation is equally important. Without this, there will be no meaning to the customer service being rendered. For example, in educational institutes, training and counselling, a customer has to dedicatedly concentrate on the sessions to bring out the best of the rendered services. Thus, customer coproduction is equally important to make customer service successful.

(F) Emotion and Mood: Emotions and moods are the most important factors that play a major role in influencing the purchase decision of the customer. It is a person's state of mind while purchasing and consumption that decide the future decisions.

1.3.3.3 Post-experience Evaluation

Once the customer purchases and consumes a product, they form a post experience evaluation whether they will come back to purchase the same again or no. It is only after they have experienced, they evaluate the quality of the product. Generally a lot of attention is given to the pre-purchase evaluations and consumer choice. However, post purchase evaluations are equally important for organisations to understand and accept. They are typically important to judge the customer's subsequent behaviour and repurchase of the product.

Post experience evaluation is basically captured in various measures of service quality, satisfaction, emotional engagement and loyalty. Following are the specifics of service quality and customer satisfaction:

(A) Word-of-Mouth Communication: This is the most preferred option for many customers. People go by the word-of-mouth reference for any products or service. Thus, it is important for organisations to create good experience so that customers can talk positively and give a good reference to others. However, if the service is bad then it is very difficult for the company to curb the negative talking that goes around amongst people.

(B) Attribution of Dissatisfaction: When a customer is dissatisfied about a service, he may link the attributes to various sources. For example, if a customer goes to a salon for a specific haircut, but is not satisfied by the same then he/she may link it to many various factors like lack of skill of the hairstylist or inability to give clear instructions on her part as to what style she wants. Most of the time, they feel responsible for dissatisfactory services as they closely participate in almost all the stages of services.

(C) Positive or Negative Biases: Research says that it is a human tendency to remember or weigh negative experiences more than the positive ones. Thus, if there is a good experience people may not remember for a long time. However if they have had a bad experience then they will never forget the same. Similarly, negative rumours are spread and affect more easily than the positive ones.

(D) Brand Loyalty: It is the brand loyalty as well on the customer's part which decides his future buying decisions. If a customer is completely satisfied with a particular brand then he will stick to it forever no matter its price or availability. Companies also make extra efforts to retain their loyal customers as they know the hard work involved in making one.

1.4 Consumer Expectation of Service

1.4.1 Introduction

Customers recognise their needs which create a buying ability in them. In order to fulfil their needs and wants, people look for products and services which will serve the purpose. They are mentally prepared to spend a reasonable amount of money to purchase something that they desire. They also consider various options available in the market to compare and select the best one.

Similarly for services too they have high expectations. Service providers understand the importance of customer behaviour and act accordingly. They try to fulfil each and every want of a customer by rendering quality and satisfactory services. As there are multiple options available in the market even in the service sectors, it does not take long for a customer to leave one company and go for the other. Thus, it is important to maintain the quality of the services being provided because competitors are waiting to grab all the customers even in the slightest possible chance. Service sectors also means dealing with the customers directly and thus it majorly works on the two important factors that are confidence and trust.

Employees should be trained well to handle each type of customer and render him exact services that he desires. The entire service industry works on the basis of customer relationships.

1.4.2 Expected Service: Levels of Expectations

Customer's expectations embrace several elements which are desired service, adequate service, predicted service and tolerance zone which falls between the desired service and the adequate service. Every customer is different and they have different types of expectations from the service providers.

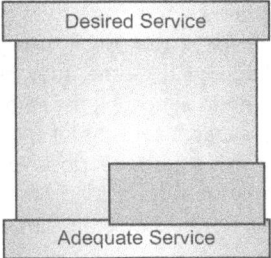

Fig. 1.2

Desired Service: This can be termed as the highest service where a customer desires, hopes or wishes the service to be. It is actually a blend of what a customer thinks it "should be" and it "can be". For example, people sign up for these online dating sites with a desire and hope to find a suitable, attractive, compatible, interesting partner to date and perhaps even marry the right one. Based on these desires they take up the service, otherwise such service providers will never make it if the desired service is not in the picture.

There are levels of expectations amongst customers due to which even two similar businesses can cater different services and still keep the customers happy. Thus, here the companies learn the desires of the customers which they can satisfy successfully. For example, Burger King and McDonald's are two major brands but still people have high expectations from McDonald's comparatively due to various reasons. Different customers have different reasons as to why they desire something from one brand and not the same from the other.

The adequate service expectation level may vary accordingly. If a customer has high expectations from McDonald's then his chances of dissatisfaction are also high as compared to Burger King even though the services of the previous ones are much better and higher.

Adequate service expectation is acceptable by the customer but not so desired.

1.4.3 Zone of Tolerance

It is not easy for organisations to make all their employees work efficiently throughout the year. The employees may have different mood swings through the year, even throughout the day. They may perform differently in different situations depending on various factors like workload, mood swings, peak time and so on. The extent to which a customer accepts this variation in employee's performance is known as the zone of tolerance or tolerance zone. If the employee's performance is too low it causes frustration and dissatisfaction amongst customers and if they perform well then it creates happy and pleased customers.

Another way of looking at this customer's zone of tolerance is to understand the range of services which the customers actually do not pay much attention to. When things fall outside this mentioned range, then the customers will definitely react, either in a positive manner or a negative manner.

The size of the tolerance zone can either be big or small for individual buyers depending upon various factors like price, competition or importance of specific service attributes, each of which has the power of influencing the level of adequate service. In short, the desired service levels move upwards very slowly in contrast to the response of the accumulated customer experiences. For example, when a businessman expects some advice from his accountant at the end of the financial year, then obviously he will have to wait as the accountants are usually busy working for various clients at this peak time of the year. In such situations, a person is mentally prepared to be patient and not to expect a quick response. Although his actual service level may not change, however his zone of tolerance may broaden up since he has a lower service threshold.

It is also very important for firms to understand how wide a customer's tolerance zone is. For example, guests will have a relatively lower zone of tolerance between desired and adequate service levels. This was found on studying individual attributes of the customers as they were being sensitive about intangibles like employee courtesy, prompt service and convenience of operating hours than about other tangibles like modern looking equipments and physical facilities.

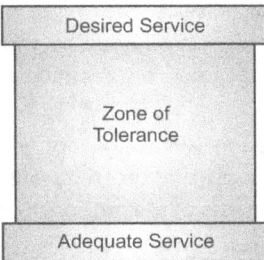

Fig. 1.3

1.4.4 Factors Influencing Consumer Expectations of Service

It is a natural tendency amongst people to keep expectations. Similarly, even with service providers, people have high expectations from them under various conditions. Marketers are working hard to find out as to what are the factors that actually shape up a buyer's expectations and in what ways they can control the same. However, it is also true that not all the factors are controllable or easy to manage.

Basically, there are three major sources of customer's expectations of service. These have been fairly further sub-divided as mentioned below:

(A) Sources of Desired Service Expectations:

Philosophies and personal needs about service are the two main influences on desired service expectations.

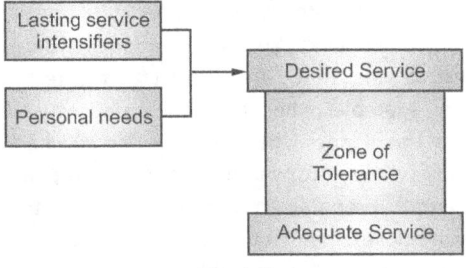

Fig. 1.4

(i) Personal Needs: Personal needs are the main factors which decide what a customer expects from the service. As per his personal needs and wants he will be demanding the desired service. It is counted under various categories like social needs, physical needs and psychological needs.

All the customers are different in nature and thus they are divided into various categories like a demanding customer, sensitive customer, angry customer, easy going ones and more. Thus based on their personal characteristics and wants they are grouped under various titles. For example, if a person who wants to watch a movie straight after work, will automatically expect a quality food and beverages counter as well to fetch when he is hungry and tired. However, a person who has eaten well before the movie may not expect such services as he will be straight going in for the movie and back home.

(ii) Lasting Service Intensifiers: Lasting service intensifiers are also known as derived service expectations because here a customer's expectations are usually derived by another customer or a group of people. It involves some stable and individual factors which leads the customer to a heightened sensitivity of service.

In an example of business-to-business service, when the software crashes or when the computer equipment is not working, the customers of the insurance company pressurize the departmental head to work on the same at the earliest. Thus, in such cases, a manager or supervisor is forced by his customers to fulfil their expectations and this brings in the desired service expectations.

In similar cases, subordinates speed up their project work when they are pressurised by their managers. The sales staff will run helter-skelter to increase their sales after being pressurised by their company. Usually, people who are in the service industry tend to have strong service philosophies and thus their expectations are also equally high. Many people also have their own personal philosophies in regards to the service industries which drive their expectations to various levels.

(B) Sources of Adequate Service Expectations:

There are various factors that affect adequate service and the level of service at which a customer finds satisfaction. Generally, these are all short-term influences and they tend to fluctuate even more than the actual desired service. Following are the five main factors that influence adequate services:

1. Temporary service intensifiers,
2. Perceived service alternatives,
3. Customer self-perceived service role,
4. Situational factors, and
5. Predicted service

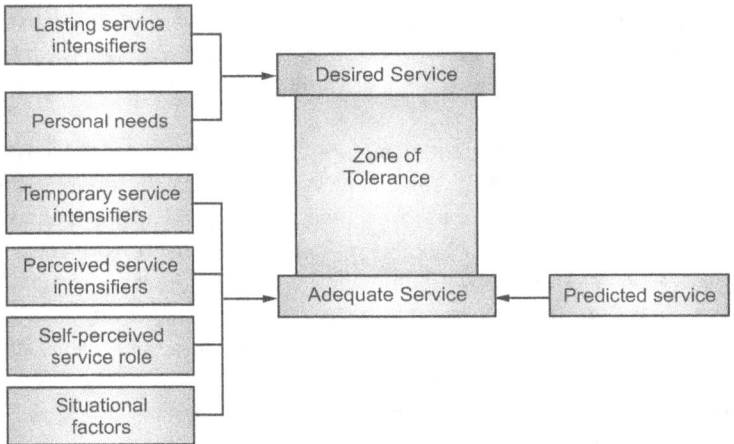

Fig. 1.5

1. **Temporary Service Intensifiers**: In temporary service intensifiers, there are individual and short-term factors that arise out of the needs for service amongst people. For example, when there is an accident, or when there is a need for car insurance or when there is a breakdown of computer systems during the peak hours of the day, then the level of adequate service expectations rises automatically. Level of responsiveness and problems with the first time service may also increase the expectations of adequate service. For example, when the service fails for the first time, then there are even higher hopes and restlessness for the second time of service. Thus, in such cases of temporary service intensifiers, there is an increase in the levels of adequate service and even the tolerance zone will narrow down.

2. **Perceived Service Alternatives**: Perceived service alternatives are the other available options that a customer can consider when in need. If there are multiple options to choose from for quality service or when a person can work for himself then they have high expectations for quality and adequate service. However, when a person does not have much option in the market to choose from, then he will not complain much and will adjust to any kind of service available for the moment. For example, a person who is staying in a small town with a nearby airport option will consider only that option as compared to a person who is from a big city and thus have multiple options to choose from.

   In this, when options are available the expectations for quality and adequate service increases and even the tolerance level zeroes down. Thus, it is very important for the marketers to understand the available options and why people will prefer them than theirs. Accordingly, they will be able to justify their services by fulfilling the demands of the customers within the expected time period.

3. **Customer's Self-Perceived Service Role**: This is a third factor, wherein a customer himself decides the adequacy level of service. If he is highly involved in the service process then his expectations also increase and gets dissatisfied if the service does not meet his expectations. Whereas, if the customer is not much involved in the service process and leaves the entire case to the service providers then his expectations will remain low and he will be mostly happy and satisfied with what he gets.

   In other words, expectations of a customer are partly shaped by how well they believe that their personal involvement is equally important. For example, when a customer in a restaurant makes special orders about how he wants his steak to be cooked then there are high chances of his dissatisfaction when it does actually turn up the way he desired. On the other hand, when a customer simply orders for what he wants and does not actually get involved as to how it is to be cooked, then his expectation levels also decreases and he will be happy the way it will be as he didn't give any special orders to cook the same.

   A customer usually takes up the responsibility of complaining if the service is poor and this factor decides the adequate levels of service. Similarly, a person who is very particular about the regular servicing of his vehicle will have high expectations from the manufacturer if anything goes wrong, whereas a person who does not follow the servicing schedule of the vehicle may not even voice his opinion or concern when things go wrong with it. Thus, a dissatisfied customer who always complains will be less tolerant as compared to the one who does not bother much about the minute details.

   Customers' tolerance zone will expand when they realise that they are not being fully responsible in the service process and not doing their part well, whereas, the tolerance zone will contract when a customer is justifying his role in the entire process. For example, when a customer says that the vehicle servicing staff does not listen to him completely which affects the work, will make a list of handwritten notes of the things to be done. By doing this, they believe that the staff will act responsibly and thus their expectation level increases as compared to the one who didn't take the same measures.

4. **Situational Factors**: Situational factors are temporary and short-term emergencies due to which a customer believes and accepts that the service quality may not be adequate as it is out of the employee's control. For example, during catastrophes (floods or storms) that affect a large number of people at the same time, the pressure on the insurance company increases which frames a picture in people's minds that the adequacy service levels drops down due to the overcrowded demand.

Customers realise that it is not the company's fault but the natural emergencies which leads to delayed or low quality service and hence they will automatically lower their expectation levels. In general, when the expectation levels are lowered down the tolerance levels increase simultaneously.

5. **Predicted Service**: In predicted service, a customer predicts as to what kind of service he will get and thus his expectation levels fluctuate accordingly. For example, a customer will expect poor service from the no-frill airlines as compared to the full-cost airlines. Thus, he predicts the situation and is mentally prepared to receive poor service. Similarly, during festival times, a customer is mentally prepared that the call centre of mobile phone companies will render poor service at the said time as compared to the other regular days. This is because during the festival times, a lot of people are setting in their new services for mobiles which they have received as gifts.

Thus, in such cases the tolerance zone widens and the level of adequate service also decreases.

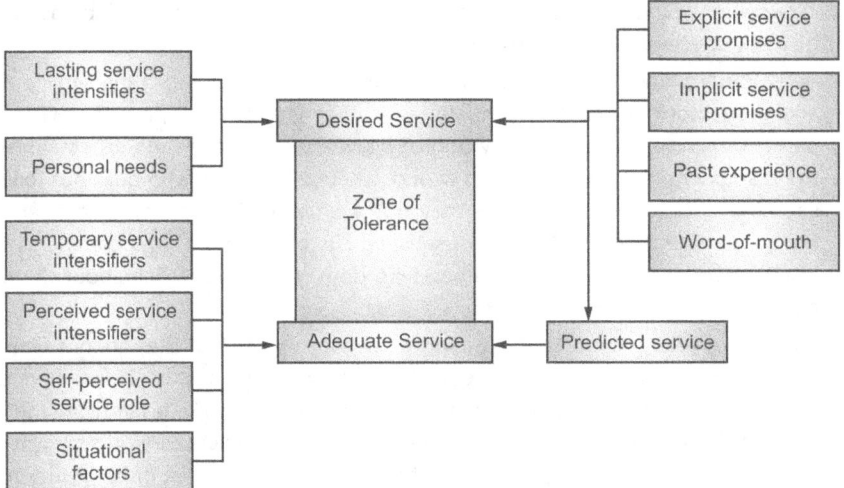

Fig. 1.6

(C) Sources of both Desired and Predicted Service Expectations:

Considering the above illustration, it highlights a group of four factors on the right-hand side that influence both the desired as well as predicted service expectations. They have been explained below:

    (i) **Explicit Service Performances**: An organisation advertises and promises a lot by making face-to-face and indirect statements to their customers. Face-to-face statements are the ones that act as personal communication with customers like a salesperson or a help-desk or a receptionist of the company giving out information.

Indirect promises are non-personal communications with customers like TV advertisements, newspaper articles, mass media and public speech. It is obvious, that the statements made by the organisation, whether personal or non-personal, is surely under their control. These explicit service promises made by the organisations actually influence the desired service expectations in customers.

Many a times, organisations make big promises in public but fail in fulfilling them. Explicit service promises influence both the levels of desired service as well as the predicted service thus also influencing the adequate service level expectations.

(ii) **Implicit Service Performances**: Various service related cues like price of the product decides the expectation levels about the quality of its services. Many a times, people believe that higher the price of the product or service better will be the quality of the same. Thus, they relate such factors to each other which form a base for driving the desired service level.

(iii) **Word-of-Mouth Communications**: People believe a lot in taking feedbacks from others before buying anything. Thus references and word-of-mouth communications amongst buyers influences the expected service levels to a great extent.

(iv) **Past Experience**: Past experience of buyers also majorly influences the desired and predicted service levels. This is a form of direct comparison which a buyer makes with his past experience if he has received poor services. For example, if a patient has had a bad experience with some medical practitioner then he may have low desires and can predict his future visit based on the last one.

1.5 Moment of Truth: Service Encounters

1.5.1 Introduction

Once the customer purchases a product, he automatically gets connected with the company. He gets a couple of contact people from the company with whom the customer can talk to regarding any queries or suggestions. Right from filling up the form, submitting the application and purchasing the goods, there are multiple employees who service the customer. These are known as service encounters which may take place in various forms like indirect encounter, telephonic encounter and face-to-face encounters. Since technology is fast booming, most of the companies do prefer telephonic or indirect encounters wherein they can give quick service to the customers.

Service environments speak a lot about the quality of service being provided by the company. Since it has all the tangible characteristics like furnishings, noise, interiors, exteriors, odour and cleanliness, a customer can very well relate to the quality based on the above mentioned elements. Moreover, depending on these elements customers also start framing their expectations and hopes accordingly.

Service personnel are employees of the company who matter equally throughout the process. The way they behave with their customers, their body language, knowledge and appearance make a lot of difference both to the company as well as the customers. Mistakes and faulty services do happen, however, how the employee handles the situation will actually decide its customer retention. If the employee remains in constant touch with the customers, listens to him patiently and works on the given feedback then the customer will surely feel confident and important. Moreover, based on the above mentioned factors, even the customers start expecting quality service and treatment from the responsible employees.

Support services are the ones which are made for supporting the services being provided to the customers. They include the equipments, materials and all the backstage process which forms the backbone for these front stage employees to function smoothly and efficiently. This part of service encounter is very important because without them, employees won't be able to provide quality service to the customers which will result in losing them completely.

Other Customers

For a customer, feedback and reaction of other customers is very important while making any purchase decisions. Thus, people always look for a feedback from others before buying anything or signing for any service provider. This forms a mental belief amongst all the buyers that if everyone is buying one thing then there is something really good about it.

Thus, places like restaurants, cinema halls, medical clinics, transport service providers and others must pull in a good crowd and maintain the same so that every customer believes that it is worth the cost. Similarly, when a customer behaves badly, even the other customer gets affected thinking that the services or the products are not good. So basically the situation is that one customer leads to the other and thus it is very important to give quality service to everyone as every customer is important!

1.5.2 Types of Service Encounter

All service firms have their own unique way of delivering services to their customers. However, one basic thing that remains common for all is an encounter of delivering services. There are three types of encounters for service delivery, as mentioned below:

(a) **Remote Encounters**: In today's fast paced age, the growing technology has added a lot of boon to the service sectors. It has made remote encounters possible with the customers, which means that companies can sell their products and services remotely to their customers without even meeting them face-to-face. This is possible due to high-end technology like an ATM machine where interaction is happening between a customer and a bank without any person being physically present for the same. Similarly, railway tickets, air tickets, money transfers, movie tickets and much more can be generated online without personally getting in touch with any of the employees of the company.

Firms try to encounter customers remotely by sending brochures, leaflets and e-mails. These types of encounters are easier to manage and control because everything is process-oriented based on the latest technology. Thus, any services and faults can be tested and corrected for efficient performance. This also helps in maintaining the right quality throughout.

(b) Phone Encounter or Indirect Personal: Phone encounters also known as indirect personal encounter is fast gaining popularity in the service field. In this, there is a contact between two people, not face-to-face but over the phone. Many companies and service providers prefer this type of an encounter with their customers because of its various benefits like easy availability, quick service, low cost, personal interaction and more. For example, insurance companies, banks, information bureaus, matrimonial services, friendship firms and others always make use of telephone encounters while dealing with their customers.

Apart from the service providers, even the customers prefer this type as it offers quick service to them. Since they can actually talk to the authorised person, they feel confident in the quality of the service being provided to them. Thus, even though there is no face-to-face interaction with the firm, the customer can still form an impression about the quality of the services rendered. It is very important for the employees to understand the importance of this encounter. Various factors like employee knowledge, their voice tone, efficiency and effectiveness in handling customer's queries can actually speak a lot about the company and its services. Thus, phone encounter has its own benefits where the service provider can make a lasting impression on the customers mind by dealing with them in the right way.

(c) Direct Face-to-Face: This type of encounter facilitates direct and personal interaction between the customers and the service providers. For example, beauty parlours, amusement parks, hospitals, educational institutions and more facilitate direct interaction between the two parties.

Like other types of encounters, even this one has its own pros and cons to it. Due to the personal interaction with the customers, employees have to be really careful of their body language, facial expressions and attitude. Since employees act as the face of the company they speak volumes about the quality and service that their company renders and customers can easily make it out. Thus, they should always be humble and best behaved with the customers to create confidence in their minds. Even if there is a fault in providing services to the customers, a polite and well behaved employee can still retain the customer in his own ways. Listening patiently to them is very important here since the customers will speak their heart out during a personal conversation. This can save the company from losing its loyal customers due to some minor faults.

It also has its own complications wherein, lack of knowledge about the service, can actually ruin the relations between the customers and the company. Thus, employee should always be updated with the latest knowhow about his company and its services. Regular training and counselling must be provided to the employees to polish their soft skills and behavioural attitude.

1.5.3 Factors Leading to Satisfaction or Dissatisfaction in Service Encounters

It is the quality of the service that creates a satisfied or an unsatisfied customer. If the quality of the product is good then there are many happy and satisfied customers; however if the quality falls then these happy customers immediately turn into the most unsatisfied ones. Following are the points that can influence customer perceptions about the services of the company:

(a) Recovery: Service failures do happen and it is important on a company's part to listen to the customers patiently. This is called the recovery process where the mistake is done, but now the company has to concentrate on creating its image back on the customer's mind. Thus, working closely with the customers by implementing their suggestions can help the company regain its original image and quality of service.

(b) Adaptability: Sellers must be adaptable in nature to work with the changing needs of the customers. Right from the retailers to the wholesalers and the manufacturers, everyone has to work backwards to produce a desired service that matches up with the requirements of the customers. It is the flexible service delivery system that helps the employees of the service.

(c) Spontaneity: Sellers must maintain spontaneity while rendering their services. If they behave well with the customers during the start but at a later stage they disrespect them in any way, then the customers start losing interest in their services. Thus, sellers have to be spontaneous enough with all their customers throughout the dealing process in order to maintain long lasting and healthy relationships.

(d) Coping: It is important for the employees to cope up with stressful situations with ease and respect. There will be problems with the customers; however, employees should know how to deal with them successfully in a peaceful manner without hurting anyone's sentiments.

1.6 Services Marketing

Services marketing refer to the marketing of services as against tangible products. Services are inherently intangible, are consumed simultaneously at the time of their production, cannot be stored, saved or resold once they have been used. Service offerings are unique and cannot be exactly repeated even by the same service provider.

Services marketing typically refer to both business to consumer (B2C) and business to business (B2B) services, and include marketing of services like telecommunications services, financial services, all types of hospitality services, car rental services, air travel, health care services and professional services. The range of approaches and expressions of a marketing idea developed with the hope that it will be effective in conveying the ideas to the diverse population who receive it is, in short, the gist of it.

1.6.1 Importance of Services Marketing

As service is an intangible product, its marketing becomes a difficult task. However, the marketing of such intangible services is extremely important in order to sustain and survive in the market. Following points are listed, to explain the importance of services marketing:

(a) **A Key Differentiator**: Most of the consumers consider the services as an important element in order to judge the product or a service. For example, Dominos and Pizza Hut are known to sell similar products in the market; however the service that they provide to their customers matter a lot. Since there is not much difference in the product of the above mentioned two brands, at such times their services create an impact on the customer's mind. Hence, "service" is defined as a key differentiator where a company can provide excellent customer services to retain their old customers and to attract new ones.

(b) **Importance of Relationship:** Since service is an intangible product, customers will be able to buy such services based on mutual trust and confidence in the seller. Hence, it is important for the seller to maintain good relationships with the customers by listening to their needs properly and delivering exactly what they want. Hence, relationship is considered very important in a service sector, which will help the seller to retain loyal customers and also attract the new ones.

(c) **Customer Retention**: In today's highly competitive environment, it is very important to retain old customers than to attract new ones. This is because there are a lot of sellers trying to catch from the same pool of buyers. Thus, sellers must concentrate on retaining the customers by fulfilling their changing needs. They must promote feedback amongst customers and must work on the given feedback in order to match up to their wants. This way they will be able to retain their loyal customers by offering increasing satisfaction.

(d) **Multiple Touch Points**: Service sector does not provide any tangible services to the customers. Thus customers have to depend on intangible services like talking to many people about the services before buying the same. This creates a perception in the customer's mind whether to go ahead with the purchase or not. These multiple touch points are important to motivate the customers to trust them and make the purchases.

(e) Services Proliferate: Since it is a challenge to market the intangible services to the customers, marketers should find various ways and means to market the product in such a way that it stands out from the rest of the crowd. They should invent various ways to communicate the benefits of the services to the customers in such a language which they find easy to reflect to their needs and value.

(f) Feedback Improves Services: Since it is difficult to match up the marketing concepts of the service sector with the needs of the customers, sellers must work on the feedback given by the customers. These feedbacks are genuine suggestions and tips given by the customers and if the seller works on the same, it will help him to match up with the changing needs and desires of the customers. Sellers must cultivate the habit of collecting regular feedbacks from the customers and working on the same.

(g) Technology Impacts: Technology is a big boon for the service sectors. People like to collect information on the services before actually purchasing them. Thus, internet plays a very important role here to flash the required details of the services so that customers can directly visit the website for details and this will also prevent them from talking to many other people. Service sellers must take full advantage of the growing technology and reach out to maximum customers with the required knowledge and quality.

1.6.2 Service Marketing Mix

In today's competitive environment, organisations are trying their best to succeed and sustain in the market. They are busy innovating ways and means to increase the quality of the service which will make them stand out from the crowd. Many organisations consider their employees as a part of the service process. Employees are known as the face of the company and thus their satisfaction and efficiency will directly impact the quality of the service being offered in the market. It is important to control and maintain the good behaviour of the employees so that they can put in their heart and soul into the services rendered.

Based on the above mentioned information, Bernard H. Booms and Mary J. Bitner worked together in developing the traditional familiar marketing mix, in the year 1981. An American professor of marketing named Jerome McCarthy has developed the traditional marketing mix; however Booms and Bitner added the extension to the same thus making it as the 7 Ps of the marketing mix. This service marketing mix is also known as the 7 Ps model. This extension of further 3 Ps to the already existing ones helps in the useful application of the same to the knowledge intensive environments and service companies.

The initial four Ps of the marketing mix are meant for the product industry whereas the extended version of it is meant for the service sectors in the market. People, process and physical evidence are known as the extended elements of the marketing mix to the traditional one. Since, service is an intangible product and has unique characteristics like heterogeneity, intangibility, perishability and inseparability, the new elements of the marketing mix were closely worked upon to match the service sectors in a valuable manner.

The service marketing mix depends upon either of the elements or may be a mixture of all to match the service sectors. Though the initial four elements of marketing mix were meant for the product-oriented industry and the recent three elements are meant for the service-oriented industry; however, depending upon the positioning of the product/service, any elements can be utilised for the same. These elements are basically useful to communicate the brand and organisational message to its customers. Hence, it is totally a company's call as to how and which elements of the marketing mix should be utilised to serve the above mentioned purpose successfully.

Some Facts about Services Marketing Mix
- Concept marketing mix was first coined by Neil Borden in his article in 1962.
- Company marketing mix as the basis of designing strategy of sketching marketing plan.
- Traditionally: Product, Price, Place and Promotion are 4 elements of a mix.
- An organisation should analyse, which element is important at a given point of time. (Hotels focus on promotion during peak demand and on pricing in off season)
- Four Ps fall short while designing marketing strategy for services, three more Ps: People, Process and Physical evidence have been added.

1.6.2.1 Traditional Marketing Mix

One of the most basic concepts in marketing is the marketing mix elements by which an organisation controls, satisfies or communicates with customers. The traditional marketing mix is composed of the four Ps: Product, Price, Place and Promotion. These elements are the core decision variables in any marketing plan. The notion of a mix implies that all of the variables are interrelated and depend on each other to some extent. Further, the marketing mix implies that there is an optimal mix of the four factors for a given market segment at any given point in time.

Careful management of the 4 Ps will, clearly, also be essential to the successful marketing of services. However, the strategies for the four Ps require some modifications when applied to services. For example, traditionally promotion is thought of as involving decisions related to sales, advertising, sales promotions, and publicity. In services, these factors are also important, but because services are produced and consumed simultaneously, service delivery people like delivery boys, clerks, conductors, doctors, cleaners, are involved in promotion of the service, even if their jobs are being carried out in terms of the operational function they perform. Pricing also becomes very complex in services where unit costs need to be calculated, prices may be difficult to determine, and where the customer frequently uses price as a cue to quality.

- **(a) Products:** Products are the means by which firms seek to satisfy consumer needs. A product in this sense is anything which the firm offers to potential customers, whether it is tangible or intangible. After initial hesitation, most marketers talk about an intangible service as a product. Thus bank accounts, insurance policies and holidays are frequently referred to as products including stars and politicians as even they are referred to as a product to be marketed. Product mix decisions facing a services marketer can be very different from those dealing with goods. Fundamentally pure services can only be defined using process descriptions rather than tangible descriptions of outcomes. Quality becomes a key element defining a product. Other elements of the product mix such as design, reliability, brand image, and product range may sound familiar to a goods marketer. There is a significant difference with goods wherein new service developments cannot be protected by patent.

- **(b) Price:** Price mix decisions include strategic and tactical decisions about the average level of prices to be charged, discount structures, terms of payment and the extent to which price discrimination between different groups of customers is to take place. Differences do however occur where the intangible nature of a service can mean that price in itself can become a very significant indicator of quality. The personal and non-transferable nature of many services presents additional opportunities for price discrimination within service markets, while the fact that many services are marketed by the public sector at a subsidised or no price can complicate price setting.

- **(c) Promotion:** The traditional promotion mix includes various methods of communicating the benefits of a service to potential consumers. The mix has been traditionally consisting of advertising, sales promotion, personal selling and public relations. The promotion of services often needs to place particular emphasis on increasing the apparent tangibility of a service. Also, in the case of services marketing, production personnel can themselves become an important element of the promotion mix.

- **(d) Place:** Place refers to the ease of access which potential customers have to a service. Place decisions can involve physical location, decisions about which intermediaries to use in making a service accessible to a consumer and non-location-decisions which are used to make services available. For pure services, decisions about how to physically move a good are of little strategic relevance. However, most services involve movement of goods of some form. These can either be materials necessary to produce a service or the service itself as its whole purpose is the movement of goods.

1.6.2.2 Extended Marketing Mix

Because services are usually produced and consumed simultaneously, customers are often present in the firm's location, interact directly with the firm's personnel and are actually part of the service production process. As services are intangible, customers will often be looking for any tangible cue to help them understand the nature of the service experience. These facts have led marketers to conclude that they can use additional variables to communicate with and satisfy their customers. For e.g. in banks the design, layout and decor of the branch as well as the appearance and attitudes of its employees will influence customer perceptions and experiences.

Acknowledgment of the importance of these additional variables has led services marketers to adopt the concept of an expanded marketing mix for services to include Process, Physical evidence and People.

(a) **People:** For most services, people are a vital element of the marketing mix. All of the participants who play a part in service delivery influence the buyer's perceptions, namely, the firm's personnel, the customer and other customers in the service environment.

The participants in the delivery of a service provide clues to the customer regarding the nature of the service itself. How these people are dressed, their personal appearance, and their attitudes and behaviours all influence the customer's perceptions of the service. Gummeson calls everyone **'part-time marketer',** in that their actions have a direct effect on the output received by customers. In fact for services like consulting, counselling, training, teaching and other professional relationship based services, the provider is the service. In other cases, the contact person plays what appears to be a relatively small part in service delivery like a courier delivery boy. Even these providers may be the focal point of service encounters that can prove critical for the firm.

In many service situations, customers themselves can also influence service delivery thus affecting service quality and their own satisfaction. In case of weight loss customers, it greatly affects the quality of service they receive when they either comply or don't comply with health regimens prescribed by the service provider.

Customers not only influence their own service outcomes, but they can influence other customers as well. In a classroom, customers' students influence the quality of service received by others – either enhancing or detracting from other customers' experiences.

People management in improving the quality of people planning, assumes greater importance within the service sector. This is especially true for those services where staff have a high level of contact with customers. For this reason, it is therefore essential that services firms clearly specify what is expected from personnel in their interaction with customers. To achieve these specified standards, methods of recruiting, training, motivating and rewarding staff are not personnel decisions but they are important marketing mix decisions. People planning within the marketing mix also involves developing a pattern of interaction between customers themselves, which can be very important where service consumption takes place in public. An important way in which a corporate executive will judge a club might be the kind of people who frequently visit it. An empty club may convey no atmosphere while a bubbly one may convey that this is just the place. Marketers must also develop strategies for producing favourable interaction between its customers; for example by excluding certain groups and developing a physical environment which affects customers' behaviour.

Given the strong influence they can have on service quality and service delivery employees, the customer and other customers are included within the people element of the services marketing mix.

(b) Physical Evidence: The intangible nature of a service means that customers are unable to judge a service before it is consumed, increasing the risk inherent in a purchase decision. An important element of marketing planning is therefore to reduce this level of risk by offering tangible evidence of the nature of the service. At its simplest, a brochure can describe and give pictures of important elements of the service product: a pictorial evidence of students, faculty, and infrastructure, in which the service is delivered and where the firm and students interact, and any tangible components that facilitate performance or communication of the service. The physical evidence of service includes all of the tangible representations of the service such as letterheads, business cards, report formats, signage etc.

In some cases it includes the physical facility where the service is offered e.g. the retail bank branch facility while in telecommunication services; the physical facility may be irrelevant. In case of repairs, tangibles such as billing statements and appearance of the car after repair may be important indicators of quality.

Since consumers have little knowledge on how to judge the actual quality of service, they will rely on these cues or they rely on the cues provided by the people and the service process.

A clean and bright environment used in a service outlet can help reassure potential customers at the point where they make a service purchase decision. Hence, fast food and photo processing outlets use red and yellow colour schemes to convey an image of speedy service.

Physical evidence cues provide excellent opportunities for the firm to send consistent and strong messages regarding the organisation's purpose, the intended market segments and the nature of the service.

(c) Process: The actual procedures, mechanisms, and flow of activities by which the service is delivered comprise the service delivery and operating systems. The actual delivery steps up the customer experiences or the operational flow of the service will also provide customers with evidence on which to judge the service.

Some services are very complex, requiring the customer to follow a complicated and extensive series of actions to complete the process.

Highly bureaucratised services frequently follow this pattern, and the logic of the steps involved often escapes the customer. Another distinguishing characteristic of the process that can provide evidence to the customer is whether the service follows a production line, standardised approach or whether the process is an empowered or customised one. None of these characteristics of the service is inherently better or worse than another but these process characteristics are another form of evidence used by the consumer to judge service.

Processes are often of critical concern to consumers of high contact services where the consumers can be seen as a co-producer of the service. A customer of a fast food joint is affected by the manner by which the staff serves them and the amount of waiting which is involved during the production process. The boundary between the producer and consumer in terms of the production functions like customers to collect their meal from a counter, or to deposit their own rubbish; it is not specific and varies as per service provider. Hence, with services, a clear distinction cannot be made between marketing and operations management.

Within the service sector, customer service is the total quality of the service as perceived by the customer. This element of the marketing mix cannot be isolated within a narrowly defined customer services department, but becomes a concern of all production personnel, for both those directly employed by the organisation and those employed by suppliers. Managing the quality of the service offered to the customer becomes closely identified with policy on the related marketing mix, elements of product design and personnel.

Expanded Marketing Mix For Services			
Product	**Place**	**Promotion**	**Price**
Product	Outlet Location	Advertising	Flexibility
Range	Accessibility	Personal selling	Level
Features	Channels	Sales promotion	Payment terms
Quality level	Coverage	Publicity	Differentiation
Accessories	Transportation	Public relations	Discounts
Warranties	Storage		Allowances
Branding	Managing channels		Quality/price
Service line			
After sales service			
People	**Physical Evidence**	**Process**	
Employees	**External**	Policies	
Recruitment	Signage	Procedures	
Training	Parking	Mechanisation	
Motivation	Environment	Employee discretion	
Reward	Location	Customer involvement	
Team work	Noise level		
Appearance	Clean, cool air	Customer direction	
Interpersonal behaviour	Facilitating goods	Flow of activities	
	Tangible clues		
Customer contact	Brochure		
	Documents		
	Notices for dues		
	Statements		
	Reports		
Customers			
Education			
Training			

(**Source:** Derived from Booms, B. H. and Bitner, M. J. Marketing Strategies and Organisation Structures for Service Firms')

Expanded Marketing Mix For Services		
7 Ps of Services Marketing		**Measurement**
1. Product 2. Price 3. Promotion 4. Place	5. People 6. Physical evidence 7. Process	Quality Customers' satisfaction Loyalty Profitability
	Service Characteristics Control	
Intangibility Inconsistency	Inseparability Inventory	Ownership

To use this screen, just mark the area where problems exist in a service firm, formulate a plan and then action the activities to ensure resolution. This screen is useful to solve case studies and monitor the operations of the service firm.

1.6.2.3 Need for Additional Three Marketing Mix Elements in Service

The concept of marketing mix is not actually based on any type of a theory; in fact it is based on the requirement of the marketing managers to put down their decision-making process into some valuable and productive actions. The familiar 4Ps of marketing mix that is the product, price, promotion and place is known to put limitations when it comes to applying these concepts in services. Hence, the need was identified to expand the concepts of marketing mix in order to assist valuable utilisation of the same. Following are a couple of problems that were limiting the usefulness of the familiar 4Ps into services:

- At first, the concept of old marketing mix was initiated to define the manufacturing sectors. Thus, this concept suited well only to this sector where the product is tangible. However, with the growth of services sector, the usage of these concepts became practically difficult as service is an intangible product. Thus, the usage of place and product were the most inappropriate Ps from the old marketing mix.
- Another reason was that there is a vast difference between service products and physical goods. This difference was not allowing the old marketing concepts and models to match up with the changing needs of the service sectors. Hence, this created a need for separate marketing models and concepts which will also concentrate on the service sector needs.
- The marketing managers of the service sectors found it difficult to match up their needs with the old marketing mix. The basic characteristics of physical goods and service goods did not match with each other at any level. This was creating ample problems in proceeding ahead with the concepts of service sector in terms of marketing mix. Thus, the need of these marketing managers gave development to the extension of the marketing mix to match up to their needs.

The above mentioned points, gave enough reasons to concentrate on the growth and development of the marketing mix especially for the service sector. Since service sector is meant for providing services to satisfy the customer's needs, it demands for add on concepts to the familiar 4Ps of the marketing mix. Thus, "people" and "processes" were developed as the 5th and 6th Ps of the marketing mix. Booms and Bitner went on further to add "physical evidence" as the 7th P of the marketing mix. And finally, today, professor Lovelock has been successful to give the latest addition of "productivity" as the 8th P of the marketing mix.

These additional Ps along with the familiar old 4Ps are also known as the **Augmented or Extended Marketing Mix**. The importance of each of these elements in the marketing mix will vary as per the product and the service. Decisions for the product or service sectors can be made either by referring to any one element or a blend of them in order to achieve successful product positioning in the market. For example, the element of "people" will be considered less important in case of a highly automated service like vending machine dispensing. However, the same element will be considered important in case of a people-intensive business like a restaurant.

Points to Remember

- Services marketing concepts and strategies have developed in response to the tremendous growth of service industries. The economic importance of services can be seen by the fact that trade in services is growing worldwide.
- The services literature highlights differences in the nature of services versus products which are believed to create special challenges for services marketers and for consumers buying services. To help understand these differences a number of characteristics that describe the unique nature of services have been proposed.
- Service products are mostly intangible but are marketed with tangible evidence. This is referred to as **tangibilising the intangibles**. While services often are accompanied with physical evidence that enables the consumer to make the product less abstract and more tangible, there will always be an intangible element to the service product.
- Inseparability has a number of important marketing implications for services. Firstly, whereas goods are generally first produced, then offered for sale and finally sold and consumed, inseparability causes the process to be different for services.
- The perishability of services describes the real time nature of the product. Unlike goods, the consumer cannot store the service and the absence of the ability to build and maintain stocks of the product means that sudden demands cannot be accommodated as it can be done in case of goods.
- **Ownership** is another distinguishing feature of service. The inability to own a service is related to the characteristics of intangibility and perishability. In case of service, when it is performed, no ownership is transferred from buyer to seller.
- For marketing professionals, it is very important to understand the customer's behaviour. If employees fail to understand this, then they never create and deliver quality services that result in happy and loyal customers.

- While purchasing any goods or services, customers actually go through a complex purchase process. This process has three major stages known as the pre-experience evaluation, consumer experience and post-evaluation experience.
- Due to the various choices available in the market and the credence qualities of goods, it is difficult to make out what decision-making process does a customer go through. It is actually a customer's experience that influences his future purchasing needs and choices. Experience plays an important role in defining the decision-making process of the customers.
- Service providers understand the importance of customer behaviour and act accordingly. They try to fulfil each and every want of a customer by rendering quality and satisfactory services.
- Customer's expectations embrace several elements which are desired service, adequate service, predicted service and tolerance zone which falls between the desired service and the adequate service. Every customer is different and they have different types of expectations from the service providers.
- All service firms have their own unique way of delivering services to their customers. However, one basic thing that remains common for all is an encounter of delivering services.
- It is the quality of the service that creates a satisfied or an unsatisfied customer. If the quality of the product is good then there are many happy and satisfied customers; however if the quality falls then these happy customers immediately turn into the most unsatisfied ones.
- This service marketing mix is also known as the 7 Ps model. This extension of further 3 Ps to the already existing ones helps in useful application of the same to the knowledge intensive environments and service companies.
- The concept of marketing mix is not actually based on any type of a theory; in fact it is based on the requirement of the marketing managers to put down their decision-making process into some valuable and productive actions. The familiar 4 Ps of marketing mix that is the product, price, promotion and place is known to put limitations when it comes to applying these concepts in services. Hence, the need was identified to expand the concepts of marketing mix in order to assist valuable utilisation of the same.

Questions for Discussion

1. Define and explain the term 'Services'. State the broad classification of services.
2. Explain the various characteristics of services.
3. Describe the various important services.
4. Describe the importance of services marketing.

5. What do understand by search, experience and credence attributes of services?
6. Discuss the stages of consumer decision-making process and explain in detail pre and post evaluation experience.
7. Describe the factors influencing consumer expectations and perceptions.
8. What is moment of truth?
9. Explain the extended marketing mix.
10. Give reasons for additional three marketing mix elements in services.
11. Explain the financial and economic impact of service.

Multiple Choice Questions

1. Distinct characteristic of services is _____.
   - (a) intangibility
   - (b) inseparability
   - (c) variability
   - (d) perishability, inconsistency
2. Services are typically produced and consumed simultaneously. This is an example of the _____ characteristic of serices.
   - (a) intangibility
   - (b) variability
   - (c) inseparability
   - (d) simultaneously
   - (d) perishability
3. Services cannot be stored. This describes the ____ characteristic of services.
   - (a) intangibility
   - (b) variability
   - (c) inseparability
   - (d) inconsistency
   - (d) perishability
4. _____ describes the employees skills in serving the client.
   - (a) Internal marketing
   - (b) External marketing
   - (c) Relationship marketing
   - (d) Interactive marketing
   - (d) Communication marketing
5. SSTS refers to ____.
   - (a) service standards testing
   - (b) self-service technologies
   - (c) standard service technologies
   - (d) self-service treatments
6. Top firms audit service performance by collecting ____ measurements to probe customer satisfiers and dissatisfiers.
   - (a) customer satisfier
   - (b) customer complaint
   - (c) voice of the customer
   - (d) psychological

7. The services a customer expects are called the ____ service package.
   (a) expected
   (b) augmented
   (c) primary
   (d) secondary
   (f) perceived

8. Added features to an offering are called ____ service features.
   (a) expected
   (b) augmented
   (c) primary
   (d) secondary
   (f) perceived

9. The intangibility of services has implications for the choice of ____.
   (a) brand elements
   (b) location
   (c) price
   (d) product features
   (d) channels of distribution

10. ____ cost refers to the product's purchase cost plus the discounted cost of maintenance and repair less the discounted salvage value.
    (a) Total
    (b) Variable
    (c) Life cycle
    (d) Net
    (d) Out-of-pocket

11. According to Parasuraman, Zeithaml & Benny, the most important determinant of service quality is:
    (a) responsiveness
    (b) reliability
    (c) assurance
    (d) empathy
    (d) tangibles

Answers

1. (a)	2. (c)	3. (d)	4. (d)	5. (b)	6. (c)	7. (c)	8. (d)	9. (a)	10. (c)
11. (b)									

Project Questions

1. Imagine you are the owner of a new service business. What is your service? What are some of the most important considerations in developing the service, training salespeople, and communicating about your service to potential customers?

2. The characteristics of services affect the development of marketing mixes for services. Choose a specific service and explain how each marketing mix element could be affected by these service characteristics.

■■■

Chapter 2...

Traditional Marketing Mix Elements in Services

Contents ...

2.1 Service Product
    2.1.1 Customer Perception, Customer Satisfaction and Service Quality
    2.1.2 Customer Perception of Services
    2.1.3 Customer Satisfaction
    2.1.4 Tolerance Zone
    2.1.5 Service Quality
    2.1.6 Customer Loyalty
    2.1.7 Service Recovery
    2.1.8 Customer Complaint
2.2 Service Pricing
    2.2.1 Approaches to Pricing Services
    2.2.2 Pricing Strategies
    2.2.3 Costs of Service Delivery
    2.2.4 Customer Profitability Measurement
    2.2.5 Revenue Management
    2.2.6 Segmented Pricing
    2.2.7 Price Discrimination
2.3 Service Place
    2.3.1 Delivering Services through Intermediaries
    2.3.2 Delivering Services through Electronic Channel
2.4 Service Promotion
    2.4.1 Objectives of Service Promotion
    2.4.2 Role of Marketing Communications
    2.4.3 Marketing Communications Planning
    2.4.4 Integrated Services Marketing Communication
    2.4.5 Referrals: Using Power of Word of Mouth
    2.4.6 Visual Merchandising
    2.4.7 Challenges of Service Communication
- Points to Remember
- Questions for Discussion
- Multiple Choice Questions
- Project Questions

Learning Objectives ...

- To understand the concept of traditional marketing mix elements in services.
- To identify the relationship between customer perception, customer satisfaction and service quality.
- To discuss the steps involved in servqual, gap, and critical incident model.
- To describe the process of creating customer loyalty programme.
- To understand the nature of complaining behaviour and handling customer complaints.
- To explain the service recovery process.

2.1 Service Product

A service cannot be touched, verified, photographed or tried out. It is an intangible product. A service product is a bundle of features and customer benefits. It is very difficult to describe what a service product is.

According to **Lynn Shostack**, there are four risks of attempting to describe services in words alone:

(i) over simplification

(ii) incompleteness

(iii) subjectivity (based on personal experience and exposure)

(iv) biased interpretation.

It often becomes difficult to translate customer experience into words. Differences in attitudes, exposure and ability to participate and perceive make the consumers subjective and biased while describing a service. After a customer sees a movie, he will not be able to relate the minute by minute movement in detail. While designing the product, service organisations have to consider these four risks which influence both the customers and the service providers. It is very difficult to produce good quality products, unless the employees of the organisation as well as the customers understand the service product properly. Processes, people, and experiences along with outputs and benefits have to be thought while designing new services.

2.1.1 Customer Perception, Customer Satisfaction and Service Quality

Often to know the customer's point of view, companies carry out customer surveys and using these surveys, improvements are made to achieve the competitive position of the firm which gives better offerings and better customer service. Services are distributed regionally, nationally, and globally and are earning a larger portion of an organisations' revenues and the quality of their services plays a very important role in customer satisfaction, with the growth in the size of the service sector of the global economy. Businesses compete to satisfy customers and economic prosperity is based on increase in customer satisfaction, according to a market economy. The suppliers compete for shoppers, but shoppers do not fight for products. Customer satisfaction is divided into three determinants:

- perceived service quality
- perceived value
- customer expectations

Perceived service quality is expected to have a direct and positive influence on customer satisfaction. The standard against performance outcomes is the concept of expectations, hence if the consumer's actual outcomes go beyond the expectations, the customer is considered to be satisfied, else if expectations shoot above the outcomes, the consumer will be dissatisfied. Service providers are laying more emphasis on service quality to achieve market leadership, due to the intense competition in the service sector. The customer value is high when the perceived quality is more than the perceived costs; but if cost is more than quality, then customer value is low. If price will be high, the satisfaction with price will be high. If there are no hidden costs and if prices do not change unexpectedly customers will perceive high price reliability. Hence, measurement of perceived value (i.e. price to quality ratio) is very important. This concept is also known as **price-quality ratio**.

The perceived value both directly and indirectly influences customer satisfaction which is an important factor for customer satisfaction. In some industries quality may have a significant positive relationship on customer satisfaction which may not be the case in other industries. The perceived value and perceived service quality should exert a positive influence on customer satisfaction as evident from literature.

2.1.2 Customer Perception of Services

For gaining sustainable competitive advantage these perceptions are becoming much more important, in today's competitive marketplace. The perceptions of the customers are influenced by a variety of factors.

The perceptions of the customer will shift from fact-based judgements to a more general. Meaning the whole relationship gains for him once he gains more experience. Over time, he puts a stronger focus on the consequence of the product or service consumption.

When moving from the area of goods to services, handling of consumer preception becomes more complex. It has been researched that it becomes difficult for consumers to evaluate "quality" when it comes to service. Since services are intangible, perishable, and have no preset physical standards, the customer may form perceptions based on ideal expectations. The supplier too forms a perception of what is adequate.

Take for example a family booking a holiday with a tour operator. The tour operator did not inform the customer of some exclusions and limitations in the package before the tour commenced. The consumer on his part had his own high expectations. When he found out once the tour commenced that there were limitations to the package, he perceived the entire tour as unsatisfactory. Tourists who had earlier experiences along these lines however did not have such expectations and their perceptions were positive.

Perceptions and Brand: Brand identity helps in making the consumer remember the association of the brand with quality and speeds up the purchase decision. This sets high expectations from the customers as he wants to make sure the service is the same or higher and any shortcoming will not be forgiven or forgotten by the customer. The golden principle in this for marketers is that they should offer only quality products when a brand is invoked.

Consumer Perception of Risks: Customers recognise some amount of risks when purchase decisions are taken, though concerns about these risks are not often expressed. Even after a transaction is completed without any risks materialising, the consumer may carry the perception that there were risks. Some of these risks are:

- Functional risk of the product not performing as expected.
- Financial risk of having paid a higher price than necessary.
- Risk of effort and time being wasted consequent to a possible product failure.

  Sellers must follow up any successful transaction so that a repeat purchase is in store in the future.

Playing Trumps: One is bound to find consumers who have difficulty in making choices due to the risks which are involved,, hence in these cases, it is up to the sales executive to be able to guide the consumer. He could:

- Ascertain their real needs and suggest products that can meet these needs.
- Encourage consumers to rely on the brand.
- Give honest brand comparisons.
- Explain the scope and limitations of after-sales-service and warranties.
- When in doubt, play trumps. Recommend only the best, setting aside the cost factors.

2.1.3 Customer Satisfaction

Customer satisfaction is defined as an "*evaluation of the perceived discrepancy between prior expectations and the actual performance of the product*". The most important factor leading toward competitiveness and success, is the satisfaction of customers with products and services of a company.

Customer satisfaction is the main outcome of marketing practices and occupies an important position in both theory and practice. The judgement between good vs. bad, is decided by satisfaction. Technology and tangible aspects of service quality are the attributes of the service firm as 'hard quality'. Customers' satisfaction is a combination of two responses such as cognitive and affective response to service encounters while, service quality is the overall assessment of a firm's service delivery system. So, service quality is the delivery of services while satisfaction is customers' experiences with services. Depending on its demand and the availability of alternative services in the market and information available to the customer, the customer makes his assessment of the product or service. Comparison will then be made on the basis of these factors. During the evaluation process if customers' expectations are met with the service; they are more likely to feel satisfied with the service. Positive perception of service quality is the indication of the customers' satisfaction. Generally, customer satisfaction is affected by customer expectations or hopes prior to receiving a service and can be calculated by the following equation given by **Parasuraman et al, (1988):**

"Customer Satisfaction = Perception of Performance – Expectations"

Service expectations are an amalgamation of a customer's predictions about what is likely to happen during a service transaction as well as the wants and desires of that customer and hence differentiation between service expectations and service perceptions must be made. Service perceptions can be defined as a customer's judgements, which narrate to the superiority of a service. **Reimann et al, (2008)** concluded this complex concept into an equation which is

Service Perception – Service Expectation = Perceived Service Quality→ Customer satisfaction.

This equation makes the concept of perceived service quality and customer satisfaction very simple. It also shows that both the apparent service quality and customer satisfaction can be managed and controlled by the service provider.

Factors Determining Customer Satisfaction

Apart from the customer's satisfaction being influenced by specific product and service features, perceptions of product and service quality, and price, personal factors such as the customer's mood or emotional state and situational factors such as family member opinions influence satisfaction.

1. **Product and Service Features:** Customer satisfaction with a product or service is influenced significantly by the customer's evaluation of product or service feature. For a service such as a resort hotel, important features might include the pool area, access to golf facilities, restaurants, room comfort and privacy, the helpfulness and courtesy of staff, room price, and so forth.

In conducting satisfaction studies, most firms determine through some means (often focus groups) what the important features and attributes are for their service and then measure perceptions of those features as well as overall service satisfaction. Research has shown that customers of services make trade-off, among different service features (e.g., price level versus quality versus friendliness of personnel versus level of customisation), depending on the type of service being evaluated and the criticality of the service.

2. **Perceptions of Equity or Fairness:** Customer satisfaction is also influenced by perceptions to equity and fairness. The satisfaction with a service provider following a service failure is largely determined by perceptions of fair treatment. The example of Sears Auto Centers division illustrates consumers' strong reactions to unfair treatment. Over a decade ago the division was charged with defrauding customers in 44 states by performing unnecessary repairs, Sears employee rewards had been based on the quantity of repairs sold, resulting in substantial unnecessary charges to customers. The $27 million that Sears paid to settle complaints and the additional loss of business all resulted from extreme dissatisfaction of its customers over the unfair treatment.

3. **Other Customers, Family Members, and Coworkers:** In addition to product and service features and one's own feelings and beliefs, customer satisfaction is often influenced by other people. Example, family decisions about a vacation destination and satisfaction with the trip are dynamic phenomena, influenced by the reactions and emotions of individual family members. Later, what family members express of satisfaction or dissatisfaction with the trip will be influenced by stories retold among the family and selective memories of the events. In a business setting, satisfaction with a new service or technology for example, a new customer relationship management software service will be influenced not only by individuals' personal experiences with the software itself but also by what others say about it in the company, how others use it and feel about it, and how widely it is adopted in the organisation.

4. **Attributions for Service Success or Failure:** Attributions - the perceived causes of events - influence perceptions of satisfaction as well. When customers have been surprised by an outcome (the service is either much better or much worse than expected), they tend to took for the reasons, and their assessments of the reasons can influence their satisfaction. For example, if a customer of a weight-loss organisation fails to lose weight as hoped for, she will likely search for the causes, was it something she did, was the diet plan ineffective, or did circumstances simply not allow her to follow the diet regimen - before determining her level of satisfaction or dissatisfaction with the weight-loss company. For many services, customers take at least partial responsibility for how things turn out.

Even when customers do not take responsibility for the outcome, customer satisfaction may be influenced by other kinds of attributions. For example, research done in a travel agency context found that customers were less dissatisfied with a pricing error made by the agent if they felt that the reason was outside the agent's control or if they felt that it was a rare mistake, unlikely to occur again.

5. **Customer Emotions:** Customers' emotions can also affect their perceptions of satisfaction with products and services. These emotions can be stable, preexisting emotions - for example, mood state or life satisfaction. Think (if times when you are at a very happy stage in your life (such as when you are on vacation), and your good, happy mood and positive frame of mind have influenced how you feel about the services you experience. Alternatively, when you are in a bad mood, your negative feelings may carry over into how you respond to services, causing you to overreact or respond negatively to any little problem.

2.1.4 Tolerance Zone

The **Tolerance zone or zone of tolerance** (ZOT) is defined as *"the difference between desired service and the level of service considered adequate"*. Consumers come to service encounters with different expectation levels and this is recognised by ZOT.

Desired service is *"the level of service the customer hopes to receive"*.

Adequate service is *"the level the customer will accept"*.

The difference between these two expectation standards is the zone of tolerance.

Desired service – Adequate service = Zone of tolerance

As long as customer perception of service performance falls in this zone of tolerance, the customer satisfaction will show results. ZOT varies across customers and can expand /contract with the same customer. They also propose that adequate service expectations are subject to change, while desired service expectations are relatively enduring.

2.1.5 Service Quality

When defining the concept of service quality, one should always start with customers, as quality is the most important factor for customers and also it is their basis of their opinion, which will then result in the fact that service quality is achieved if the customer expectations are achieved.

While doing the service product design process, a significant element is the service quality, as it influences the volume of demand for a given service product, as well as customer profile of this service product. The most significant positioning tool of service providers and their offer on the contemporary service market is the service quality.

The impact of quality service on profit and financial indicators of business performance is an important aspect to understand in services marketing. Service quality must be viewed as a strategic force, but also as the key problem of service marketing management. As it affects the constant improvement of service performance by increasing market share and profit growth, keep in mind that service quality is a significant source of sustainable competitive advantage. This will yield an increase in financial results and will achieve sustainable competitive advantage.

Quality-based service marketing strategy is sustainable, as not all competitors can achieve the service quality expected by the consumers. Hence those service companies that base their strategies on the quality have an excellent reputation, and this feature of their quality poses a barrier to developing competitive copycat marketing strategies.

Service providers define and attain the service quality, while consumers perceive quality during the service delivery process. The way consumers perceive moments of truth is directly reflected on the evaluation of total quality service, especially in services whose deliveries are repeated, which implies a highly professional approach to moments of truth, aimed at building and maintaining long-term consumer relations. Improving service quality and building long-term consumer relations requires good knowledge of moments of truth, i.e. activities carried our within those, as well the customer perception of those.

Quality-based service company management should especially focus on four key areas important for achieving quality:
- Service encounters (moments of truth);
- Service design;
- Service productivity; and
- Service provider's corporate culture.

Without the appropriate design of service provision systems, service exchange on the market is not possible as its functioning enables efficient service delivery. In service design decision-making, the key problem is related to the choice between the *service personnel* and the *technological support* to the service delivery process, depending on whether the service provider is focused on achieving maximum efficiency.

The main understanding of service quality is the customer's view of service quality is connected to certain benchmarks, if a given service can be standardised. Disagreements regarding the nature of service quality are mostly related to the relationship between satisfaction and service quality, and in addition to quality, satisfaction is affected by a larger number of factors.

2.1.5.1 Principles of Service Quality

The process used for goods in evaluating services differs from the process used by consumers. Goods tend to be high in search qualities whole services tend to be high in accepted quality and experience.

1. **Search Qualities:** Search qualities are attributes that consumers can evaluate prior to purchasing a service or good. Items such as colour, style, fit, feel, smell, and price, are found included in the search qualities. Some products such as shoes, jeans, washing machines, cars are high in search qualities. Raw materials, component parts, and office supplies (business goods) also tend to be high in search qualities. Consumers can easily evaluate the quality of goods prior to purchase since they are high in search qualities.

2. **Experience Qualities:** Experience qualities are attributes that consumers can evaluate only during or after the consumption process. Food, catering services, meals, entertainment, and cosmetic surgery are services high in experience qualities. Under the business services, some services which are high in experience include lawn services, delivery services etc. Only after the service has been consumed or during the process of consumption, evaluation takes place. For example, a meal at a restaurant can only be evaluated once it is eaten and not before.

3. **Credence Qualities:** Credence qualities are attributes that consumers have difficulty evaluating even after the consumption is complete. Consumer services such as accountant services, funeral services, education, and veterinarian care are examples of services high in credence qualities. Examples in the business sector would include financial advice, and advertising services. Few consumers have the medical knowledge or tax knowledge to judge if the service provider performed the service properly. The same is true for a business trying to evaluate consulting or advertising services. Clearly, evaluating services high in credence qualities is difficult.

2.1.5.2 Methods of Measuring Service Quality

Different measurement criteria are required for different concepts such as service quality, customer satisfaction, customer perceptions, expectations and loyalty. While assessing these concepts, they will need to use different measuring scales, scope of opinions, attitudes and behaviour Some current methods of measuring customer expectations and customer perceptions are SERVQUAL, SERVPERF, Critical Incidents Technique, observation studies, focus group discussions and in-depth interviews and evaluate these methods in terms of their relevance and appropriateness for services marketing in different contexts.

Table 2.1: Methods of measuring service quality

1. SERVQUAL
2. SERVPERF
3. Scales for measuring customer satisfaction and loyalty
4. Critical incidents technique
5. Observation studies
6. Focus group discussion
7. In-depth interviews

2.1.5.3 Gap Model

Parasuraman et al., developed a conceptual model of service quality where they identified five gaps that could impact the consumer's evaluation of service quality in four different industries:

- retail banking
- credit card
- securities brokerage
- product repair and maintenance.

These gaps were:

Gap 1: Consumer Expectation - Management Perception Gap

Service firms may not always understand what features a service must have in order to meet consumer needs and what levels of performance on those features are needed to bring deliver high quality service. This results in affecting the way consumers evaluate service quality.

Gap 2: Management Perception - Service Quality Specification Gap

This gap arises when the company identifies what the consumers want but the means to deliver to expectation does not exist. Some factors that affect this gap could be resource constraints, market conditions and management indifference. These could affect service quality perception of the consumer.

Gap 3: Service Quality Specifications – Service Delivery Gap

Companies could have guidelines for performing service well and treating consumers correctly but these do not mean high service quality performance is assured. Employees play an important role in assuring good service quality perception and their performance cannot be standardised. This affects the delivery of service which has an impact on the way consumers perceive service quality.

Gap 4: Service Delivery – External Communications Gap

External communications can affect not only consumer expectations of service but also consumer perceptions of the delivered service. Companies can neglect to inform consumers of special efforts to assure quality that are not visible to them and this could influence service quality perceptions by consumers.

Gap 5: Expected Service – Perceived Service Gap

From their study, it showed that the key to ensuring good service quality is meeting or exceeding what consumers expect from the service and that judgement of high and low service quality depends on how consumers perceive the actual performance in the context of what they expected.

Parasuraman et al., later developed the **SERVQUAL** model *which is a multi-item scale developed to assess customer perceptions of service quality in service and retail businesses.*

2.1.5.4 SERVQUAL Model

The SERVQUAL model of measuring service quality is based on the pioneering work of *Parasuraman, Zeithaml and Berry*. The model talks about the way a customer distinguishes the service quality by comparing the expected service with the perceived service.

Service = Service expectations - Service perceptions

The outcome of such comparisons can take three forms,

- Confirmed or met expectations,
- Unmet expectations
- Exceeded expectations.

Service quality is perceived to be:

1. **Satisfactory** when service delivery = the expected service.

   In this customer is happy and there is no situation of surplus or deficit.

2. **Poor** when customer expectations are not met.

   The perceived service falls short of expected service.

3. **Surplus**: Customer expectations are exceeded, then the service quality is good. This comparison is the key building block of this model.

One must make sure to understand what is measured before starting the measuring process. When doing a comparison between expected and perceived service, it is important to find out what is the measure used in the expected service that becomes the basis of such a comparison.

Customers use five principal dimensions to judge service quality:
- reliability
- responsiveness
- assurance
- empathy
- tangibles.

The **ServQual** instrument is used to obtain *customer expectations and perception scores on these five dimensions of service.*

Two scores of perception scores are compared to the two scores of customer expectations. *The gaps so obtained are aggregated to obtain a composite score of service quality.*

Below are the dimensions in more detail:

- **Assurance:** It includes knowledge, competence and courtesy of employees and their ability to convey trust and confidence in the customer towards the service firm. Competency refers to the possession of required skills and knowledge to perform the service. Courtesy involves politeness, respect, friendliness, honesty and trustworthiness of contact personnel.

- **Tangibles:** Tangibles include appearance of physical facilities, equipment, personnel and communication materials. The organisation's physical facilities, their equipments appearance of their personnel and appearance of communication materials used to promote their products/ services are also included.

- **Responsiveness:** It refers to the willingness of the organisation's employees to help customers by providing them with prompt service.

- **Reliability:** The organisation promises to perform the service dependably and accurately. The service is performed right the first time itself and honours its commitments.

- **Empathy:** The attention which the firm provides to the customer is known as empathy. The attention should be caring and individualised, including approachability, ease of contact of service providers and making of efforts to understand the customer needs.

The designers observed that these dimensions capture the key features of service quality and these dimensions are also known as SERVQUAL dimensions.

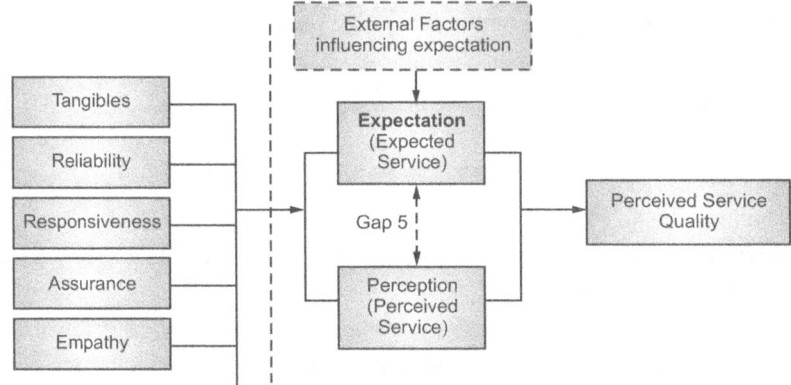

Fig. 2.1: SERVQUAL Model

2.1.5.5 Critical Incident Model

Critical incident as described by **Lovelock, Patterson and Walker**, is a technique designed to elicit details about services that "*particularly dissatisfy or delight customers*". The information can either be collected by in-house comment cards as found in hotels or through one to one interviews. The information and comments which are obtained from the interviews identify the common problems or the praises showered on the company. Unlike other qualitative methods of collecting feedback, customers are not forced to give answers to predetermined potential problems. Infact, customers are asked to jot down the more memorable incidents from the service. According to **Hope** and **Muhlemann** the technique is useful in a number of respects:

- It facilitates the identification (if specific attributes of service which have a significant impact upon customers).
- This can be used to redesign the service delivery system around the more important customer-perceived quality attributes.

2.1.6 Customer Loyalty

The term **customer loyalty** is defined as *the behaviour of repeat customers, as well as those that offer good ratings, reviews, or testimonials*. The customers can rate the service by offering a good word. It is a process, a programme, or a group of programmes geared toward keeping a guest happy so he or she will provide more business.

According to **Iddrisu, A. M.**, "*loyalty is developed over a period of time from a consistent record of meeting, and sometimes even exceeding customer expectations*". Some of the types of customer loyalty programmes can be discounts, free offers, coupons, low interest rates on financing, high value trade-ins, extended warranties, rebates, and other rewards and incentive programmes. The ultimate goal of these is to develop happy customers who will return to purchase again and persuade others to use that company's products or services. This equates to great cost savings and profitability to the company through the keeping of current customers as against attracting new ones as well as making stakeholders happy. Loyal customers are those who are not easily swayed by price inducement from competitors, and they usually purchase more than those less loyal customers.

The service provider's ability to maintain its customers' loyalty and persuade them to recommend its services to potential customers, is customer loyalty. There are six points that measure customer loyalty:
- share information
- say positive things
- recommend friend
- continue purchasing
- purchase additional service
- test new service

Customer retention programmes give encouragement to customers to remain active and ensuring that they choose their brand as the exclusive brand. It is a strategy that creates rewards to profit customers and the firms. With loyalty customers, companies can maximise their profit because loyal customers are willing to purchase more frequently, spend money on trying new products or services, recommend products and services to others, and give companies sincere suggestions.

2.1.6.1 Significance of Customer Loyalty

Customer loyalty is very essential for the growth of an organisation because loyal customers:
1. Purchase products and services again and again over time.
2. Increase the volume of their purchases and buy beyond traditional purchases, across product-lines.
3. The company's sales are increased through word of mouth.
4. Become immune to the pull of the competition.
5. If something goes wrong, the customer gives the benefit of doubt to the company.

2.1.6.2 Creation of Customer Loyalty Programmes

The manner in which a customer can be loyal to a firm and the way marketers can increase their loyalty can be divided into the following:
1. The Foundations of Customer Loyalty
2. Creating Bonds with Customers
3. Managing and Curtailing Drivers of Customer Defections

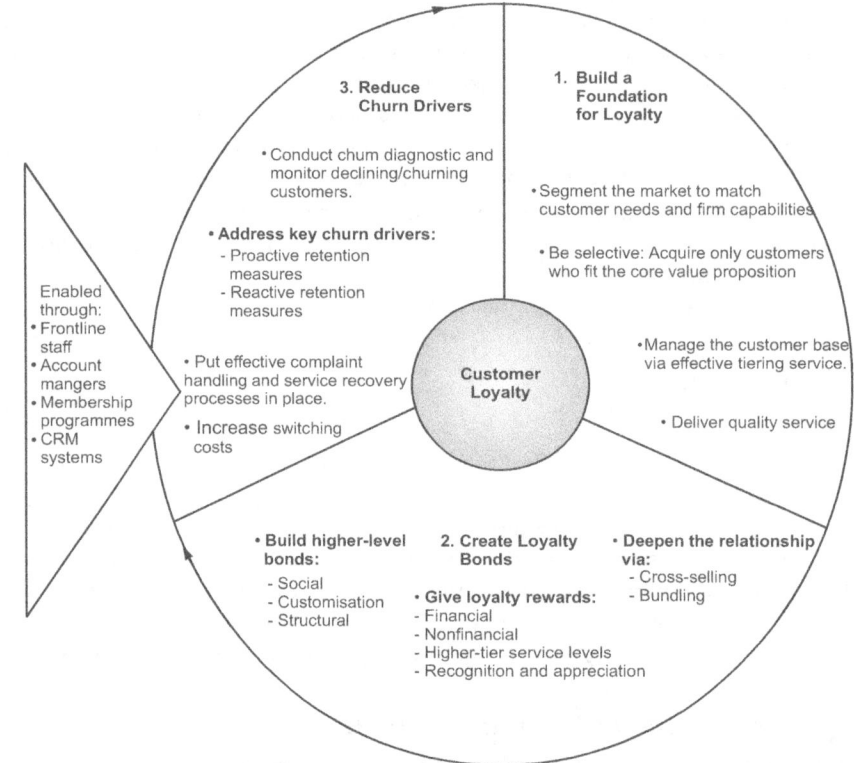

Fig. 2.2: Customer Loyalty

1. **The Foundations of Customer Loyalty:** The foundation for true loyalty lies in customer satisfaction.
   (a) **A Delighted Happy Customer:** A customer who is fully satisfied with the service offered by the organisation and the kind of customer who will talk about their experience to their friends and basically be an unpaid salesperson.
   (b) **A Satisfied Customer:** When the experience is not better or worse but is equal to their experience. this does not seem to enter the customer's memory for any long period of time.
   (c) **A Dissatisfied Customer:** When the experience of what you get as a customer is less than the expectations, causing frustration, annoyance or impatience. Many organisations are actually safe from extinction and possible ruin because they have such low expectations within their customers that their experience, whilst falling below many other standards, managed to escape dissatisfaction

Fig. 2.2 above divides the satisfaction loyalty relationship into **three main zones**.

(a) The zone of defection is at low satisfaction levels. Customers will switch unless switching costs are high or there are no viable or convenient alternatives. Extremely dissatisfied customers provide an abundance of negative word of mouth for the service provider.

(b) The zone of indifference is at intermediate satisfaction levels. Here, customers are willing to switch if they find a better alternative.

(c) The zone of affection is at very high satisfaction levels, and customers here can have such high attitudinal loyalty that they do not look for alternative service providers. Customers who praise the firm in public and refer others to the firm are described as "apostles."

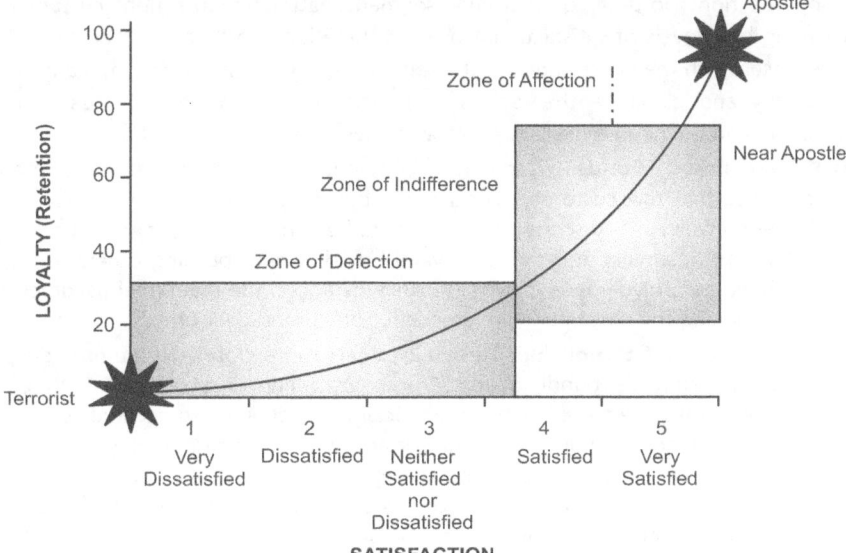

Fig. 2.3: The Customer / Loyalty Relationship

Dissatisfaction drives customers away and is a key factor in switching behaviour whereas highly satisfied or even delighted customers are more likely to become loyal apostles of a firm, consolidate their buying with one supplier, and spread positive word of mouth in contrast.

The customers' expectations should be built with a buffer of at least 50% into all time deadlines.

2. **Managing and Curtailing Drivers of Customer Defections:** So far, we have discussed drivers of loyalty and strategies to the customers more closely to the firm. An alternative approach is to understand drivers of customer defections, or churn, and work on eliminating or reducing those drivers. For example, in the mobile phone industry, players regularly conduct "churn diagnostics" the analysis of data warehouse information on churned and declining customers, exit interviews (call center staff often have a short set of questions they ask when a customer cancels an account, to gain a better understanding of why customers defect), and in-depth interviews of former customers by a third-party research agency, which typically yield a more detailed understanding of churn drivers.

3. **Creating Bonds with Customers:** A solid foundation for creating customer loyalty are having the right portfolio of customer segments, attracting the right customers, and delivering high levels of satisfaction. However, there is more that firms can do to "bond" more closely with their customers. At the same time, service marketers should be working to identify and eliminate the factors that result in "churn," or the loss of existing customers and the need to replace them with new ones.

    (a) **Reward-Based Bonds:** Within any competitive product category, managers recognise that few customers consistently buy only one brand, especially if service delivery involves a discrete transaction rather than being continuous. In many instances, consumers are loyal to several brands while spurning others—sometimes described as "polygamous loyalty". In such instances, the main goal becomes one of strengthening the customer's preference for one brand over others.

    (b) **Deepening the Relationship:** To tie customers more closely to the firm, deepening the relationship via bundling and / or cross-selling is an effective strategy. For example, banks like to sell as many financial products into an account or household as possible. Once a family has its current account, credit card, savings account, safe-deposit box, car loan, mortgage, and so on, with the same bank, the relationship is so deep that switching becomes a major exercise and is unlikely unless, of course, the customer is extremely dissatisfied with the bank.

    Incentives that offer rewards based on the frequency or value of purchase or combination of both represent a basic level of customer bonds. Reward-based bonds can be financial or non-financial. Financial bonds are built when loyal customers are rewarded with incentives that have a financial value, such as discounts on purchases and loyalty-program rewards, such as frequent flier miles or the cash-back programmes provided by some credit card issuers, based on the level of spending charged by card members.

    Non-financial rewards provide customers with benefits or value that cannot be translated directly into monetary terms.

Important intangible rewards may take the form of special recognition and appreciation. Customers tend to value the extra attention given to their needs, as well as the implicit service guarantee offered by higher-tier memberships, including efforts to meet special requests. One objective of reward-based bonds is to motivate customers to consolidate their purchases with one provider or at least make it the preferred provider. Tiered loyalty programmes often provide direct incentives for customers to achieve the next higher level of membership. However, regard-based loyalty programmes are relatively easy for other suppliers to copy and rarely provide a sustained competitive advantage. By contrast, the higher-level bonds that we discuss next tend to be more sustainable.

Creation of Customer Bonds through Membership Relationships and Loyalty Programs: As a marketing strategy, many businesses seek ways to develop formal, ongoing "membership" relations with customers. Hotels, for instance, have developed "frequent-guest programmes" offering priority reservations, upgraded rooms, and other rewards for frequent guests. Many nonprofit organisations, such as museums, create membership programmes in order to reinforce the links with their most active supporters, offering them such extra benefits as private showings and meetings with curators or artists as a reward for annual donations. The marketing task here is to determine how to build sales and revenues (or, in the case of nonprofits, donations) through such "memberships," while avoiding the risk of freezing out a large volume of desirable casual business. A number of other service businesses have sought to copy the airline industry with loyalty programmes of their own. Hotels, car rental firms, telephone companies, retailers, and even credit card issuers have been among those that seek to identify and reward their best customers.

Although some provide their own rewards—such as free merchandise, class of vehicle upgrades, or free hotel rooms in vacation resorts—many firms denominate their awards in miles that can be credited to a selected frequent flyer programmed. In short, air miles have become a form of promotional currency in the service sector. In large companies with substantial customer bases, transactions can still be transformed into relationships by implementing loyalty-reward programmes, which require customers to apply for membership cards with which transactions can be captured and customers' preferences communicated to the front line. Account management programmes may be added to the loyalty programme by offering a special telephone number to call for assistance or even naming a designated account representative. Long-term contracts between suppliers and their customers take the nature of relationships to a higher level, transforming them into partnerships and strategic alliances.

Of course, rewards alone will not suffice to retain a firm's most desirable customers. If customers are dissatisfied with the quality of service they receive or believe that they can obtain better value from a less expensive service they may quickly become disloyal. No service company that has instituted an awards programme for frequent users can ever afford to lose sight of its broader goals of offering high service quality and good value relative to the price and other costs incurred by customers.

One of the risks associated with emphasising relationships with high-value customers is that a firm may allow service to other customers to deteriorate.

(c) **Social Bonds:** Have you ever noticed how your favourite hairdresser addresses you by name when you go for a haircut or asks why you haven't been in for a long time and hopes everything went well when you were away on a long business trip? Social bonds are typically based on personal relationships between providers and customers. Alternatively, they may reflect pride or satisfaction in holding membership in an organisation. Although social bonds are more difficult to build than financial bonds and may require considerable time to achieve, they are, for that same reason, also more difficult for other suppliers to replicate for that same customer. A firm that has created social bonds with its customers has a better chance of retaining them for the long term.

Common Churn Drivers

To understand why customers' defect, many surveys have been carried out. The answers may vary by customers and organisation, but the surveys can highlight similar trends and reasons:

(a) **Price:** Price may attract new customers but looking at the larger picture, it may be a minor issue when looking at loyalty and customer retention.

(b) **Physical Factors:** Physical factors such as location, invention are also ranked low. Marketing and competitor activity and a relationship with a competitor are about 15 per cent. The competitor product's advantages can often account for the further 10 to 15 per cent.

(c) **Customer Sophistication:** Customers want more and they are always very clear about that. With the dramatic change in housing, education, travel etc. has changed the way the service is selected these days.

(d) **Complexity:** Buying even the simplest product or service can be a very complex decision-making process. These days there are so many brands, products and companies that it makes it difficult to isolate the buying motivations and criteria.

(e) **Costs:** Cost has significant role to play in understanding the economic trends and changes of recent years. The economic downturn of the early nineties gave both the business customer and personal consumer a sharp jab in the ribs to remind them that markets can indeed go down as well as up. The experience and the lingering memory of it has made us all the more aware of cost, the value of managing cost, and the importance of getting greater value for money when purchasing and choosing suppliers.

(f) **Competition:** Competition has increased dramatically in the last ten years, around the world. Factors such as globalisation, advanced manufacturing technology, etc., has led to business becoming faster, of higher quality and quick to innovate and more price-competitive.

(g) **Indifference:** One of the most common and significant reasons for customer switching and disloyalty is the indifference and inattention of the business - from the customer's point of view, the lack of any reason to stay. Most surveys highlight poor service as a more common reason for switching suppliers than price advantage. This can also be supported by the general observations of marketing specialists, who detect the following changes in consumer and business purchasing behaviour.

If we look in more detail at what is meant by 'indifference', both through the research statistics and our own experience, it becomes clear that there are many critical aspects behind any customer defection, including:

- Too little contact
- Too little individual attention
- Poor quality attention-especially when problems are encountered
- Generally poor service levels and standards

2.1.7 Service Recovery

To reduce the effect of service failure on business interests of service companies, service recovery concepts came into force. The emergence of service companies leads to increased customer expectations and thus increased service failure. Due to this, the concept of service recovery has gained importance. Service recovery has been perceived as a satisfactory solution to the problem of service failure.

Grönross found *service recovery to be the Service provider's response in case of service failure*. Doing the service right the second time is known as service recovery. Some of the service recovery methods are refunds, compensation, apologies and excuses.

2.1.7.1 Guidelines for Effective Service Recovery

A service provider can consider the following aspects for effective service recovery:

1. **Measure the Costs:** As opposed to chasing new customers, the cost of losing and the benefits of keeping existing customers should be evaluated.

2. **Encourage Complaints:** Complaints from customers which can be found in customer surveys, monitoring the service delivery process ensures proper customer satisfaction during the service encounter.
3. **Anticipation:** Services are made of critical incidents where the customer and the service provider interact. The service provider should anticipate where failures might occur in the service delivery process and attempt to minimise the same.
4. **Quick Response:** Whenever a service failure occurs, the company should respond quickly and then only the recovery effort will be successful.
5. **Employee Training:** Training should be given to employees to handle the customer needs effectively.
6. **Empowerment:** Instead of waiting for managerial approval, the frontline service personnel have authority to attend to customer complaints.
7. **Close the Loop:** Provide feedback to the customer about his complaints and assure him that such failures will not occur in future.

2.1.7.2 Service Recovery Process

There are five logical steps in the service recovery process:
1. **Acknowledging their Feelings:** Anticipating means *understanding customer expectations at key points along the experience pathway*. If there is a clear idea about what the customer expects at each junction, one can anticipate and prepare for them. Dissatisfaction results, when we fail to understand and manage the expectations. The key to success is being able to anticipate the customers' needs at each step and strive to ensure that processes are in place that will meet and exceed their expectations.
2. **Apologising and Owning the Responsibility:** The moment we come to know that expectations are not met, service recovery begins. It is vital that we acknowledge the problem and the customer's feelings, at that particular point. Perception is the stark reality and it is not the time to argue and explain your position but to accept the responsibility responsibly.
3. **Offering Alternatives:** An apology, as simple as it may seem, is an important step in moving the situation away from the negative and into the positive, action-focused arena. An apology is not an admission of guilt.
4. **Making Amends:** Offering alternatives whenever possible is a method for helping dissatisfied customers regain a sense of control. Rather than telling customers what they cannot have, focus on options for what is possible. Put them back into the driver's seat.
5. **Anticipating Customer Needs:** Making amends corrects the mistake being made. Simple things like sending a follow up letter, making a sincere apology, a small token or appreciation is all it takes to satisfy the customer.

2.1.7.3 Impact of Service Failure versus Product Failure: Service Recovery Paradox

There has been substantial research in traditional services on the effect of service failures and recovery on customer loyalty.

First, service failures have a negative effect on loyalty and have been found to be a driving factor in customer switching.

Second, in the event of a service failure, customers expect effective recoveries and their satisfaction with the recovery increases customer loyalty.

Third, a "recovery paradox" has been proposed where customers who experience a service failure followed by superior recovery exhibit behavioural intentions towards the service provider which are more favourable than they would be had no failure occurred.

A situation where the levels of satisfaction of customers who received good or excellent recoveries are actually higher than those of customers who have not experienced any problem, leading to exceptional service recovery efforts can produce a service **"recovery paradox"..** On the other hand, it is clear that an inappropriate response or no response to a service failure, complaint will result in a magnification of negative evaluation, also referred to as "double deviation".

Magnini et al. presented a notion called the *'service recovery paradox'*. *This idea is a good service recovery strategy that enables a firm to build goodwill than if the service failure had never occurred. Initial researchers approved service recovery paradox. But this did not have uniform acceptability and service researches found no relevance of this concept.* **Smith and Bolton** *perceived service recovery paradox as a condition when an effective service recovery results in greater post-recovery satisfaction than that prior to the service failure.* Alternative opportunity of increasing customer retention to the service provider as it may result in greater customer satisfaction than in the cast of a failure-free service is offered by the service recovery situation.

Product failure exists when the competitive outcome of markets is not efficient from the point of view of society as a whole. This is usually because the benefits that the free-market confers on individuals or businesses carrying out a particular activity diverge from the benefits of society as a whole.

2.1.8 Customer Complaint

It only takes one unsatisfied person to shatter a perfectly good day at work for everyone and to steer many more prospective customers away from you. Unhappy customers have their reasons for being discontent. Some may not feel well, some have unrealistic expectations and others may just have angry dispositions.

Its difficult to do everything right all the time since often businesses are complex. Many things can go wrong and some issues, such as weather, are beyond a person's control. Complaints coming from customers are often a challenge to handle.

A basic approach would be to ask the customer how they would like the problem to be rectified. The customer may agree for the job to be redone or by replacing the item. If a customer will only accept a full or partial refund, it may be in the firm's best interest to honour the request, even when it is not written in in the guidelines to do so.

Unarticulated complaints are evident in many ways such as unpaid invoices, negative word of mouth, bad treatment to sales representatives etc. Establish firm guidelines regarding customer response times and stick to them.

2.1.8.1 Nature of Complaining Behaviour

The definitions of customer complaint behaviour have generally been based on dissatisfaction and a goods-dominant logic perspective, and are outcome-oriented; consequently, complaint behaviour becomes per definition a post-purchased activity. **Landon** defines customer complaint behaviour as *"an expression of dissatisfaction by individual consumers (or on a consumer's behalf) to a responsible party in either the distribution channel or a complaint handling agency"*.

Day extended this definition *to exclude false claims by including only those claims that are honest and reasonable.* **Oliver** notes *that complaint behaviour is dissatisfaction which is caused by negative disconfirmation of purchase expectations.* **Jacoby and Jarrard** defined complaining as *"action taken by an individual which involves communicating something negative regarding a product or service, either the firm manufacturing or marketing that product or service, or to some third-party organisational entity"*.

These key phrases can be explained as follows:
- "Process that emerges" – is a series or chain of progressive and interdependent activities that spread from a source and appear as networks of activities, rather than as sequences, although they are still linked in an orderly way. The process has a certain starting point while it does not always have a definite end point.
- "Unfavourable service experience" – is knowledge or practical wisdom gained from what the customer has observed, understood, and remembered as it occurred at the time. This causes the customer to form a negative cognitive and emotional impression, which ultimately results in a negative mental 'mark' (or memory).
- "Outside the acceptance zone" – is an experience that is beyond the boundary or limit of what is tolerable.
- "Service interactions" – is the co-creation process consisting of a series of moment-of-truth activities where the customer meets the resources of the service provider or

his network. The main rationale for interaction between the customer and provider is to communicate about, coordinate and adapt the activities and resources the provider is allocating to and/or using in the relationship. During these interactions, the service comes alive, within the relationship and in a service environment. The interaction is considered to be a crucial part of the service experience and will influence the relationship with the service company. The service interaction may therefore contain several phases and each phase may have different dominant service interaction forms. The service interactions are embedded in the interaction platforms and may include interaction with products/goods, service employees, technical systems, and/or service environment. The service interaction is the generator of service experience.

- "and/or in the evaluation of the value-in-use" – is a judgement or assessment the customer does during and/or after the service interaction. Value becomes something that is assessed and develops over time during and/or after the service interaction. It starts as an impression through the exchange of value and is a judgement of desirability and preference, ending as a total evaluation of the interaction including an assessment of the process. Value can only be created with and determined by the user in the 'consumption' process and through use or what is referred to as value-in use. The customer's value-in-use begins with the enactment of value propositions and offers some thoughts on the development and practical use of reciprocal value propositions for generating sustainable betterment. The service provider can only make value propositions (offerings), since it is the customer who determines value and co-creates it. The actual value-in-use is first evaluated during and/or after the service interaction.
- "Verbal and/or non-verbal communication" – verbal communication behaviour includes written and spoken exchanges using many channels, whereas non-verbal communication behaviour refers to physical expressions and acts (or performances).
- "May lead to a behavioural change" – is a possible response or reaction made by the customer in the specified circumstance. The definition includes incidents during the service interaction and evaluation after the interactions as motivations to complain. In addition, the definition indicates the behavioural responses that are possible and the long-term behavioural effect.

2.1.8.2 Complaint Resolution: Process of Complaints Handling

Customer complaints are never easy to hear. Thriving companies take basic steps to completely and systematically process customer complaints,

(a) Screen and Log in Information: Start the procedure by screening the call, electronically logging in the date the complaint is received and recording the customer information.

- **(b) Empathise:** After having the opportunity to express dissatisfaction, the customer wants to know that someone understands and cares about the situation. Listen and respond with empathy to acknowledge the customer's feelings (upset, frustrated, disappointed). If possible, tell the customer how long it will take to satisfy the complaint, especially if a delay might occur.

- **(c) Listen**: A disgruntled customer wants to know that someone is willing to listen. Being quiet, paying attention and listening carefully to what the customer is saying without being distracted or sounding impatient - are important. Try not to interrupt, as doing so may cause the customer to agrue, withdraw, or simply hang up or walk away. At an appropriate time during this initial contact, remember to thank the customer for bringing the problem to your attention.

- **(d) Solicit Feedback:** Try to get the customer to explain how the problem happened. By asking the customer for feedback on how the problem occured, you convey concern and a willingness to understand the problem in order to arrive at the best solution. Another way to get feedback is to ask, "What do you think would be fair in this situation?" It will appeal to the customer's sense of justice and feeling of involvement in trying to resolve the problem.

- **(e) Deliver Bad News Positively:** There may come time when you must tell a customer that you will not be able to take something back, that the item he or she ordered is out of stock or that he or she must pay in advance. The following list offers some suggestions for delivering unavoidable bad news to a customer:
    1. Look for an alternative first.
    2. Inform the customer as early in the process as possible. Even though this part of the job is unpleasant, do not put it off.
    3. Inform the customer over the phone or in person not by letter.
    4. Get to the point quickly. You can warn the customer that bad news is coming in a kind way by saying something like, "You are not going to like hearing this, but...." This can sometimes soften the subsequent distress.
    5. Treat the customer fairly. Customers remember your courtesy and professionalism long after the actual problem has been forgotten.

- **(f) Take ownership and Formulate a Solution:** If there is one thing that will frustrate a customer, it is "ping-poinging," being passed from one employee or department to another. Ping-ponging occurs when you come into contact with a customer service rep that either is not given the authority to resolve issues, is not trained properly, or both. If the problem can be fixed on the spot, take care of it. If not, call your supervisor or transfer the customer to the appropriate person who can address the situation. Take ownership of the problem and make sure that it is handled appropriately and immediatety. Any solution should conform to your established customer relations policy and take into account contractual and warranty obligations, customer expecations, your company's expectations and your ability to deliver on your decision.

(g) **Apologise:** The customer wants to hear that you are sorry about the problem or inconvenience, even if you are not necessarily the one to blame. You can apologise without accepting blame by saying, "This situation is unfortunate and I apologise for it." A genuine apology is often the key to healing wounds. An immediate, sincere apology defuses hostility, no matter how grievous the injury. An apology is not only an expected social politeness but also a practical step that helps open the door to further communication and possible resolution of the complaint.

(h) **Follow Up:** Following any action that has been taken, contact the customer to ensure that the matter has been resolved satisfactorily. Ask for a second chance by saying, "We hope we will have a chance to serve you again."

(i) **Communicate a Solution:** When you respond, make sure your message is clear and appropriate. Try to avoid technical jargon. A respectful explanation of even an adverse decision can often preserve customer goodwill.

2.1.8.3 Significance of Handling Complaints

1. **Customer Retention:** The ability to retain the loyalty of customers will be enhanced.
2. **Brand Reputation:** Implementing and certifying the complaints management system demonstrates to stakeholders that individuals have a real commitment to managing customer care issues and have processes in place to handle, analyse, and review complaints.
3. **Flexibility:** It helps in adding value and efficiency to the organisation. It also provides guidance specifically for small businesses.
4. **Improved Internal Communications and Relations:** It helps an individual to adopt a customer-focused approach to resolving complaints and encourage personnel to improve their skills in working with customers.
5. **Operational Efficiency:** Implementation and certification ensures a consistent approach to handling customer queries, enabling individual to identify trends, and eliminate the causes of complaints, as well as improve the organisation's operations.
6. **Continual Improvement:** It provides a basis for continual review and analysis of the complaints-handling process, the resolution of complaints and where improvements can be made.

2.2 Service Pricing

To manage revenues in ways that support the firm's profitability objectives is the key goal of effective pricing strategy. The firm has to have a good understanding of its costs, the value created for customers and competitor's pricing. Demand fluctuates widely, whereas capacity tends to be relatively fixed. The only function that brings revenues to the organisation is Marketing, since all other management functions incur costs. Pricing is the mechanism by which sales are transformed into revenues. As compared to manufacturing, pricing is more complex in services, since there is no ownership of services, it is more difficult for managers to determine the financial costs of creating a process or performance for a customer than to identify the costs associated with creating and distributing a physical good.

Pricing of goods is determined by the market demand in most cases, unless regulated by the government. The pricing of goods differs from the pricing of services. Price has a single name in the manufacturing sector, whereas it takes different names in the services sector. For example, the price charged for advertising is known as commission, for boarding and lodging services, as tariff; for legal services and healthcare as fees; and for share or stock services as brokerage and commission.

Price is controlled by different bodies for various services. For example, prices for government provided services like the railways are completely controlled by the government; prices for services like banking, power, telephone, and insurance are partially regulated by the government, prices in hotels, domestic services, auto servicing, personal care services, recreation, etc., vary according to the demand in the market; and prices of advertising services, hospitals, expert services like lawyers and stock brokers are determined by the service providers themselves.

2.2.1 Approaches to Pricing Services

We discuss below these differences in the context of the three pricing structures typically used to set prices: (1) cost-based, (2) competition-based, and (3) demand-based pricing.

1. Cost-Based Pricing

In cost-based pricing, a company determines expenses from raw materials and labour, adds amounts or percentages for overhead and profit, and thereby arrives at the price. This method is widely used by industries such as utilities, contracting, wholesaling, and advertising. The basic formula for cost-based pricing is

Price = Direct costs + Overhead costs + Profit margin

Direct costs involve materials and labour that are associated with delivering the service, overhead costs are a share of fixed costs, and the profit margin is a percentage of full costs (direct + overhead).

Special Challenges in Cost-Based Pricing for Services

One of the major difficulties in cost-based pricing involves defining the units in which a service is purchased. Thus the price per unit a well-understood concept in pricing of manufactured goods is a vague entity. For this reason many services are sold in terms of input units rather than units of measured output. For example, most professional services (such as consulting, engineering, architecture, psychotherapy, and tutoring) are sold by the hour.

What is unique about services when using cost-based approaches to pricing? First, costs are difficult to trace or calculate in services businesses, particularly where multiple services are provided by the firm. Consider how difficult it must be for a bank to allocate teller time accurately across its checking, savings, and money market accounts in order to decide what to charge for the services. Second, a major component of cost is employee time rather than materials, and the value of people's time, particularly non-professional time, is not easy to calculate or estimate.

An added difficulty is that actual service costs may under-represent the value of the service to the customer. A local tailor charges $10 for taking in a seam on a $350 ladies' suit jacket and an equal $10 for taking in a seam on a pair of $14 sweat shorts. The tailor's rationale is that both jobs require the same amount of time. What she neglects to see is that the customer would pay a higher price and might even be happier about the alterations-for the expensive suit jacket, and that $10 is too high a price for the sweat shorts.

Examples of Cost-Based Pricing Strategies Used in Services

Cost-plus pricing is a commonly used approach in which component costs are calculated and a markup is added. In product pricing, this approach is quite simple; in service industries, however, it is complicated because the tracking and identification of costs are difficult. The approach is typically used in industries in which cost must be estimated in advance, such as construction, engineering, and advertising. In construction or engineering, bids are solicited by clients on the basis of the description of the service desired. Using their knowledge of the costs of the components of the service (including the raw materials such as masonry and lumber), labour (including both professional and unskilled), and margin, the company estimates and presents to the client a price for the finished service. A contingency amount-to cover the possibility that costs may be higher than estimated is also stated because in large projects specifications can change as the service is provided.

Fee for service is the pricing strategy used by professionals; it represents the cost of the time involved in providing the service. Consultants, psychologists, accountants, and lawyers, among other professionals, charge for their services on an hourly basis. Virtually all psychologists and social workers have a set hourly rate they charge to their clients, and most structure their time in increments of an hour.

In the early 1900s, lawyers typically billed clients a certain fee for services rendered regardless of the amount of time they spent delivering them. Then in the 1970s, law firms began to bill on an hourly rate, in part because this approach offered accountability to clients and an internal budgeting system for the firm. One of the most difficult aspects of this approach is that recordkeeping is tedious for professionals. Lawyers and accountants must keep track of the time they spend for a given client, often down to 10 minute increments. For this reason the method has been criticised because it does not promote efficiency and sometimes ignores the expertise of the lawyers (those who are very experienced can accomplish much more than novices in a given time period, yet billings do not always reflect this). Clients also feared padding of their legal bills, and began to audit them. Despite these concerns, the hourly bill dominates the industry, with the majority of revenues billed this way.

2. Competition-Based Pricing

The competition-based pricing approach focuses on the prices charged by other firms in the same industry or market. Competition-based pricing does not always imply charging the identical rate others charge but rather using others' prices as an anchor for the firm's price. This approach is used predominantly in two situations: (1) when services are standard across providers, such as in the dry cleaning industry and (2) in oligopolies with a few large service providers, such as in the airline or rental car industry. Difficulties involved in provision of services sometimes make competition-based pricing less simple than it is in goods industries.

Special Challenges in Competition-Based Pricing for Services

Small firms may charge too little and not make margins high enough to remain in business. Many mom and pop service establishments-dry cleaning, retail, and tax accounting, among others-cannot deliver services at the low prices charged by chain operations.

Further, the heterogeneity of services across and within providers makes this approach complicated. Bank services illustrate the wide disparity in service prices. Customers buying checking accounts, money orders, or foreign currency, to name a few services, find that prices are rarely similar across providers. Banks claim that they set fees high enough to cover the costs of these services. The wide disparity in prices probably reflects the bank's difficulty in determining prices as well as their belief that financial customers do not shop around nor discern the differences (if any) among offerings from different providers. A banking expert makes the point that "It's not like buying a quart of milk". Prices aren't standardised. Only in standardised services (such as dry cleaning) are prices likely to be remembered and compared.

Examples of Competition-Based Pricing in Services Industries

Price signaling occurs in markets with a high concentration of sellers. In this type of market, any price offered by one company will be matched by competitors to avoid giving a low-cost seller a distinct advantage. The airline industry exemplifies price signaling in services. When any competitor drops the price of routes, others match the lowered price almost immediately.

Going-rate pricing involves charging the most prevalent price in the market. Rental car pricing is an illustration of this technique (and also an illustration of price signaling, because the rental car market is dominated by a small number of large companies). For years, the prices set by one company have been followed by the other companies. When Hertz instituted a new pricing plan that involved "no mileage charges, ever," other rental car companies imitated the policy. They then had to raise other factors such as base rates, size and type of car, daily or weekly rates, and drop-off charges to continue to make profits. Prices in different geographic markets, even cities, depend on the going rate in that location, and customers often pay different rates in contiguous cities in the same state. The newsletter Consumer Reports Travel Letter advises customers that the national toll-free reservation lines offer better rates than are obtained calling local rental car companies in cities, perhaps because those rates are less influenced by the going rates in a particular area.

3. Demand-Based Pricing

The two approaches to pricing just described are based on the company and its competitors rather than on customers. Neither approach takes into consideration that customers may lack reference prices, may be sensitive to non-monetary prices, and may judge quality on the basis of price. All these factors can be accounted for in a company's pricing decisions. The third major approach to pricing, demand-based pricing, involves setting prices consistent with customer perceptions of value. Prices are based on what customers will pay for the services provided.

Special Challenges in Demand-Based Pricing for Services

One of the major ways that pricing of services differs from pricing of goods in demand-based pricing is that non-monetary costs and benefits must be factored into the calculation of perceived value to the customer. When services require time, inconvenience, and psychological and search costs, the monetary price must be adjusted to compensate. And when services save time, inconvenience, and psychological and search costs, the customer is willing to pay a higher monetary price. The challenge is to determine the value to customers of each of the non-monetary aspects involved.

Another way services and goods differ with respect to this form of pricing is that information on service costs may be less available to customers, making monetary price not as salient a factor in initial service selection as it is in goods purchasing.

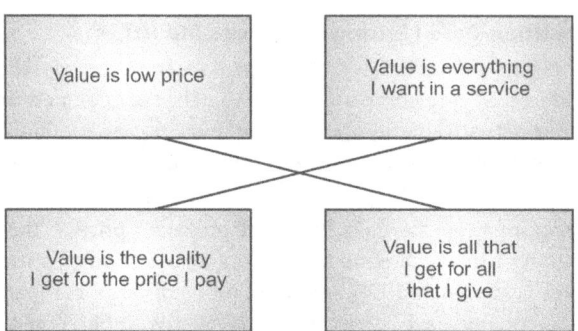

Fig. 2.4: Four Customer Definitions of Value

Source: N.C. Mohan, "Pricing Research for Decision Making," Marketing Research: A Magazine of Management and Applications 7, no. I (Winter 1995), pp. 10-19. Reprinted by permission of the American Marketing Association.

- **Value is Low Price:** Some consumers equate value with low price, indicating that what they have to give up in terms of money is most salient in their perceptions of value, as typified in these representative comments from customers:

  For dry cleaning: "Value means the lowest price."

  For carpet steam cleaning: "Value is price-which one is on sale."

  For a fast food restaurant: "When I can use coupons, I feel that the service is a value."

  For airline travel: "Value is when airline tickets are discounted."

- **Value Is Whatever I Want in a Product or Service**: Rather than focusing on the money given up, some consumers emphasise the benefits they receive from a service or product as the most important component of value. In this value definition, price is far less important than the quality or features that match what the consumer wants. In the telecommunications industry, for example, business customers strongly value the reliability of the systems and are willing to pay for the safety and confidentiality of the connections. Service customers describe this definition of value as follows:

  For an MBA degree: "Value is the very best education I can get."

  For medical services: "Value is high quality."

  For a social club: "Value is what makes me look good to my friends and family."

  For a rock or country music concert: "Value is the best performance."

- **Value Is the Quality I Get for the Price I Pay**: Other consumers see value as a trade-off between the money they give up and the quality they receive.

  For a hotel for vacation: "Value is price first and quality second."

  For a hotel for business travel: "Value is the lowest price for a quality brand,"

  For a computer services contract: "Value is the same as quality. No-value is affordable quality."

- **Value Is What I Get for What I Give:** Finally, some consumers consider all the benefits they receive well as all sacrifice components (money, time, effort) when describing value.

  For a housekeeping service: "Value is how many rooms I can get cleaned for what the price is."

  For a hairstylist: "Value is what I pay in cost and time for the look I get."

  For executive education: "Value is getting a good educational experience in the shortest time possible."

The four consumer expressions of value can be captured in one overall definition consistent with the concept of utility in economics. Perceived value is the consumer's overall assessment of the utility of a service based on perceptions of what is received and what is given. Although what is received varies across consumers (some may want volume, others high quality, still others convenience), as does what is given (some are concerned only with money expended, others with time and effort), value represents a trade-off of the give and get components. Customers will make a purchase decision on the basis of perceived value, not solely to minimise the price paid. These definitions are the first step in identifying the elements that must be quantified in setting prices for services.

2.2.2 Pricing Strategies

In this section we describe the approaches to services pricing that are particularly suited to each of the four value definitions.

(A) Pricing Strategies When the Customer Means "Value Is Low Price"

When monetary price is the most important determinant of value to a customer, the company focuses mainly on price. This focus does not mean that the quality level and intrinsic attributes are always irrelevant, just that monetary price dominates in importance. To establish a service price in this definition of value, the marketer must understand to what extent customers know the objective prices of services in this category, how they interpret various prices, and how much is too much of a perceived sacrifice. These factors are best understood when the service provider also knows the relative dollar size of the purchase, the frequency of past price changes, and the range of acceptable prices for the service. Some of the specific pricing approaches appropriate when customers define value as low price include discounting, odd pricing, synchro-pricing, and penetration pricing.

1. **Discounting:** Service providers offer discounts or price cuts to communicate to price-sensitive buyers that they are receiving value. Colleges are now providing many forms of discounting to attract students. For example, University allows top students to get a fifth year of undergraduate or graduate education free, and also offers

scholarships based on criteria other than financial need. The business school also cut tuition 22 per cent for its master's programmeme and allows graduates to take two-thirds off the regular tuition price. Discount pricing has become a creative art at other educational institutions.

2. **Odd Pricing:** Odd pricing is the practice of pricing services just below the exact amount to make buyers perceive that they are getting a lower price. Dry cleaners charge ₹ 2.98 for a shirt rather than ₹ 3.00, health clubs have dues priced at ₹ 33.90 per month rather than ₹ 34, and haircuts are ₹ 9.50 rather than ₹ 10.00. Odd prices suggest discounting and bargains and are appealing to customers for whom value means low price.

3. **Synchro-Pricing:** Synchro-pricing is the use of price to manage demand for a service by capitalising on customer sensitivity to prices. Certain services, such as tax preparation, passenger transportation, long-distance telephone, hotels, and theatres, have demand that fluctuates over time as well as constrained supply at peak times. For companies in these and other industries, setting a price that provides a profit over time can be difficult. Pricing can, however, play a role in smoothing demand and synchronising demand and supply. Time, place, quantity, and incentive differentials have all been used effectively by service firms. Place differentials are used for services in which customers have sensitivity to location. The front row at concerts, the 50-yard line in football, center court in tennis or basketball, ocean-side rooms in resort hotels-all these represent place differentials that are meaningful to customers and that therefore command higher prices.

4. **Penetration Pricing:** The price charged for products and services is set artificially low in order to gain market share. Once this is achieved, the price is increased. Penetration pricing is a strategy in which new services are introduced at low prices to stimulate trial and widespread use. The strategy is appropriate when:

   (a) Sales volume of the service is very sensitive to price, even in the early stages of introduction;

   (b) It is possible to achieve economies in unit costs by operating at large volumes;

   (c) A service faces threats of strong potential competition very soon after introduction; and

   (d) There is no class of buyers willing to pay a higher price to obtain the service.

   Penetration pricing can lead to problems when companies then select a "regular" increased price. Care must be taken not to penetrate with so low a price that customers feel the regular price is outside the range of acceptable prices.

(B) Pricing Strategies When the Customer Means "Value Is Everything I Want in a Service"

When the customer is concerned principally with the "get" components of a service, monetary price is not of primary concern. The more desirable intrinsic attributes a given service possesses, the more highly valued the service is likely to be and the higher the price the marketer can set.

(C) Prestige Pricing

Prestige pricing is a special form of demand-based pricing by service marketers who offer high-quality or status services. For certain services-restaurants, health clubs, airlines, and hotels-a higher price is charged for the luxury end of the business. Customers of service companies who use this approach, may actually value the high price because it represents prestige or a quality image. Others prefer purchasing at the high end because they are given preference in seating or accommodations and are entitled to other special benefits. In prestige pricing, demand may actually increase as price increases because the costlier service has more value in reflecting quality or prestige.

(D) Skimming Pricing

Skimming, a strategy in which new services are introduced at high prices with large promotional expenditures is an effective approach when services are major improvements over past services. In this situation, customers are more concerned about obtaining the service than about the cost of the service, allowing service providers to skim the customers most willing to pay the highest prices.

(E) Pricing Strategies When the Customer Means "Value Is the Quality I Get for the Price I Pay"

Some customers primarily consider both quality and monetary price. The task of the marketer is to understand what quality means to the customer (or segments of customers) and then to match quality level with price level. Specific strategies are shown in Fig. 2.

1. **Value Pricing:** The widely used term value pricing has come to mean "giving more for less." In current usage it involves assembling a bundle of services that are desirable to a wide group of customers and then pricing them lower than they would cost alone. For example, in the US Taco Bell pioneered value pricing with a $0.59 Value Menu.

    After sales at the chain rose 50 per cent in two years to $2.4 billion, McDonald's and Burger King adopted the value pricing practice. The menu at Taco Bell has since been reconfigured to emphasise plain tacos and burritos (which are easier and faster for the chain to make) for less than a dollar. Southwest Airlines also offers value pricing in its airline service: a low, cost for a bundle of desirable service attributes such as frequent departures, friendly and funny employees, and on-time arrival. The airline offers consistently low fares with bare-bones service.

2. **Market Segmentation Pricing:** In market segmentation pricing, a service marketer charges different prices to groups of customers for what are perceived to be different quality levels of service, even though there may not be corresponding differences in the costs of providing the service to each of these groups. This form of pricing is based on the premise that segments show different price elasticity's of demand and desire different quality levels.

(F) Pricing Strategies When the Customer Means "Value Is All That I Get for All That I Give"

Some customers define value as including not just the benefits they receive but also the time, money, and effort they put into a service. Fig. 2.5 illustrates the pricing strategies described in this definition of value.

1. **Price Framing:** Because many customers do not possess accurate reference prices for services, services marketers are more likely than product marketers to organise price information for customers so they know how to view it. Customers naturally look for price anchors as well as familiar services against which to judge focal services. If they accept the anchors, they view the price and service package favorably.

2. **Price Bundling:** Some services are consumed more effectively in conjunction with other services; other services accompany the products they support (such as extended service warranties, training, and expedited delivery). When customers find value in a package of services that are interrelated, price bundling is an appropriate strategy. Bundling, this means pricing and selling services as a group rather than individually, has benefits to both customers and service companies. Customers find that bundling simplifies their purchase and payment, and companies find that the approach stimulates demand for the firm's service line, thereby achieving cost economies for the operations as a whole while increasing net contributions. Bundling also allows the customer to pay less than when purchasing each of the services individually, which contributes to perceptions of value.

The effectiveness of price bundling depends on how well the service firm understands the bundles of value that customers or segments perceive, and on the complimentarily of demand for these services. Effectiveness also depends on the right choice of services from the firm's point of view. Because the firm's objective is to increase overall sales, the services selected for bundling should be those with a relatively small sales volume without the bundling to minimise revenue loss from discounting a service that already has a high sales volume.

3. **Complementary Pricing:** Services that are highly interrelated can be leveraged by using complementary pricing. This pricing includes three related strategies-captive pricing, two-part pricing, and loss leadership. In captive pricing the firm offers a base service or product and then provides the **supplies** or peripheral services needed to continue using the service. In this situation the company could off load some part of the price for the basic service to the peripherals. For example, cable services often drop the price for installation to a very low level, then compensate by charging enough for the peripheral services to make up for the loss in revenue. With service firms, this strategy is often called two-part pricing because the service price is broken into a fixed fee plus variable usage fees (also found in telephone services, health clubs, and commercial services such as rentals). Loss leadership is the term typically used in retail stores when providers place a familiar service on special largely to draw the customer to the store and then reveal other levels of service available at higher prices.

4. **Results-Based Pricing:** In service industries in which outcome is very important but uncertainty is high, the most relevant aspect of value is the result of the service. In personal injury lawsuits, for example, clients value the settlement they receive at the conclusion of the service. From tax accountants, clients value cost savings. From trade schools, students most value getting a job upon graduation. In these and other situations, an appropriate value-based pricing strategy is to price on the basis of results or outcome of the service.

The most commonly known form of results-based pricing is a practice called contingency pricing used by lawyers. Contingency pricing is the major way that personal injury and certain consumer cases are billed; it accounts for 12 per cent of commercial law billings. In this approach, lawyers do not receive fees or payment until the case is settled, when they are paid a percentage of the money that the client receives. Therefore, only an outcome in the client's favour is compensated. From the client's point of view, the pricing makes sense in part because most clients in these cases are unfamiliar with and possibly intimidated by law firms. Their biggest fears are high fees for a case that may take years to settle. By using contingency pricing, clients are ensured that they pay no fees until they receive a settlement.

5. **Money-Back Guarantees:** Vocational colleges offer one major promise: to get students jobs upon graduation. So many schools commit to this promise-often blatantly in television advertising-that prospective students have come to distrust all promises from these colleges. To give substance to its promise, a college, a for-profit vocational college, offered a tuition-back guarantee to any graduate who, after due effort, failed to obtain a suitable position within 90 days of programme completion.

Although other educational institutions cannot do this, largely because the results desired do not often arrive within a 90-day period, other results-based plans are taking shape. A future-income dependent payment plan has been considered by many schools. Under such a plan, a student would receive a full scholarship and, after graduation, pay a fixed percentage of salary for a set period-for example, 5 per cent of salary for 20 years. Under this plan, the more "value added" by education and the more money-oriented the student, the more the student and the institution would benefit financially.

6. **Commission:** Many services providers-including real estate agents and advertising agencies-earn their fees through commissions based on a percentage of the selling price. In these and other industries, commission is paid by the supplier rather than the buyer.

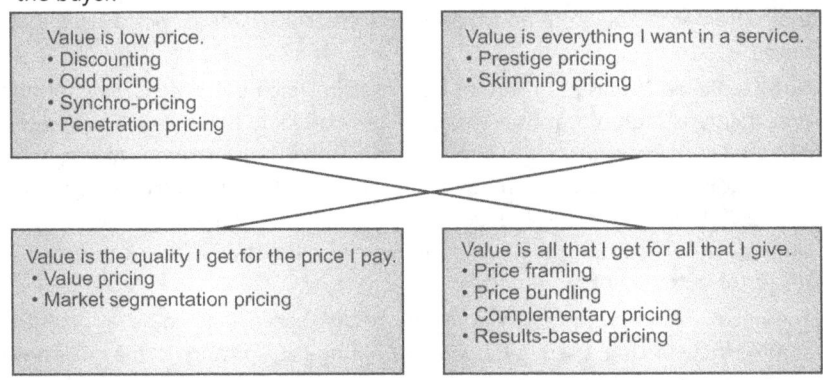

Fig. 2.5: Service Pricing Strategies for Four customer Definitions of Value

The commission approach to services pricing is compelling in that agents are compensated most when they find the highest rates and fares. It would seem that agents have an underlying motivation to avoid the lowest fares and rates for their clients.

2.2.3 Costs of Service Delivery

Service delivery incurs costs. It is necessary to collect data on unit service counts, number of beneficiaries, money spent per unit of service, the time spent on service coordination and delivery, wages and salaries of staff involved in service delivery, and the amount spent on risk/liability prevention since assessment of performance of service delivery in relation to its cost-effectiveness. The data contains information regarding the areas or the types of services and clients for which financial resources are being used. Whenever there is some inconsistency, corrective actions can be taken as it is easy to find out. If the cost of unit of service is too high, an organisation may not be able to support a loss of funding, because clients will have been accustomed to a level of service that the organisation will no longer be able to afford. An organisation may not be able to save for an unforeseen event and will be vulnerable to dissolution if funding is lost, if the cost of the unit service is too high. There is a risk of losing community support or receiving pressure to cut services at the expense of quality, if the cost of a unit of service is too high. When designing delivery systems, organisations use developments in information technology (IT) to rethink -approaches while others choose different ways to deliver the services they offer. It is fair to underline that IT developments have not only reduced costs and lead times within the systems and procedures but have enabled organisations to redesign many of these delivery systems. The internet offers a lot of capability to personalise the service to the client. Organisations will have to decide the extent to which customers can participate in the creation of the service, when the design of the delivery system takes place.

The next step would be analysis of how the organisation's current customer service delivery cost structure will be developed and the costs that will be involved for meeting the newly identified service levels by customer segment. Firms that have applied activity-based costing (ABC) will find this to be a straightforward task as without the ABC the analysis will be conducted on a project basis.

An organisation does need to put in place a costing system for analysing costs pertaining to service delivery as well as recovery. The CC can provide a cost-effective solution to service recovery and achieving customer service excellence.

2.2.4 Customer Profitability Measurement

Customer profitability measurement *refers to the allocation of revenues and costs to customer segments or individual customers; such that the profitability of those segments and/or individual customers can be calculated.*

The incentive for increasing the attention for CPA is for the following two reasons:
1. The increase of ABCs in the 1990s, led to a rise in the understanding of the extent to which the manufacturing of different products used a firm's resources.
    (a) Firms first find out the cost pools.
    (b) For each of these cost pools, cost drivers should be identified.
    (c) Costs are then allocated to the cost objects based on the extent to which these objects require certain activities
    (d) If it was accepted that not every product requires the same types and same levels of activities, it was a small step to see that customers, too, differ in their consumption of resources

2. Both in type and amount, information technology makes it possible to record and analyse more customer data, since number of sales visits, number of service calls etc. are stored at the level of the individual customer it becomes possible to actually calculate customer profitability.

It is considered good industrial marketing practice to build and nurture profitable relationships with customers. The CPA can deliver knowledge such as how current customer relationships differ in profitability, as well as what customer segments offer higher potential for future profitable customer relationships.

2.2.5 Revenue Management

Revenue management *is the collection of strategies and tactics firms use to scientifically manage demand for their products and services*. This practice was started by the airline industry but has now moved to fashion retail, energy and hospitality to name a few.

It has become more disciplined and technical in using a variety of analytics to predict consumer demand, and to optimise the inventory and price availability to maximise revenue, as revenue management has slowly developed. The essence of this discipline is in understanding the customers' perception of product value and accurately aligning product prices, placement and availability with each customer segment.

Yield management, also known as *revenue management, aims at earning the highest possible revenue in capacity-constrained services through the service-provider's operations.* To divide their customers into finer segments, which in turn help in understanding better, each segment's price sensitivity; organisations use information technology. This however will depend on the amount of past data on demand patterns that will be available with the organisation.

Service organisations often use the percentage of capacity sold as a measure of operational efficiency. Though, these figures tell us little about the relative profitability of the customer base, by themselves.

2.2.5.1 Process of Revenue Management

There are four steps involved in revenue management:

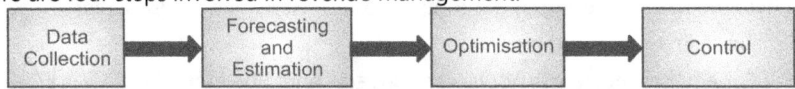

Fig. 2.6: Process of Revenue Management

1. **Data Collection:** If the company uses revenue management, they will have to store all their data about their customer behaviour, prices, demand and other factors in order to make good forecasting and estimation. The more precisely we can store our historical data, the more precise forecast we can make. This is the foundation of all yield management systems.

2. **Forecasting and Estimation:** The parameters of the model and later making predictions using these parameters have to be estimated. Companies will not only forecast demand but if there are any cancellations too. Forecasting is the basis of optimisation as data is the basis of forecasting. Optimising the controls cannot happen without a good forecast of the demand.
3. **Optimisation:** We have to find the optimal set of controls, which we are going to use. These can be booking limits, prices, discounts, etc.
4. **Control:** Finally the sale of inventory has to be controlled using the previously optimised controls.

2.2.5.2 Revenue Management Techniques

We will now talk about the different revenue management techniques:

(a) Contribution Margin: Measure used to assess the impact on profits is contribution margin, measured in an incremental fashion by assessing the increased revenues minus the increased costs. The standard measure of contribution margin is revenue minus variable costs, that is, those costs that change as output (revenue) changes. As discussed in the next section, an accurate assessment of variable costs is critical to making good revenue management decisions. Using contribution margin analysis reflects the unstated assumption that a base of business that covers all costs and earns a profit already exists, and the proposal at hand is for an incremental change that builds on that base. Thus revenue management proposals often seek to make relatively small modifications to an existing business base and existing price structure, with the goal of adding to the overall contribution margin of the organisation.

It is possible to use revenue management as a strategic approach to an entire price structure, in such cases; contribution margin is not the relevant metric. When dealing with the entire business segment, then something closer to full cost profitability should be used.

(b) Account Analysis: Estimating fixed and variable costs is a very approximate process. There are techniques of varying complexity that do exist and one of the simplest forms called as **account analysis**, includes classification of each account title as fixed, variable, or possibly mixed. Based on one's knowledge of and beliefs about cost behaviour, these classifications are judgemental. The other technique is **two-point analysis** also known as high-low anaylsis, uses the change in costs between two different output levels to estimate the fixed and variable components. The change in cost over the change in output quantity would be due to the variable cost items, as we assume no change in fixed costs.

(c) Dynamic Pricing:

The methods of dynamic pricing are:

1. **Discount Airline Pricing:** It is worth mentioning this particular case, because when it comes to airlines we have to set our prices differently. As departure day approaches (the day when our inventory loses its value), in contrast to style goods, prices become higher. There is a simple explanation to this. Airline companies prefer customers who book early, but if customers book tickets early and then see that prices dropped, they are going to be furious. It would lead to high uncertainty if everybody wanted to buy their tickets the day before departure.

2. **Consumer-Packaged Goods Promotion:** The main difference in this case is that a promotion is a short-term price reduction. Consumer-packaged goods are products that customers buy repeatedly, so they know how the prices change, and they are willing to adapt to these changes. For example, if the price of coffee drops, then customers tend to buy a lot of packages, they stockpile it. So we can see a drop in demand after the promotion ends. We have to be careful about the length of the promotion. If it is too long, our product can lose its value. But it is a great way if we want extra attention on our product and we want to advertise it.

3. **Style and Seasonal Goods Markdown Pricing:** Yield management applies to perishable assets. This means that our goods will lose their value and we cannot sell them after that, so we cannot make profit. Every company's goal is to reduce spoilage to the minimum. So before the inventory loses its value, companies will lower prices, in hope of increase in demand. It is always better to sell something for a low price, then to not sell it at all. This is a very simple, but useful use of dynamic pricing to gain more revenue. Another scenario can be that we do not have enough information about the demand of our clients. So first we need to set all prices high and as time goes by, we can observe which products are the ones for which people are willing to pay the high price. For the rest of the products we can lower our prices. Applying this kind of dynamic pricing is also a good way to learn about customer demand.

4. **Auctions:** Besides dynamic pricing, auctions are another form of tactics used in price-based revenue management. The main difference between the two is that in case of dynamic pricing companies decide about the price of their products, but when it comes to auctions, the customers are the ones offering prices. This is called bid, and companies decide which one to accept. An auction is basically a set of rules, which is called mechanism. In case of auctions, prices can easily follow the changes in the market and customer demand. One of the biggest

advantages of this kind of price-based revenue management is that we don't need much information about customer demand and their willingness to buy our product.

Types of Auctions

Here are the different types of auctions:

- **Open Ascending (English) Auction**: This method is used mainly for selling art in auction houses. In this type of auction, the pricing method the seller will offer increasing prices to the buyers. With a show of the hand, the buyer indicates that they are willing to buy the product for that price. The bidding will keep happening till only one buyer remains.
- **Open Descending (Dutch) Auction:** This method is in contrast to the open ascending method, where the seller starts with a price but once the bidding starts, the prices keep decreasing. The first customer, who is willing to pay the offered price, wins the product.
- **Sealed-bid, First Price Auction:** Sealed bids of the contract are submitted to the company by potential buyers. In this case, the buyers will not know how many customers have bidded for the contract and what amount they have offered. The customer, who submitted the highest bid, wins the product.
- **Sealed-bid, Second-price Auction (Vickrey Auction):** Similar to the previous method, the difference being that the customer who makes the highest bid and who won the product will not have to pay the highest bid but the second highest bid.

(d) **Price Discrimination:** When a seller charges competing buyers different prices for 'commodities' of like grade and quality, a pricing auction may be judged as a pricing discrimination. Discriminatory prices might be direct or indirect in the form of allowances. They are also called segmented pricing or revenue management. Price discrimination is not illegal per se and it is widely practiced as a profit-maximising pricing approach.

2.2.6 Segmented Pricing

In segmented pricing, the company sells a product or service at two or more prices, even though the differences in prices are not based on differences in costs. Companies will often adjust their basic prices to allow for differences in customers, products and locations.

There are several forms in segmented pricing:

1. **Customer Segment Pricing**: different customers pay different prices for the same product or service. Museums, for example, may charge a lower admission for students and senior citizens.

2. **Product-form Pricing**: different versions of the product are priced differently but not according to differences in their costs.
3. **Location Pricing**: a company charges different prices for different locations, even though the cost of offering each location is the same. For instance, theatres very their seat prices because of audience preferences for certain locations and state universities charge higher tuition for out-of-state students.
4. **Time Pricing**: a firm varies its price by the season, the month of the day and even the hour. Some public utilities vary their prices to commercial users by time of day and weekend versus weekday. Resorts give weekend and seasonal discounts.

Some of the terms used by various industries for segmented pricing are:
- yield management: used by airlines, hotels etc.
- According to Robert Cross, it is called revenue management:"*companies will sell the right product to the right consumer at the right time for the right price*".

Some conditions that should be met for an effective strategy:
1. The market must be segmentable and the segments must show different degrees of demand.
2. The segmenting and watching the market cannot exceed the extra revenue obtained from the price difference.
3. The segmented pricing must also be legal.
4. Segmented prices should reflect real differences in customer's perceived value. Otherwise, in the long run, the practice will lead to customer resentment and ill will.

2.2.7 Price Discrimination

Price discrimination *is selling a product at different prices for different classes of buyers based on their differing demand for the product or service; whether the product or service actually differs among the price groups is secondary, but in most cases, the different prices charged are not related to the differences in the cost of providing the underlying item.*

When identical goods or services are sold at different prices from the same provider, price discrimination occurs.

There are three types of price discrimination:
- **First Degree**: The seller must know the absolute maximum price that every consumer is willing to pay.
- **Second Degree:** The price of the good or service varies according to quantity demanded.
- **Third Degree:** The price of the good or service varies by attributes such as location, age, gender and economic status.

To capture the market's consumer surplus is the purpose of price discrimination. Price discrimination allows the seller to generate the most revenue possible for a good or service.

The monopolist struggles to charge the highest prices where demand is inelastic i.e., where higher prices lead to higher revenue in spite of the decreasing quantities sold at the higher prices — and lower prices for more price sensitive buyers, where higher prices would decrease the quantity sold, leading to lower revenue in spite of the higher prices, because the drop in quantity more than offsets the rise in price. The differences in prices are mostly motivated by a desire to earn greater profits — it does not reflect the cost-of-production differences among the products. The products sold to different classes of buyers are sometimes different, but the differences have no significant relationship to the price differentials. Businesses and enterprises have little concern for the price, which is why many items targeted for that market are more expensive than for the consumer market.

2.3 Service Place

The factors influencing distribution of tangible goods differs from services.

- In tangible goods: *production is separate from consumption.*
- In services, *production and consumption take place simultaneously.*

Linking of production with distribution makes the service distribution more complex than distribution of tangible goods. The service provider and consumer will participate in service production at a specified location.

The importance of distribution can be traced in services marketing with its presence in the name of 'place' in the services marketing mix. The intangible nature -of services would appear to make the idea of distribution inapplicable to services. But there are more than enough similarities to make distribution relevant and important to service firms (Donald H. Light).

In terms of market expansion, Business firms or social organisations, measure their growth. There are only two options before the service provider when he wants to expand his market operations:

- Start service outlets at various places offering the same package and quality
- to use private distributors for the purpose.

Maintaining standards of performance at the service outlet is always challenging for the service provider. If this job is assigned to middlemen, there may be a danger of decrease in the value of offering and bad reputation to the organisation. However, if the distributors have the ability and willingness to offer such services, the risk of failure and damage to the company image gets minimised. Quality in service is reflected in the encounter between customer and employees of the service firm.

To make services available at the right time and at the right place and accessible to consumers with ease and convenience, is the basic objective of distribution of services. All characteristics of services influence the distribution of services. The tangibles enable customers to avoid direct personal contact with their banker. The inseparability of services limits the scope of market expansion. The variability character of service limits the chances of standardisation and creates frontline management challenges. Due to the perishability of services, demand and capacity management at every service outlet becomes critical. Customer participation demands a customer friendly environment and equipment at the service distribution outlet. As services cannot be owned, the job of frontline employees becomes more critical in classifying and convincing customers. If the services are intangible such as education, consultancy and so on, the service provider needs to have more direct contact with the customer. When tangibles play a significant role in service production and delivery, the requirement of direct contact may be reduced or sometimes may be avoided.

2.3.1 Delivering Services through Intermediaries

Except for situations such as distance learning, where electronic channels can distribute services, providers and consumers come into direct contact in service provision. This is due to the inseparability of production and consumption in service, providers must either be present themselves when customer receive service or find ways to involve others in distribution. Quality in service occurs in the service encounter between company and customer and hence involving other becomes problematic. The value of the offering decreases and the reputation of the original service may be damaged, unless the service distributor is willing and able to perform in the service encounter as the service principal would. Service companies face an even more formidable task: *attaining service excellence and consistency when intermediaries represent them to customers.*

Roles of Middlemen or Intermediaries

- Information Flow
- Promotion Flow
- Pre-Sales Service
- Price Stability
- Post-Sales Service
- Title to the Goods
- **Information Flow:** The mediators like wholesalers, agents, buyers, retailers etc, are important sources of information for the marketer. The mediators have to be in constant touch with traders, competitors, customers. The information received by the mediators will then go to the service marketer with careful management. If any

change takes place with the system, the intermediaries will send out the warning signals. The changes are of the following types:

- **Customer Demographics and Psychographics:** A retailer will come to know the changes in the customer profile in his catchment area, such as their spending capability, addresses, average family size, occupation, their lifestyles and attitudes etc. Wholesalers are a source of information about the strengths and weaknesses of the retailers.
- **Media habits:** The retailers, news agents and cable operators have their fingers on the pulse of the media habits of the public, and the service firm should be smart enough to tap this source.
- **Entry of a New Competition, Brand or the Practice of a New Marketing Method or Promotion:** The retailers, wholesalers and agents are also the most important sources for any changes or entry in the composition of competitors. If a new brand or service product enters the marker, the service firm, could be alerted by its distribution chains. If a competitor tries out a new promotion scheme and if it happens to be effective or ineffective the service firm would be better off being warned than taken by surprise.

Due to the intangibility factor, the service marketer avoids the use of middlemen like dealers, stockists, warehouses and wholesalers, etc. Service retailing would entail servicing the consumer with information or the service itself.

- **Promotion Flow:** By using the mass media or through direct marketing, the channel or the intermediaries are an essential route for promotional information to travel from the former to the latter. The service firm uses the channel to implement its 'push' and 'pull' promotion strategy. The channel is also the source of information on the effectiveness of the promotions.
- **Pre-Sales Service:** The manufacturers of the service firms have been able to reduce the number of contacts with the customers and concentrate on their core offers, with the help of the channel members. Other marketing activities preceding sales such as packaging, marking, pricing and assembling goods which suit the final consumer are also performed by the channel members and other facilitators.
- **Price Stability:** To give an image of stability to the customer, the intermediaries absorb price hikes. The continuity of price is an attempt at overcoming intra-intermediaries competition.
- **Post-Sales Service:** Post-sales services like home delivery, installation and maintenance and repairs are given by the intermediaries. They direct the money received as payment in the reverse direction.

- **Title to the Goods:** It is very relevant in retailing, although this does not really work in services. Intermediaries like retailers take title to the goods and services and do transactions in their own name. The intermediaries share the risks with the vendors and the physical ownership of the goods will enable them to service the consumer's needs on time.

Strategies for Effective Service Delivery through Intermediaries

Service companies often face the question of how their intermediaries should be treated. If an effective service delivery is needed, then an effective management of the channels used for distribution should be in place. Whether the intermediaries should be treated as customers, partners or a part of the company should be decided by the service companies. Below are the strategies used by service companies to control the intermediaries effectively:

(A) Intermediary Control Strategies: By using control strategies, service companies can offer unique services, and enjoy high demand and customer loyalty. The basic principle is that intermediaries perform best when they are given standard instructions on the service quality and revenue generation, and are rewarded for their performance. These strategies require the active participation of the service principal. The two important aspects of a control strategy are:

1. **Review:** Franchisers can exert control over franchisees through non-renewals, restricted supplier resources, quotas and terminations. Franchisers can also offer price breaks to franchisees for achieving a certain volume of sales quota.

2. **Measurement:** The service principal (service provider) should find ways to measure the performance of the intermediaries on a regular basis. Conducting customer surveys provides feedback on the level of service provided by the franchisees. Franchisers may choose to reward the intermediaries based on their performance.

(B) Empowerment Strategies: If the service company uses the empowerment strategy, they follow the principle that the participative style of intermediary management delivers the best results. The different activities involved in adopting and implementing the empowerment strategy are discussed below:

1. **Enabling Intermediaries to Develop Customer-Oriented Service Processes:** Here, necessary support is provided to the intermediaries to set and maintain the service standards, as they lack the funds to conduct customer research or impart training to their employees.

2. **Providing Required Support Systems:** By offering them the support systems required for efficient performance, the service principal should help the intermediaries. Some of these are standard processes, quality standards which will help in improving, implementing and measuring services.

3. **Adopting Cooperative Management Structure:** This strategy aims at adopting a cooperative management structure by reducing the number of management levels at the service outlets and empowering franchisees to develop their own methods of hiring and training employees. This motivates the franchisees and improves their morale. This, in turn, results in increased revenues and profits as happy employees make customers happy.

4. **Motivating Intermediaries to Deliver Consistent Quality Service:** In this strategy, the service principal aims to provide training or implement other development programmes for service personnel of intermediaries to enhance their skills and knowledge on delivering quality service consistently. This includes rewarding the desired performance.

(C) **Partnering Strategies:** Since the relationship between the service principal and the intermediaries are improved, partnering strategies are considered very effective. Both the service principal and the intermediaries collectively learn new ways to improve the service delivery, and understand the changing tastes of target customers to change the service offering accordingly.

1. **Participation and Cooperation:** In this strategy, a service principal consults his intermediaries before introducing any new policies or policy changes. The views and opinions of intermediaries are considered important in decision-making. This strategy makes the intermediaries feel that they are also part of the business. They are motivated and offer innovative ideas for improving the system of service delivery.

2. **Alignment of Goals:** This strategy aims at aligning the goals of the service principal and those of the intermediaries. Intermediaries can set their individual targets to deliver quality service to the customers and to achieve their target revenues and profits. The principal does not interfere in the process and steps in only when the intermediary desires.

2.3.2 Delivering Services through Electronic Channels

Electronic channels are the only service distributors that do not require direct human interaction. What they do require is some pre-designed service and an electronic vehicle to deliver it. Most of the people are all familiar with telephone and television channels and the internet and web and may be aware of the other electronic vehicles that are currently under development.

The consumer and business services that are made possible through these vehicles include movies on demand, interactive news and music, banking and financial services, multimedia libraries and databases, distance learning, desktop videoconferencing, remote health services, and interactive, network-based games. The more a service relies on technology and/or equipment for service production and the less it relies on face-to-face contact with service providers, the less the service is characterised by inseparability and non-standardisation. Using electronic channels overcomes some of the problems associated with service inseparability and allows a form of standardisation not previously possible in most services.

More recently, entrepreneurs have taken advantage of the Internet to create new services. Four innovations of particular interest are

- Usage of voice-recognition technology that allows customers to give information and request service simply by speaking into a phone or microphone.
- Creation of websites that provide information, take orders, and even serve as a delivery channel for information-based services.
- Commercialisation of "smart cards" containing a microchip that can store detailed information about the customer and act as an electronic purse containing digital money. The ultimate in self-service banking will be when you can only use a smart card as an electronic wallet for a wide array of transactions, but also refill it from a special card reader connected to your PC
- Development of "smart" mobile telephones and PDAs (personal digital assistants), and Wi-Fi speed Internet technology that can link users to the Internet wherever they may be.

As a distribution channel, the Internet facilitates categories of "flow" information:

- negotiation
- service
- transactions
- promotion.

It is a good method to help market goods and services by helping researchers create online communities, obtain their feedback soon from consumers and collect data on consumer information instead of the traditional methods.

There are a lot of online communities all over the world though the first one was Amazon.com. Ease of search, 24/7 service, comfort of their homes or offices, convenience, a bigger selection, prompt delivery and a better price are the factors that attract consumers to online stores.

Apart from the physical stores, many chains are opening online stores, in an effort to counter competition from "cyberspace retailers". However high capital setup costs, and no one can be sure whether the investment will lead to long-term profits and high growth when adding an internet channel . In India, Amazon.com, flipkart.com, jabong.com, myntra.com are good examples of online stores.

Online stores are becoming more user friendly and sophisticated. They replicate the services of a sales associate so that customers are likely to purchase the product online. Online live chat is also available which provides the customer with a helpful customer service personnel. Facilitating searches is another useful service on many sites ranging from looking at what books are available by a particular author to finding schedules of flights between two cities on a specific date.

Recent developments, such as, customer relationship management (CRM) systems, mobile telephony, integrating mobile devices into the service delivery infrastructure can be used as a means to:

1. access services,
2. alert customers to opportunities or problems by delivering the right information or interaction at the right time,
3. update information in real time to ensure that it is continuously accurate and relevant.

2.4 Service Promotion

The customer buys a combination of product, price and place not having been convinced of the availability of all these factors to his satisfaction he then buys an image, when he buys the services and the attached products. The promotion mix is the creation of the perception building activities and exercises and it is a part of the marketing mix and cannot be separated from it. The consumer while buying identical services may buy different things for this personal satisfaction. Some of the things he buys:

- The image of the service in relation to other service brands on the offer.
- The image of the service provider in relation to other service providers.
- And the self-image created by him through the use of marketing and other promotional efforts adopted by the service providers.

2.4.1 Objectives of Service Promotion

Service promotion as we have learnt, is a part of the marketing mix and cannot be separated from the other elements of the marketing mix. When a service organisation speaks of the service promotion, the act will involve promoting all elements of the marketing mix comprising the tangible and the intangible essentials of materials of material service, the price and the service delivery place along with its physical evidence, the personnel involved in service and the perception that the service provider wants to create about the service he is selling. By following the below objectives of sales promotion the firm will be able to achieve all these:

1. **Motivating Intermediaries:** Intermediaries play a very significant role in promoting services in services marketing. The service items many a times carry out promotion campaigns to motivate the intermediaries and promote their service facilities to gain better customer patronage of the service delivery points.

2. **Increasing Awareness of New Service:** All promotions are directed at the initial stage to create awareness about the service provider amongst the targeted universe of customers and prospects. The entire effort of the firm at this level is to make sure that new customers are not only informed of the service but they are also attracted to visit the service administrative points and buy the services of the firm.

3. **Competitive Sales Strategy:** The campaigns can be directed at the trading intermediaries, customers and prospects to inform them about the competitive strengths of the services marketing firm. The firms can go outright offensive against the claims by being competitive in its campaigns or it can adopt a defensive strategy depending on the strategy so decided. Promotion many a times is directed towards taking a stand against the strategies adopted by the competitors selling similar or identical services.

2.4.2 Role of Marketing Communications

The following points are the roles that the marketing communication follows:

1. **Add Value through Communication Content:** Information and consultation are important ways to add value to a product. Potential customers may need information and advice about what service options are available to them; where and when these services are available; how much they cost, and what features, functions, and service benefits there are.

2. **Position and Differentiate the Service:** Communication efforts serve not only to attract new users but also to maintain contact with an organisation's existing customers and build relationships with them. Marketing communications is used to convince potential and current customers about the firm's superior performance on determinant attributes. Firms must use marketing communications to persuade target consumers that their service offers the best solution in meeting the consumer's needs.

3. **Facilitate Customer Involvement in Service Production:** Customers need training to help them perform well, when they are actively involved in service production. The company also benefits, when customers perform well since its productivity increases. By showing service delivery in action, is a good way to train customers. Television and videos are effective because of their ability to interest the viewer and to show a sequence of events in visual form.

4. **Stimulate of Dampen Demand to Match Capacity:** Many life service performances, such as a "buy 1 get one 1 free" haircut on Wednesdays, are time specific and they cannot be used at a later time. Advertising and sales promotions can help to change the timing of customer use and thus help to match demand with the available capacity at a given time.

2.4.3 Marketing Communications Planning

There are five essential W's which will help the service provider to gather a lot of information regarding the consumer. A useful checklist for marketing communication planning is provided by the "5 Ws" model:
- Who is our target audience?
- What do we need to communicate and achieve?
- Why should we communicate this?
- Where should we communicate this?
- When do the communications need to take place?

The first part to review is defining **WHO** is the target audience

Defining the Target Audience

The three broad target audiences for any service communication strategy are:
- **Prospects:** Marketers of consumer services do not usually know prospects in advance. Therefore, they typically use a traditional communications mix, like media advertising, public relations, and use of purchased lists for e-mail campaigns, direct mail, or telemarketing.
- **Employees:** Employees serve as a secondary audience for communication campaigns through public media. A well designed campaign targeted at users, nonusers, or both can also be motivating for employees, especially those in frontline roles. In particular, it may help to shape employees' behaviour if the advertising content shows them what is promised to customers. However, there is a risk of demotivating employees if the communication promotes levels of performance that they feel are unrealistic or even impossible to achieve.
- **Users:** In contrast to prospects, more cost-effective channels can be used to reach existing users. These include cross- or up-selling efforts by frontline employees, point-of sale promotions, and other information distributed during service encounters. If the firm has a membership relationship with its customers and has a membership database containing contact and profiling information, it can distribute highly targeted information through e-mail, text messages, direct mail, or telephone.

Specifying Communication Objectives

Once the target audience is defined, we have to define what has to be achieved with this audience. Communications objectives answer the question of what we need to communicate and achieve. Marketers need to be clear about their goals; otherwise, it will be difficult to formulate specific communications objectives and select the most appropriate messages and communication tools to achieve them. Common educational and promotional objectives for service organisations include:

- Create memorable images of companies and their brands.
- Build awareness and interest in an unfamiliar service or brand.
- Compare a service favourably with competitors' offerings.
- Build preference by communicating the strengths and benefits of a specific brand.
- (Re)position a service relative to competitive offerings.
- Reduce uncertainty and perceived risk by providing useful information and advice.
- Provide reassurance, such as by promoting service guarantees.
- Encourage trial by offering promotional incentives.
- Familiarise customers with service processes in advance of use.
- Teach customers how to use a service to their best advantage.
- Stimulate demand in low-demand periods and shift demand during peak periods.
- Recognise and reward valued customers.

Elements of Service Promotion: Service Promotion Mix

Once the target audience and the objectives are in place, the next step would be to select a mix of cost effective communications channels. Most service marketers have access to numerous forms of communication, referred to collectively as the marketing communications mix. Different communication elements have distinctive capabilities relative to the types of messages they can convey and the market segments most likely to be exposed to them. The mix includes personal communications, advertising, sales promotion, publicity and public relations, instructional materials, and corporate design.

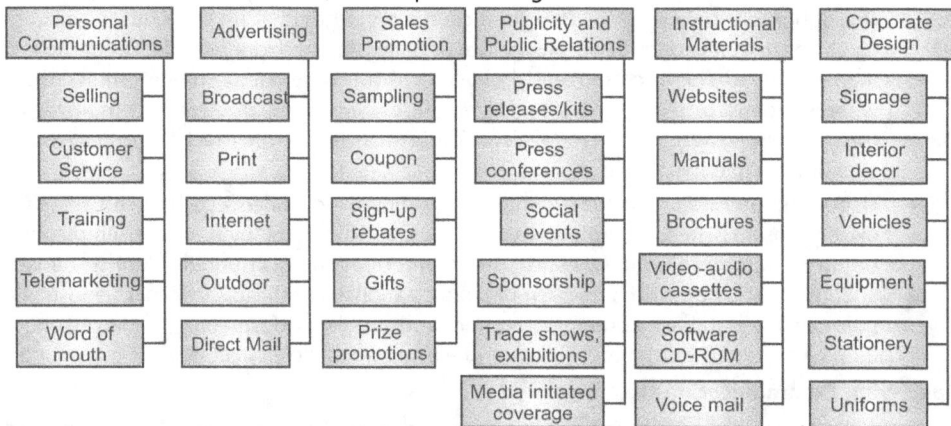

Fig. 2.7: The marketing communications mix for services

As shown in the figure two main channels can be categorised as those controlled by the organisation and those that are not. Not all communications messages originate from the service provider. Rather, some messages originate from outside the organisation. Messages from an internal source can be further divided into those:

- transmitted through marketing channels (traditional media and the Internet).
- transmitted through the service firm's own service delivery channels.

Messages Transmitted through Traditional Marketing Channels

The principal elements of messages transmitted through marketing channels are:

1. **Advertising:** The most commonly used form of communication in consumer marketing and is often the first point of contact between service marketers and their customers is advertising. It informs, persuades, reminds and builds awareness and plays an important role in providing factual information about services and educating customers about product features and capabilities. The most important challenge facing the advertisers is getting the consumer's attention.

2. **Public Relations:** Public relations (PR) involves efforts to stimulate positive interest in an organisation. A basic element in PR strategy is the preparation and distribution of press releases (including photos and/or videos) that feature stories about the company, its products and its employees and the organisation. PR is done by sending out news releases, holding press conferences, staging special events, and sponsoring newsworthy activities put on by third parties. These tools can help a service organisation build its reputation and credibility; form strong relationships with its employees, customers, and the community; and secure an image conducive to business success.

    Other widely used PR methods include recognition and reward programmes, obtaining testimonials from public figures, community involvement and support, fundraising, and obtaining favourable publicity for the organisation through special events.

3. **Direct Marketing:** Tools such as mailings, email and text messaging are included in this channel. These channels offer the potential to send personalised messages to highly targeted micro segments. Commercial services are available that combine company collected data with rich, third-party online and offline data sources. When marketers possess a detailed database of information about customers and prospects, direct strategies will succeed.

4. **Sales Promotion:** Looking at sales promotions as a communication with an incentive is a good way. Sales promotions usually are specific to a time period, price, or customers group-sometimes all three. Typically, the objective is to get customers

to make a purchase decision faster or encourage customers to use a specific service sooner, in greater volume with each purchase, or more frequently. Used in these forms, they increase sales during periods when demand would otherwise be weak, speed up the introduction and acceptance of new services, and generally get customers to act faster than they would in the absence of any promotional incentive.

5. **Personal Selling:** This refers to interpersonal encounters in which efforts are made to educate customers and promote a particular brand or product. Many firms, especially those marketing business-to-business services, have a sales team or employ agents and distributors to undertake personal selling efforts on their behalf.

6. **Trade Shows:** Trade shows are a popular form of publicity that also include important personal selling opportunities in the business to business marketplace. Trade shows receive a lot of media coverage and offer business customers an opportunity to find out about the latest offerings from a wide variety of suppliers in the field, in many industries. Trade shows can be very productive promotional tools because they are among the few opportunities in which large numbers of potential buyers come to the marketer rather than the other way around. A sales representative who usually reaches four to five prospective clients per day may be able to generate five useful leads per hour at a show. Service vendors provide physical evidence in the form of exhibits, samples, demonstrations, and brochures to educate and impress these potential customers.

Messages Transmitted through the Internet

Advertising on the Internet allows companies to complement and sometimes even substitute traditional communications channels at a reasonable cost. Remember Internet advertising should be part of an integrated, well-designed communication strategy.

1. **Company's Website:** Marketers use their own websites for a variety of communications tasks, including promoting consumer awareness and interest, providing information and consultation, facilitating two-way communications with customers through email and chat room, stimulating product trial, enabling customers to pace orders etc.

2. **Online Advertising:** Banner advertising and search engine advertising are the two main options of online advertising. By advertising online, It provides a very clear and measurable return on investment, especially when compared to other forms of advertising.

    - **Search Engine Advertising:** Search engines are a form of a reverse broadcast network. Instead of advertisers broadcasting their messages to consumers, search engines let advertisers know exactly what consumers want through their keyword

search. Advertisers can target relevant marketing communications directly at these consumes. One of the phenomenal success stories of search engine advertising has been Google with firms like Yahoo!, QOL, MSN seeking to become major players in this field.
- **Banner Advertising:** Many firms pay to place advertising banners and buttons on portals like Yahoo or CNN as well as on other firms' websites. The usual goal is to draw online traffic to the advertiser's own site. In many instances, websites include advertising messages from other marketers with related but non-competing services. For example, Yahoo's stock quotes page features a sequence of advertisements for various financial service providers.

Moving from Impersonal to Personal Communication:

Communication experts divide impersonal communications. Technology has created a gray area between personal and impersonal communication.

With the advances of on-demand technologies, consumers are increasingly empowered to decide how and when they like to be reached. This development is transforming marketing communications not only on the Internet but also on TV and radio.

Messages Transmitted through Service Delivery Channels

Unlike most goods marketers, service firms typically control the point-of-sale and service delivery channels, which offer service firms particularly powerful and cost-effective communications opportunities. Specifically, messages can be transmitted through service outlets, frontline employees, self-service delivery points, and even customer training.

1. **Frontline Employees:** Employees in frontline positions may serve customers face-to-face by telephone, or via e-mail. Communication from frontline staff takes the form of the core service and a variety of supplementary services, including providing information, taking reservations, receiving payments, and solving problems. New customers, in particular, often rely on customer service personnel for help in learning to use a service effectively and to solve problems. The frontline staff has a very important part to play. Brand equity is created very much through a customer's personal experience with the service firm. In comparison, mass communications are more suitable for creating awareness and interest.

2. **Service Outlets:** Both planned and unintended messages reach customers through the service delivery environment. Impersonal messages can be distributed in the form of banners, posters, signage, brochures, video screens, and audio. As we will discuss in Service Environment, the physical design of the service outlet -what we call the servicescape sends important messages to customers. Interior architects and corporate design consultants can design the servicescape to coordinate the visual

elements of both interiors and exteriors in such a way that they communicate and strengthen the positioning of the firm and shape the nature of the customers' service experiences in positive ways.

3. **Self-Service Delivery Points:** ATMs, vending machines, and websites are all examples of self-service delivery points. Promoting self-service delivery requires clear signage, step-by-step instructions on how to operate the equipment, and user-friendly design. Self-service delivery points often can be effectively used in communications with current and potential customers and to cross-sell services and promote new services.

Messages Originating from Outside the Organisation

Messages about a company and its products come from outside the organisation and are not controlled by the marketer. They include word-of-mouth, blogs, Twitter, and media coverage.

1. **Word-of-Mouth:** Word-of-mouth (WOM) has a powerful influence on people's decisions to use (or avoid using) a service. Recommendations from other customers are generally viewed as more credible than a firm's promotional activities. In fact, the greater the risk customers perceive in purchasing a service, the more actively they will seek and rely on WOM to guide their decision making. In addition, WOM has been found to be an important predictor of top-line growth. There are now ways to measure WOM and these allow firms to test the effect of WOM on sales and market share for brands, individual promotional campaigns, and also for the company as a whole.

Positive WOM is particularly important for service firms, as services tend to have a high proportion of experience and credence attributes and are therefore associated with high perceived risk by potential buyers.

These include:

- Offering promotions that encourage customers to persuade others to join them in using the service (for instance, "bring two friends, and the third eats for free" or "subscribe to two cell phone service plans, and we'll waive the monthly subscription fee for all other immediate family members").
- Presenting and publicising testimonials. Advertising and brochures sometimes feature comments from satisfied customers
- Referencing other purchasers and knowledgeable individuals, for instance: "We have done a great job for ABC Corp., and if you wish, feel free to talk to Mr. Cabral, their MIS manager, who oversaw the implementation of our project."

- Developing referral incentive schemes, such as rewarding an existing customer with units of free service, a voucher, or even cash for introducing new customers to the firm.
- Creating exciting promotions that get people talking about the great service the firm provides. Richard Branson of Virgin Atlantic Airways has repeatedly got people talking about his airline. For example, Branson abseiled (climbed down) off a 407 feet Las Vegas hotel dressed like James Bond in a tuxedo to promote his, then new, Virgin America airline. More and more firms are running creative promotions on social media that can get global attention in a few days.

In addition to WOM, we also have "word-of-mouse." Viral marketing has spread so fast online that firms cannot ignore it. One of the early success stories of online viral marketing was Microsoft's free e-mail service, Hotmail.

2. **Blogs - A Type of Online WOM:** Blogs also know as Web logs are seen everywhere today. They can be modified, web pages and their entries are listed in reverse chronological sequence. Best described as online journal, news listing or diaries where people can post anything. Bloggets, who are authors, usually focus on narrow topics, and quite a few love become de facto watchdogs and self-proclaimed experts in certain fields. Some sites, such as the travel-focused tripadvisor.com, allow users to post their own reviews or ask questions that more experienced travelers may be able to answer. There are a growing number of travel-oriented sites.

Blogs have evolved into a new form of social interaction on the web, and this what marketers are interested in: a massively distributed but completely connected conversation covering every imaginable topic, including consumers' experiences with service firms and their recommendations on avoiding or patronising certain firms.

3. **Twitter:** Created in 2006 by Jack Dorsey, Twitter has gained in popularity worldwide and was the fastest-growing social networking service in 2009. Service firms have started using Twitter in various ways. Twitter is a social networking and microblogging service that allows its users to send and read other users updates, which are up to 140 characters in length and can send and **receive** via the Twitter web site

4. **Media Coverage:** Although the online world is rapidly increasing in importance, coverage on traditional media cannot be neglected, especially as newsworthy events often are first discussed in the online world, but then are picked up and reported in the traditional media that then, reach the broad masses. Media coverage of firms and their services is frequently stimulated by PR activity, but broadcasters and publishers also often initiate their own coverage. In addition to news stories about a company and its services, editorial coverage can take several other forms.

2.4.4 Integrated Services Marketing Communication

Accurate and appropriate communications, that do not overpromise or misrepresent are essential in delivering services that customers perceive as high in quality. One of the major difficulties associated with these types of communications is that they involve issues that cross disciplinary boundaries, since, service advertising promises what people do, and because what people do cannot be controlled in the same way as machines that produce physical goods, this type of communication involves functions other than the marketing department. Marketing must accurately but charmingly reflect what happens in actual service encounters set-up unrealistic expectations for customers, the actual encounter will disappoint the customer.

The difference between what a firm promises about a service and what it actually delivers, is a major cause of poorly perceived service. Customer expectations are shaped by both uncontrollable and company-controlled factors. Customer needs are key factors that influence customer expectations but are rarely controllable by the firm, customer experiences with other service providers, and word of mouth. Company advertising, personal selling, and the promises made by service personnel, which are controllable factors influence the expectations that customers hold for a service. Accurate, coordinated, and appropriate company communication is essential to delivering services that customers perceive as high in quality.

This concept includes many online and offline marketing channels. Offline marketing channels are traditional print (newspaper, magazine), mail order, public relations, industry analyst relations billboard, radio, and television. Online marketing channels include any e-marketing campaigns or programmes, from search engine optimisation (SEO), pay-per-click, affiliate, email, banner to latest web-related channels for webinar, blog, RSS, podcast, and Internet TV.

An integrated communications programme is the coordinated use of the various communication mediums to accomplish a central objective. Communications include the promotional options of advertising, sales promotion, and personal selling. Communications within the marketing context involves informing, persuading, and influencing consumer behaviour.

Importance of Integrated Marketing Communications
1. Greater communication consistency.
2. Improved creative integrity.
3. Improved use of media.
4. Increased overall impact.

5. Underlines increased importance of brand image.
6. Improves marketing precision.
7. Enables greater client control over marketing communications.
8. Helps eliminate misconceptions between multiple agencies.
9. Provides more client control over parties involved.
10. Provides clients with greater professional expertise.
11. Improves operation efficiency.
12. Reduced cost of marketing communications programmes.
13. Provides method for effective measurement.
14. Creates opportunity for greater agency accountability.

2.4.5 Referrals: Using Power of Word of Mouth

One of the most powerful sources of leads is through referrals, when it comes to getting new customers. The old fashioned way is word of mouth as compared paid advertisement.

Chances are that the customers are spreading the word anyway, if the firm keeps quality services and products.

Word-of-mouth is characterised as oral, person-to-person communication between a receiver and a communicator whom the receiver perceives as non-commercial, regarding a brand, product or service. This was an attempt to identify the domain of WOM research.

Stern defined word-of-mouth by drawing on its distinctiveness from advertising. WOM involves the exchange of ephemeral oral or spoken messages between a contiguous source and a recipient who communicate directly in real life. Consumers are not assumed to create, revise and record pre-written conversational exchanges about products and services.

However, we've come a long way from leads exchange networking groups where participants were actively encouraged to refer new business to each other. Those groups still have their place.

Word-of-mouth marketing, which occurs when others tell each other about a business, is also considered a form of referral marketing. Referral marketing is spreading the word about a product or service through a business' existing customers, rather than traditional advertising.

Taxonomy of Referrals

A.F.T. Payne developed taxonomy of referral types, broadly split into two groups:

1. **Customer referrals** may be either customer initiated or company initiated.
   (i) **Customer-initiated referrals** originate from current or former customers who have been satisfied or delighted with their experiences. They act as unpaid advocates.

(ii) **Company initiated referrals:** A number of companies are attempting to harness the power of WOM by giving customers incentives to refer their friends and family.

2. **Non-customer referrals:** Companies may benefit from a number of other referral sources, in addition to these customer referrals. ***Reciprocal referrals*** *occur when two or more organisations agree to cross-refer customers to each other.* Examples of reciprocal referrals are law firms, estate agents and building societies. Divisionalised organisations, such as accounting firms, may cross-refer clients between divisions, for example audit customers might be targeted for consultancy services. Referrals from current or past employees may also benefit a company.

Importance of Referrals
- Customer defections are kept to a minimum.
- The most powerful fact associated with customers making referrals is that they are willing to put their reputations on the line, When this happens, the customers are basically becoming the practice's external marketing department.
- Customers are retained longer and customer acquisition costs are minimised
- Most telling indicator of a practice's growth potential is the propensity of its customers to refer its services to their friends and family

Two Factors Related to Referrals
1. **Trust:** Being referred to someone comes with an implied endorsement. People don't like risks, and they don't want to belong to the burned buyers club. So by simply opening, themselves to the idea of asking others who they recommend, they move closer to acceptance and action required to make a buying decision.
2. **Risk Elimination:** Essentially the recommendation eliminates the need for the potential client to look at normal depths with your products and services. Of course, the risk is not entirely eliminated, granted. But the normal methods of sales channels and marketing methods designed to influence, a decision, those are typically side-stepped.

2.4.6 Visual Merchandising

Visual merchandising, briefly defined, *is the presentation of a store and its merchandise in ways that will attract the attention of potential customers and motivate them to make purchases.* The role of the visual merchandiser in this effort is to carry out the merchandising concepts as formulated by management. These merchandising plans include what items are to be featured and in which locations they should be housed. The visual merchandiser, guided by these decisions and using all of his or her creative talents, sets out to present the best possible visual effects.

It involves artistic talent and training and also knowledge of tools, lighting, construction of backgrounds and props, and a complete understanding of store design. A position as a visual merchandiser involves a combination of skills, including creativity; a sense of order; dedication to design principles; and the discipline to follow directions, stay within budgets, and complete paperwork. Other important skills include the ability to create signs, write copy, and create and choose appropriate graphics.

2.4.6.1 Components of Visual Merchandising

A variety of different components must be successfully coordinated, in order to bring the retail premises to its highest level of visual appeal, and to effectively differentiate one retail facility from another. Visual merchandisers must be constantly aware of what's taking place in each of these visual segments and must be prepared to make any necessary changes. The following sections represent an overview of the various components.

1. **Mannequins:** While traditional mannequins are still often featured, many stores have replaced them with, to name a few, wire mannequins, soft sculptured types, stylised forms, and motorised models. With the increasing cost of traditional mannequins, many merchants have opted for forms that represent mannequins and are created by visual merchandisers.

2. **Store Design**: There is no longer a typical store design. Merchants employ the services of architects and designers who, along with visual merchandisers, create environments that are both unique and functional. The space that was once allocated to store windows has been minimised and replaced with more selling floor space. In place of the traditional windows, large panes of glass are used to allow shoppers to see a large portion of the store. The interiors range from natural settings using stone and hand-hewn woods to elegant environments with atriums, majestic staircases, marble flooring, and other touches of grandeur. Many of the major department stores are reducing the appearance of vast selling floors with the construction of individual shops or boutiques to house their special designer collections. This approach gives the customer the feeling of shopping in smaller stores rather than the cold feeling of the large department store.

   Food stores are abandoning the sterile looks long associated with them in favor of surroundings that feature espresso and juice bars, preparation areas that allow shoppers to see how the products are prepared, areas that offer "prepared meals," and a host of kiosk fixtures scattered throughout the store.

3. **Sound Usage:** Sound is not a visual element, but it is being used to enhance visual presentation. Professionals in the field agree that shoppers can turn away from visual elements, but sound is inescapable. The first early venture into sound for visual enhancement was made by Disney. In its Main Street environment in Disneyland, Disney determined that the attractions alone were not sufficiently stimulating. The incorporation of sound made them come to life. Sound is being used abundantly by

retailers today to set moods and give shoppers news. More and more retailers are using music to put shoppers in a buying frame of mind.

4. **Graphics and Signage:** Although traditional two-dimensional signs are still used abundantly, signage and graphics have taken on new looks. Airbrushed murals celebrating local landmarks, multilevel murals featuring a variety of montages, animated cartoon characters that move throughout the signage, backlit transparencies, light walls, prismatic displays, and digitally produced huge photographic blowups that rival outdoor billboards are just a few of the exciting approaches now used in retail environments.

   Electronics continue to pervade retailers' premises. In addition to in-store video, retailers are using other electronic formats to capture shoppers' attention. The system highlights store sales and promotions and gives previews of upcoming events. It also automatically dispenses individual retailer coupons. The customer inputs his or her size and selects an outfit, which is then displayed on the person's image on a computerised screen.

5. **Lighting:** Although fluorescents are still used by retailers like supermarkets and warehouse clubs for general illumination, this form of lighting is no longer in great prominence in most retail stores. Today, halogen and quartz lighting and high-intensity discharge lamps are the products of choice. They not only serve the functional needs of illumination but can be used to achieve dramatic effects. Numerous types of cans or holders are being used to house these light bulbs, supplying a variety of looks to augment the many types of store fixtures.

6. **Props and Materials:** The list of materials and props used by today's visual merchandisers seems to be endless. Although conventional store-bought props are available at various resource centers, more and more retailers are making use of things found in nature (such as tree branches, rocks, and sand) and found objects once reserved for the junk pile (such as old chairs, worn picture frames, and rusty farm tools). With fresh coats of paint and new finishes, found display objects can be used dramatically in displays. Not only do they provide for effective visual presentations, they also enable budgets to go further. Antiques and antique reproductions are also being used extensively. Of course, at Christmas time, animated displays and glittery props are still of paramount importance. Shoppers line up along the major department store windows to enjoy the creative offerings of companies.

7. **Point of Purchase:** In addition to the signage that abounds in retail establishments, there are point-of-purchase programmes developed by manufacturers for retailer use. The point-of-purchase merchandising is defined as "displays, signs, structures and devices that are used to identify, advertise and/or merchandise an outlet, service or product and which serve as an aid to retail selling". Industry reports revealed that whenever these programmes were in evidence for specific brands, sales increased significantly.

2.4.6.2 Trends in Visual Merchandising

Companies are undertaking changes in visual programmes and directions to maintain their places in this highly competitive business arena. Visual merchandisers have come up with new approaches to planning as sometimes the visual budgets have strained. Others without the constraints of limited funds have also embarked upon new approaches to their programmes that they hope will generate excitement and transform "lookers" into customers. By all accounts, there are many trends, no matter what the budget, that are making headlines in the area of visual merchandising and environmental design, such as:

1. **Directional Signage:** It has become essential for retailers to create directional signage that quickly directs the customer to the right place to find the desired products. To achieve this there is a trend toward greater use of hanging and framing systems. Companies are addressing retailer needs with a wealth of new signage products that will more than likely become part of the interior landscape of the vast majority of large retail spaces
2. **Increased use of Graphics:** In just about every retailing venue, and in the stores that house them, the use of graphics is reaching new heights. Everything from the digitally produced "billboards" to graphics that feature motion is being utilised to capture the attention of the shopper.
3. **Resurgence of Mannequins:** In the past few years, many retailers have opted for less costly, more practical mannequins on which to display their merchandise. Today, however, and for the foreseeable future, companies are following the trend of relying upon unique mannequins to enhance their facilities in place of the less costly "torso" and "headless" types that made their way into visual merchandising during the close of the twentieth century.
4. **Opulence in Store Design:** Throughout the country, upscale retailers are investing in store designs that are more extravagant than ever before. Companies have taken facilities design to new heights in City emporiums with extravagant fixtures, lighting, and other amenities to capture the upper-class market. This is only the beginning and that retailers will be likely to continue these design endeavors for the foreseeable future.
5. **Innovative Lighting:** A wealth of new ideas is now vastly improving lighting for interiors and visual presentations. Included are advances in color kinetics, new lensing systems that give a smoother appearance to the light beam, new lighting control systems, and greater energy efficiency in white-light LEDs.

2.4.7 Challenges of Service Communication

Traditional marketing communication strategies were shaped largely by the needs and practices associated with marketing manufactured goods. However, several of the differences that distinguish services from goods also have a significant effect on the ways we approach the design of service marketing communication programmes.

Problems of Intangibility

Services are performances rather than objects, their benefits can be difficult to communicate to customers, especially when the service in question does not involve tangible actions to customers or their possessions. Intangibility creates four problems for marketers seeking to promote its attributes or benefits. **Banwari Mittal** and **Julie Baker** highlight the implications of each of these four problems as follows:

1. **Generality refers** to items that comprise a class of objects, persons and events - for instance, airline seats, flight attendants and cabin service. These general classes have physical analogues and most consumers of the service know that they are. However, a key task for marketers seeking to create a distinctive value proposition is to communicate what makes a specific offering distinctly different from and superior to competing offerings.
2. **Abstractness:** Because abstract concepts such as financial security, expert advice or safe transportation do not have one-to-one correspondence with physical objects, it can be challenging for marketers to connect their services to those concepts.
3. **Nonsearchability:** It refers to the fact that intangibles cannot be searched or inspected before they are purchased. Physical service attributes, such as the appearance of a health club and the type of equipment installed, can be checked in advance, but the experience of working with the trainers can only be determined through extended personal involvement.
4. **Mental impalpability:** Many services are sufficiently complex, multidimensional or novel that it is difficult for consumers - especially new prospects - to understand what the experience of using them will be like and what benefits will result.

Points to Remember

- Service is an intangible product.
- The customer satisfaction is divided into three determinants:
    1. perceived service quality,
    2. perceived value and
    3. customer expectations
- Customer satisfaction is defined as an "evaluation of the perceived discrepancy between prior expectations and the actual performance of the product".
- "Customer Satisfaction = Perception of Performance – Expectations"
- Service Perception – Service Expectation = Perceived Service Quality → Customer satisfaction.
- The Tolerance zone or zone of tolerance (ZOT) is defined as "the difference between desired service and the level of service considered adequate".
- Desired service – Adequate service = Zone of tolerance.

- Methods of measuring customer expectations and customer perceptions are current methods of measuring customer expectations and customer perceptions, SERVQUAL, SERVPERF, Critical Incidents Technique, observation studies, focus group discussions and in-depth interviews.
- The ServQual model of measuring service quality is based on the pioneering work of Parasuraman, Zeithaml and Berry. The model talks about the way a customer distinguishes the service quality by comparing the expected service with the perceived service.
- Service = Service expectations - Service perceptions.
- Critical incident as described by Lovelock, Patterson and Walker, is a technique designed to elicit details about services that "particularly dissatisfy or delight customers".
- The term customer loyalty is used to describe as the behaviour of repeat customers, as well as those that offer good ratings, reviews, or testimonials.
- To reduce the effect of service failure on business interests of service companies, service recovery concepts came into force.
- Landon defines customer complaint behaviour as "an expression of dissatisfaction by individual consumers (or on a consumer's behalf) to a responsible party in either the distribution channel or a complaint handling agency".
- Price = Direct costs + Overhead costs + Profit margin.
- Revenue management is the collection of strategies and tactics firms use to scientifically manage demand for their products and services.
- Yield management, also known as revenue management, aims at earning the highest possible revenue in capacity-constrained services through the service-provider's operations.
- Process of revenue management: data collection, forecasting, optimisation, control.
- In segmented pricing, the company sells a product or service at two or more prices, even though the differences in prices are not based on differences in costs.
- Price discrimination is selling a product at different prices for different classes of buyers based on their differing demand for the product or service; whether the product or service actually differs among the price groups is secondary, but in most cases, the different prices charged are not related to the differences in the cost of providing the underlying item.
- A useful checklist for marketing communication planning is provided by the "5 Ws" model:
  1. Who is our target audience?
  2. What do we need to communicate and achieve?
  3. Why should we communicate this?
  4. Where should we communicate this?
  5. When do the communications need to take place?

- Reciprocal referrals occur when two or more organisations agree to cross-refer customers to each other.
- Visual merchandising, briefly defined, is the presentation of a store and its merchandise in ways that will attract the attention of potential customers and motivate them to make purchases.

Questions for Discussion

1. Discuss the concept of traditional marketing mix elements in services.
2. What is the relationship between customer perception, customer satisfaction and service quality?
3. Discuss the steps involved in SERVQUAL, GAP, and critical incident model.
4. Describe the process of creating a customer loyalty programme.
5. Elaborate the nature of complaining behaviour and handling customer complaints.
6. Explain the service recovery process.

Multiple Choice Questions

1. The difference between desired service and the level of service considered adequate is known as
   - (a) Service Quality
   - (b) Tolerance zone
   - (c) GAP
   - (d) SERVQUAL
2. The difference between which two expectation standards is the zone of tolerance?
   - (a) Desired service, adequate service
   - (b) Professional service, adequate service
   - (c) Desire service, adequate service
   - (d) Desired service, advance service
3. Perception of Performance – Expectation gives us
   - (a) Customer motivation
   - (b) Customer service
   - (c) Customer satisfaction
   - (d) Customer performance
4. Attributes where consumers can evaluate only during or after the consumption process is known as:
   - (a) Credence qualities
   - (b) Experience Qualities
   - (c) Search Qualities
   - (d) None of the above
5. What are the five principal dimensions to judge service quality?
   - (a) Reliability, responsiveness, assurance, empathy, tangibles
   - (b) Reliability, response, assurance, empathy, tangibles
   - (c) Reliability, responsiveness, assurance, empathy, targets
   - (d) Reliability, responsiveness, aspects, empathy, tangibles

6. What is the sequence of steps for the service recovery process?
    (a) Anticipating customer needs, acknowledging their feelings, Apologising and Owning the Responsibility, Offering alternatives, making amends,
    (b) Acknowledging their feelings, Apologising and Owning the Responsibility, making amends, anticipating customer needs, Offering alternatives
    (c) Acknowledging their feelings, Apologising and Owning the Responsibility, Offering alternatives, making amends, anticipating customer needs
    (d) Acknowledging their feelings, Offering alternatives, Apologising and Owning the Responsibility, making amends, anticipating customer needs
7. The collection of strategies and tactics firms use to scientifically manage demand for their products and services is known as:
    (a) Customer profitability measurement
    (b) Costs of service delivery
    (c) segmented pricing
    (d) Revenue management
8. Which is a type of auction?
    (a) Open descending
    (b) Open Close
    (c) Sealed price
    (d) Sealed ascending
9. How many types of price discriminations are there?
    (a) 1
    (b) 3
    (c) 2
    (d) 4
10. Text messaging is a type of which promotion strategy?
    (a) Personal Selling
    (b) Sales Promotion
    (c) Direct Marketing
    (d) Public relations

Answers

1. (b)	2. (a)	3. (c)	4. (b)	5. (a)	6. (c)	7. (d)	8. (a)	9. (b)	10. (c)

Project Questions

1. Evaluate the service quality that you received from the institution you have studied from, by using the five dimensions mentioned.
2. A number of supply and demand strategies were presented as possible solutions to offset the challenges created by the perishability of services.
    (a) Discuss the major objective of demand strategies in comparison to supply strategies.
    (b) To which group of strategies does "increasing consumer participation" belong?
    (c) How does "increasing consumer participation" solve potential problems caused by the perishability of services?

■■■

Chapter 3...

Service Process

Contents ...
3.1 Introduction
3.2 Service Process
    3.2.1 Introduction
    3.2.2 Steps for Managing Service Processes
3.3 Service Design
    3.3.1 Introduction
    3.3.2 Service Blue Printing
    3.3.3 Quality Function Deployment
3.4 Demand and Capacity Management
    3.4.1 Introduction
    3.4.2 Level of Demand
    3.4.3 Managing Fluctuations in Service Demand
    3.4.4 Waiting Lines
3.5 Standardisation: Customer Defined Service Standards
    3.5.1 Introduction
    3.5.2 Factors Necessary for Appropriate Service Standards
    3.5.3 Types of Service Standards: Hard and Soft Measures
3.6 Service Delivery
    3.6.1 Introduction
    3.6.2 Designing Service Delivery System
    3.6.3 Self Service Technologies
- Points to Remember
- Questions for Discussion
- Multiple Choice Questions
- Project Questions

Learning Objectives ...
- To understand the concept of service process
- To explain the service design and the types of standards involved
- To describe the process of service blue print
- To discuss the strategies involved in managing demand and capacity
- To identify the aspects of service delivery and understand the meaning of self-service technologies

3.1 Introduction

The seventh "P" of the marketing mix of services is **PROCESS**. The manner, in which the services are delivered, including the steps, procedures and mechanisms, is referred by the Process. The process of services cannot be exclusive of the customer, in fact it involves the customer, the intermediaries, the service delivery provider, and the technology that is adopted to process and deliver the quality service. The production process and the delivery become inseparable and often it becomes difficult to differentiate one form from the other, due to the vague nature of services.

To satisfy a customer, one must start with the product and the service design, keeping in mind that the decisions that are made in this area influence the operations, including the overall success of the organisation.

3.2 Service Process

3.2.1 Introduction

When manufacturing goods, the process involved takes place in the factory's premises, keeping the customers at bay. The customer rarely comes in contact with the manufacturing process, as those processes that lie with the factory premises, lie in the sole domain of operations. Interaction of the customers with the system should be a part of the service creation and hence this makes the customer be a part of the service process. The service failures often are the result of inadequately and inappropriately designed service processes. Services which depend on customer contact or customers are the recipient of service actions, the customer side of the process can be mapped by identifying service delivery process. A chart that draws and lists the various contact points when the system and the customer come in contact to create a value is known as a **flow chart.**

Service production and consumption are inseparable, and therefore the customer acts as a co-producer of many services. The service delivery is the outcome of the service process. The process constitutes the service itself. The service characteristics of inseparability and participation often make the customer, interact and become a part of the process. Despite such importance of the service process, sometimes service organisations pay very little systematic attention to this aspect of business. As a result, service processes evolve on their own with internal bias or no focus at all. Therefore, it is not surprising that many service organisations are not adequately equipped to serve the customer well and such processes limit the efficiency of the operations.

3.2.2 Steps for Managing Service Processes

Services are experiences from the customer's point of view. Services are processes that have to be designed and managed to create the desired customer experience from the organisation's viewpoint. Hence processes become the plan of the services. **Processes** *describe the method and sequence in which the service operating systems work and specify how they link together to create the value proposition promised to customers*. Customers are an integral part of the operation, and the process becomes their experience, in high contact services. If the process has been designed up to the customer's standards, this will frustrate the customers as the process are often slow and of poor quality.

If the process is not designed properly, it affects the frontline employees also in doing their jobs well, which then results in poor productivity, with an increase in the risk of service failures.

While designing and managing a service process, keep in mind the following steps:

(a) **Flowcharting:** Flowcharting, *a technique for displaying the nature and sequence of the different steps involved in delivering a service to customers, offers an easy way to understand the totality of the customer's service experience*. We can gain valuable insights into the nature of an existing service by flowcharting the sequence of encounters customers have with a service organisation. Recognising that a value proposition may embrace all or part of the whole cluster of benefits a firm offers to its target market, service marketers need to create a coherent offering in which each element is compatible with the others and all are mutually reinforcing.

(b) **Service Blueprinting:** It is important for an organisation to gain a holistic view of how the elements of the service relate to each other, when the service production processes are complex and involve multiple service encounters.

'**Blueprinting**' according to **Shostack,** *is a graphical approach, designed to overcome problems that occur where a new service is launched without adequate identification of the necessary support functions.*

The three main elements in a customers's blueprint are:
1. All of the principal functions required to make and distribute a service are identified, along with the responsible company unit or personnel.
2. Timing and sequencing relationships among the functions are depicted graphically.
3. For each function, acceptable tolerances are identified in terms of the variation from standard that can be tolerated without adversely affecting customer's perception of quality.

(c) **Identify Failure Points:** A good blueprint will bring out the key elements in service delivery, highlighting risks which can go wrong. The most serious fail points are those that will result in failure to access or enjoy the core product, from the customer's view point. They involve:
- the reservation (could the customer get through by phone? Was a table available at the desired time and date? Was the reservation recorded accurately?)
- seating (was a table available when promised?).

There is also the possibility of delays between specific actions, requiring the customers to wait, since service delivery takes place over time. Too much waiting can irritate customers. Failures often lead directly to delays, reflecting orders that were never passed on, or time spent correcting mistakes.

(d) **Failure Proofing:** Once the points that seem negative have been identified then a careful analysis for the reasons for failure need to be evaluated in service processes. The analysis done often points outs the prospect for "failure proofing" certain activities in order to reduce or even eliminate the risk of errors. **Poka-Yoke** technique is widely used in fail-safe service processes.

(e) **Setting Service Targets:** Service managers can learn the nature of customer expectations at each step in the process, through both formal research and on-the-job experience. The expectations of customer's vary from the desired level to the threshold level of merely adequate service. At each step service providers should design standards to satisfy and make the customers happy else they will have to modify the customer's expectations. These standards might include time parameters, the script for a technically correct performance, and prescriptions for appropriate style and demeanor.

(f) **Service Process Redesign:** The processes that have been out dated, get a fresh lease of life but this does not mean that in the first place the processes were poorly designed. Rather, changes in technology, customer needs, added service features, and new offerings may have made existing processes crack and creak. Instead of getting rid of outdated services and replacing them with a new innovations, redesigning of existing services should be considered. These are the following types of service redesign:

1. **Eliminating Non-value Adding Steps:** With the goal of focusing on the benefit-producing part of the service encounter, some activities at the front-end and back-end processes of services can be streamlined. By trying to eliminate non-value-adding steps, service redesign streamlines these tasks. The outcomes are typically increased productivity and customer satisfaction.

2. **Physical Service:** Physical re-design involves changing the customer's experience through the tangibles associated with the service or the physical surroundings of the service. Midway Express Airlines has changed the entire airline flight experience primarily through re-designing the interior of its airplanes. Leather seats, two-by-two seating, China plates, and cloth napkins are all ways of creating a new experience through tangibles and services cape re-design.

3. **Pre-Service:** This type of re-design involves streamlining or improving the activation of the service, focusing on the front-end processes. An example can be express check-in at a hotel or car rental, pre-admission processes at a hospital and pre-payment of tolls on highways. Making the front-end of the service more efficient can dramatically change the customer experience during actual service delivery.

4. **Direct Service:** Direct service means bringing the service to the customer rather than asking the customer to come to the provider. This might mean delivering the service to the customer in his or her home or workplace. Restaurant food and dry cleaning delivery to the office, pet grooming in the home, auto repair in one's driveway, and computer distance education and training services are examples of firms bringing services directly to their customers rather than customers travelling to the service provider.

5. **Self-Service:** Moving the customer into a production mode rather than a passive, receiving mode is another approach to redesign. Re-designing the service process in this way increases benefits for the customer in terms of personal control, accessibility, and timing. Prime examples of self-service occur when companies offer their services via the Internet, as in the case of Internet banking.

6. **Bundled Service:** Grouping, or bundling, multiple services together is another way to re-design current offerings. The benefit to customers is in receiving greater value, combined with convenience, than they might have received by hiring each service independently.

(g) **Managing Customers Effectively:** Managing customers effectively as partial employees is another way to enhance customer performance in service processes and to reduce customer-induced service failures. The following steps need to be followed:

1. **Recruitment and Selection:** For a human resource management to be effective, the first plan is to start with recruitment and selection. The same approach should hold true for "partial employees". So if co-production requires specific skills, firms should target their marketing efforts to recruit new customers who have the competency to perform the necessary tasks.

2. **Job Analysis:** A "job analysis" of the customer's roles in the business needs to be in place, which should be compared against the roles that the firm wants them to play. Find out if the customers are capable enough to have the skills needed to perform.

3. **Education and Training** Once the job has been analysed, the next step would be education and training, especially if the job analysis identified significant misalignment of customers' role perceptions. If the customers are expected to work more, then the information which be needed by them to perform better would be greater. This type of training and education can be given to them in different ways. Automated machines often contain user-friendly operating instructions. Many websites include a Frequently Asked Questions (FAQ) section. Advertising for new services often contains significant educational content, and brochures and posted instructions are two widely used approaches.

4. **Motivate:** Motivation is an essential part for managing customers effectively. They must be motivated by rewarding them for performing well.

5. **Appraise:** Appraisals should be done at regular intervals. If the performance is unsatisfactory, then make sure to improve the customer's knowledge by giving him proper training.

6. **Ending:** When a relationship is not working out, ending it remains an option of last resort. Physicians have a legal and ethical duty to help their patients, but the relationship will succeed only if it is mutually cooperative. Having to terminate customer relationships may indicate problems in the recruitment process that needs to be addressed.

3.3 Service Design

3.3.1 Introduction

Though there are a lot of similarities between a product and the service design, at the same time there are some major differences involved too. One feature that distinguishes the two is that services are created and delivered simultaneously, whereas in manufacturing production and delivery are usually separated in time.

'Service refers to an act, something that is done to or for a customer (client, patient, etc.). It is provided by a service delivery system, which includes the facilities, processes, and skills needed to provide the service.' The service component in products is increasing. The ability to create and deliver reliable customer oriented service is often a key competitive differentiator. Successful companies combine customer-oriented service with their products.

System design involves development or refinement of the overall service package:
1. The physical **resources** needed.
2. The accompanying goods that are **purchased or consumed** by the customer, or provided with the service.
3. **Explicit services** (the essential/core features of a service, such as tax preparation).
4. **Implicit services** (ancillary/extra features, such as friendliness, courtesy).

Start a service design by the choice of a service strategy. This will determine the nature and focus of the service including the target market This requires an assessment by top management of the potential market and) or a particular service and an assessment of the organisation's ability to provide the service.. Once the important decisions have been made, then the requirements and expectations of the customer must be evaluated.

Two key issues in service design are:
- The degree of variation in service requirements,
- The degree of customer contact and customer involvement in the delivery system.

This will have an impact on how the service can be standardised. The lower the degree of customer contact and service requirement variability, the more standardised the service can be. Conversely, high variability and high customer contact generally mean the service must be highly customised.

3.3.2 Service Blue Printing

The **Service Blueprinting** method is applied mainly in the *Service Design* phase. Once the previous stages are completed in order to apply this method, and the outcomes should be integrated into the service Blueprinting. *Service-Blueprinting is a service planning help tool. It can be used for developing new innovative services as well as for improving existing services.* This method also ensures the quality of the service processes and can be used for new employee training or for showing a client a service cycle. Blueprinting has its origins in a variety of fields and techniques, including logistics, industrial engineering, decision theory, computer systems analysis, and software engineering - all of which deal with the definition and explanation of processes.

Service Blueprinting allows for visualisation of the service development process in its early stages. *The Service Blueprinting output consists of a graphically-presented overview of the service process and its activities.* The contact points between client and firm (and physical element, if a tangible service) become visible, in each process step. Identifying failure points and discovering areas of innovation become possible. This technique eases the identification of cost saving potentials and offers an excellent base for further Service-process management.

A service blueprint is a picture or map that portrays the customer experience and the service system, so that the different people involved in providing the service can understand it objectively, regardless of their roles or their individual points of view. During the design stage of service development, Blueprints are very useful. A service blueprint visually displays the service by simultaneously depicting

- the process of service delivery,
- the points of customer contact,
- the roles of customers and employees,
- the visible elements of the service.

Blueprinting is a particularly useful technique for describing services are "experiences" rather than objects or technologies. It provides a way to break a service down into its logical components and to depict the steps or tasks in the process, the means by which the tasks are executed, and the evidence of service as the customer experiences it.

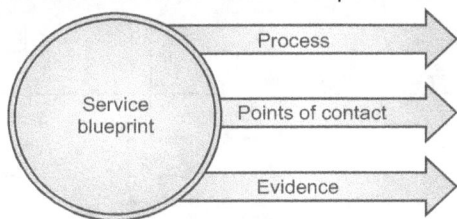

Fig. 3.1: Service Blueprinting

3.3.2.1 Components of Service Blueprinting

The key components of service blueprints are shown in Fig. 3.1.

They are:

- Customer actions,
- Onstage/visible contact employee actions,
- Backstage/invisible contact employee actions,
- Support processes.

Principles of drawing the service blueprints have not been defined and hence the particular symbols used, the number of horizontal lines in the blueprint, and the labels for each part of the blueprint may vary somewhat depending on the complexity of the blueprint being described. As long as you keep in mind the purpose of the blueprint and view it as a useful technique rather than as a set of rigid rules for designing services, these variations will not pose a problem. *Flexibility* is one of the major strengths of service blueprinting.

1. **Customer Actions**: The steps, choices, activities, and interactions that the customer performs in the process of purchasing, experiencing, and evaluating the service are covered in the customer action area. In this area of the blueprint, the total customer experience is apparent. In a legal services example, the customer actions might include a decision to contact an attorney, phone calls to the attorney, face-to-face meetings, receipt of documents, and receipt of a bill.

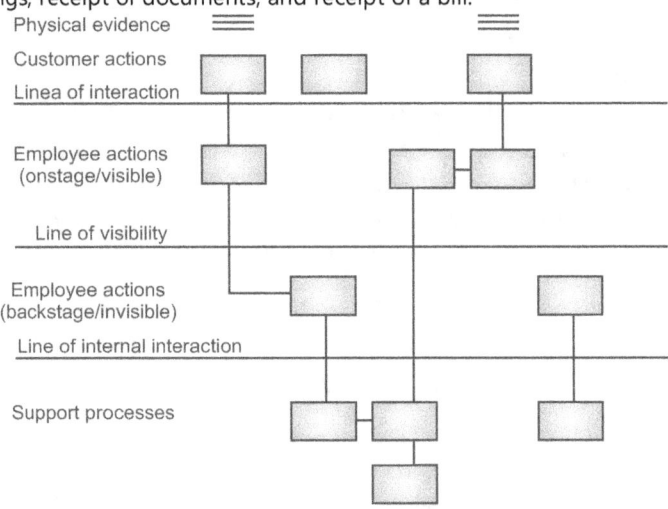

Fig. 3.2: Service Blue Print Components

2. **Contact Employee Actions:** Matching the customer actions are two areas of contact employee actions:

    (i) **Backstage/Invisible Contact Employee Actions**: Those contact employee actions that occur behind the scenes to support the onstage activities are the backstage/invisible contact employee actions. In the example, anything the attorney does behind the scenes to prepare for the meetings or to prepare the final documents will appear in this section. All contact employee actions are shown in this area of the blueprint.

    (ii) **Onstage/Visible Contact Employee Actions**: The activities that the contact employee performs that are visible to the customer are the *onstage/visible contact employee* actions. In the legal services setting, the actions of the attorney visible to the client are, for example, the initial interview, intermediate meetings, and final face-to-face delivery of legal documents.

3. **Support Processes**: In delivering the service, the support processes section of the blueprint covers the internal services, steps, and interactions that take place to support the contact employees. Again, in our legal example, any service support activities such as legal research by staff; preparation of document and secretarial support to set up meetings will be shown in the support processes area of the blueprint.

At the very top of the blueprint you see the physical evidence of the service. Typically, above each point of contact the actual physical evidence of the service is listed.

The key action areas are separated by three horizontal lines:

1. The line of interaction, representing direct interactions between the customer and the organisation. Anytime a vertical line crosses the horizontal line of interaction, a direct contact between the customer and the organisation, or a service encounter, has occurred.
2. Is the critically important line of visibility. This line separates all service activities visible to the customer from those not visible. In reading blueprints, it is immediately obvious whether the consumer is provided with much visible evidence of the service simply by analysing how much of the service occurs above the line of visibility versus the activities carried out below the line. This line also separates what the contact employees do onstage front what they do backstage.
3. The third line is the line of internal interaction, which separates customer-contact employee activities from those of other service support activities and people. Vertical lines cutting across the line of internal interaction represent internal service encounters.

In designing effective service blueprints, it is recommended that the diagramming start with the customer's experience and then work into the delivery system. The boxes shown within each action area depict steps performed or experienced by the actors at that level. The most significant differences between service blueprints and other process flow diagrams is the primary focus on customers and their experience with the service process.

3.3.2.2 Process of Service Blueprint

Many of the benefits and purposes of building a blueprint evolve from the process of doing it. The development or the blueprint needs to involve a variety of functional representatives as well as information from customers. Drawing a blueprint is not a task that should be assigned to one person or one functional area. Fig. 3.3 identify the basic steps in building a blueprint.

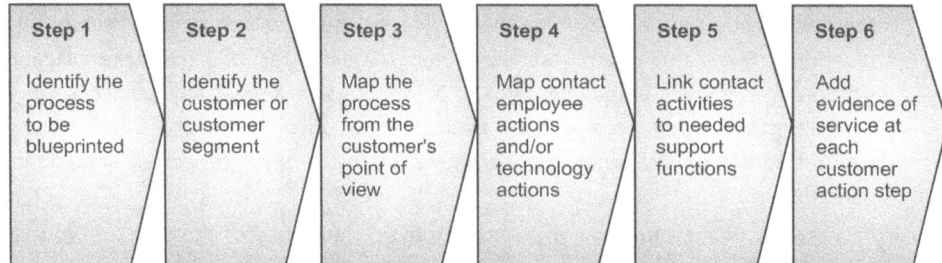

Fig. 3.3: Building a Service Blueprint

Step 1: Identify the Service Process to be blueprinted: Since blueprints can be built at a variety of levels, the starting point has to be identified. Specific blueprints could be developed for two-day express mail, large accounts, Internet-facilitated services, and/or storefront drop-off centers. Each of these blueprints would share some features with the concept blueprint but would also include unique features.

Step 2: Identify the Customer or Customer Segment Experiencing the Service: In market segmentation each segment's needs are different and hence a variation of services in the service or product features. When a service is developed for a particular customer, blueprints are the most useful. It may be possible to combine customer segments on one blueprint at the conceptual level. However, once almost any level of detail is reached, separate blueprints should be developed to avoid confusion.

Step 3: Map the Service Process from the Customer's Point of View: Chart the choices and actions that the customer performs or experiences in purchasing, consuming, and evaluating the service. Sometimes the beginning and ending of the service from the customer's point of view are not obvious. Identifying the service from the customer's point of view first will help avoid focusing on processes and steps that have no customer impact. This step forces agreement on which customer it is and may involve considerable research and observation to determine exactly how the customer experiences the service.

Step 4: Map Contact Employee Actions and/or Technology Actions: The lines of interaction and visibility are drawn, and then the process from the customer contact person's point of view is mapped, distinguishing visible onstage activities from invisible backstage activities. For existing services, this step involves questioning or observing frontline operation employees to learn what they do and which activities are performed in full view of the customer versus which activities are carried out behind the scenes.

If no employees are involved in the service, the area can be relabeled "*onstage technology actions*." If both human and technology interactions are involved, an additional horizontal line can separate "*visible contact employee actions*" from "*visible technology actions*". Using the additional line facilitates reading and interpretation of the service blueprint.

Step 5: Link Contact Activities to Needed Support Functions: In this process, the direct and indirect impact of internal actions on customers becomes apparent. Internal service processes take on added importance when viewed in connection with their link to the customer. Alternatively, certain steps in the process may be viewed as unnecessary if there is no clear link to the customer's experience or to an essential internal support service.

Step 6: Add Evidence of Service at Each Customer Action Step: A photographic blueprint, including photos, slides, or video of the process, can be very useful at this stage to aid in analysing the impact of tangible evidence and its consistency with the overall strategy and service positioning.

3.3.3 Quality Function Deployment

Quality Function Deployment (QFD) *is a structured approach for defining customer needs or requirements and translating them into specific plans to produce products to meet those needs.* The "*voice of the customer*" describes the stated and unstated customer requirements. The voice of the customer is captured in a variety of ways:

- direct discussion or interviews,
- surveys,
- focus groups,
- customer specifications,
- observation,
- warranty data,
- field reports, etc.

The needs of the customer are then summed up in a product planning matrix or "house of quality". These matrices are used to translate higher level "what's" or needs into lower level "how's".

The Quality Function Deployment matrices are a good communication tool at each step in the process, but these matrices are only the means. The process of communicating and decision-making is the real value with QFD. QFD is oriented toward involving a team of people representing the various functional departments that have involvement in product development: Marketing, Design Engineering, Quality Assurance, Manufacturing/ Manufacturing Engineering, Test Engineering, Finance, Product Support, etc..

QFD is a system with the aim of translating and planning the "voice of the customer" into the quality characteristics of products, processes and services in order to reach customer satisfaction.

QFD is an important planning as well as quality tool and it allows the consideration of the "voice of the customer" along the service development path to market entry.

3.3.3.1 Factors that Firms Need to Address by Using QFD

The factors that firms need to address for using QFD are:

1. **Competitiveness:** Three aspects are especially important for the development of firms' competitiveness:

    (i) **Cost:** To reach price competitiveness the process costs should be low, which can lead to an increase in the market share but it is not profitable in the long run.

    (ii) **Quality:** The importance that client gives is to the quality of the services and also to some different services that are offered. Sometimes a firm can lose customers due to the quality and infact often there are cases where the customers would in turn go and narrate the poor service to his acquaintances and friends.

    (iii) **Opportunities:** are directly related to "time to market". Mature processes for new service development can lead to shorter development times. Shorter times could mean a more agile response to the market and may increase the competitive ability of the company.

    In conclusion, it is desirable to have services with short "time to market", of high quality and at a low cost; this leads to a more competitive firm.

2. **Quality Lever:** A concept that help visualising the effects of the development stage and how they affect the quality of the produced service is known as the quality lever. The idea is that improvements carried out in the production phase can lead to a lower cost-benefit ratio when compared to the increase of the service's quality.

QFD is a tool that makes it possible to transform reactive service development processes into proactive processes.

3.3.3.2 Advantages of QFD

Applying QFD is quite simple. The advantages obtained from a QFD application are:

- **Reduction of Development Time:** QFD application allows reducing costs and the time needed to introduce the new service into the market.

- **Preventive Design:** One of the biggest advantages of QFD is it promotes the development of services in a practical manner. When applying QFD, more than 90% of changes on service design are performed before the market entry takes place. Since they are performed "in the worksheet", the changes are less expensive and it is possible to prevent the problems.

- **Client Satisfaction:** QFDs are oriented to the "voice of the customer" and not to the "thoughts of the developer". With the focus on the consumer, all decisions made during the service design are targeted at the customer.

3.4 Demand and Capacity Management

3.4.1 Introduction

The level of demand keys basic decisions about how much capacity to build into a service delivery system. The decision about how much and what kind of capacity has a lifelong effect on the success of a service facility and is made early in the service design process. The pattern of demand often influences the kind of capacity developed for service delivery. Relationships between demands for various parts of a multistep service suggest the amount of capacity to be provided for each step.

Its importance lies in the way in which demand and capacity characteristics relate to produce two of the most important ways of evaluating potential risk and potential return in a service business. The need for this kind of information gives efforts to assess demand special significance.

3.4.2 Level of Demand

The developer of a breakthrough service can't observe demand levels of competitors' offerings. But because service concepts are defined in terms of results produced for customers, developers can observe potential customers trying to achieve the same kind of results through other more conventional means. In order to maintain control over the process even though it may be more costly than using outside services provided by firms specialising in the work, many smaller brokerage firms process their customers' transactions in-house.

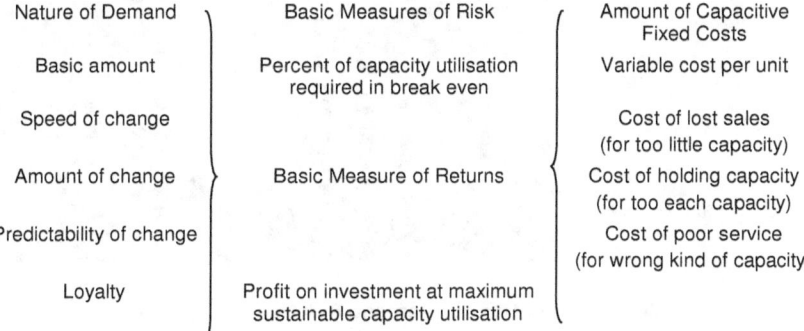

Fig. 3.4: The Importance of Demand Capacity Relationships in the Service Risk/Return Evaluation

If prospective demand levels are to be forecasted with even approximate accuracy for a previously unoffered service, then many new service concepts can be tested. For most services as compared to products, markets tests are more feasible. New services can be offered but experiences of others have suggested certain caveats in planning and measuring the results of such efforts. These include close attention to the frequency with which a service is purchased, the importance of referrals from other users in the decision to try a service, and the very nature of the innovation adoption rate for particular services.

Some responses to services may be rapid such as restaurant services or hair styling services, but these require more time as they are less frequently purchased. Other examples may include legal and medical services for individuals and industrial cleaning and advertising services for commercial customers.

A referral process for prospective customers is very important, as there is an absence of search qualities for most services.

Valarie Zeithaml has stated that consumers accept innovations in services more slowly than they accept innovations in goods and maintain greater loyalty to services they use than to products they use. These behaviours vary according to other characteristics of particular services, but they suggest extreme care in structuring a market test to allow for the referral process and for repeat usage to take place sufficiently to be able to gauge the potential level of demand for a new service.

3.4.3 Managing Fluctuations in Service Demand

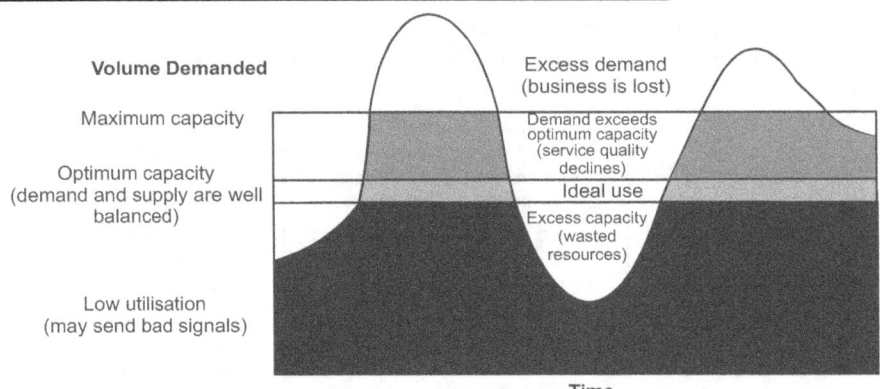

Fig. 3.5: Variations in Demand Relative to Capacity

There are four basic scenarios that may result from different combinations of supply and demand and this is represented by the middle areas in the figure:

- **Excess demand:** Demand exceeds maximum capacity; some customers may be turned away.

- **Demand exceeds optimum capacity:** No one is turned away but service quality may suffer.
- **Demand and supply balanced at an optimum level of capacity:** Staff and facilities are utilised at the ideal level.
- **Excess capacity:** Demand is below optimum capacity, and productive resources are underutilised, resulting in low productivity.

There are two types of approaches to the problem of fluctuating demand:

(i) To adjust the level of capacity to meet the variations in demand.

(ii) To manage the level of demand.

(A) Managing Capacity:

There two approaches for managing capacity:

1. **Capacity Level:** The ability to absorb extra demand, some capacity is elastic in nature, which means that the actual level of capacity remains unchanged and more people will be served with the same level of capacity.

    Take for example the Mumbai trains. The normal capacity may be for seating 40 people and 60 for standing passengers, but during rush hour you can see 200 standees being accommodated in the train. Yet another strategy for stretching capacity is to utilise the facilities for longer periods.

2. **Adjusting Capacity to Demand Patterns:** This strategy known as chasing demand, involves tailoring the overall level of capacity to match variations in demand a strategy. There are several actions that managers can take to adjust capacity as needed.

    - **To ensure that 100 percent capacity** is available during peak periods, maintenance, repair and renovations should be conducted when demand is expected to be; Schedule downtime during the periods of low demand.
    - **Use part-time employees:** Many organisations hire extra workers during their busiest periods. For example, additional hotel employees during vacation periods and for major conventions.
    - **Ask customers to share:** Capacity can be stretched by asking customers to share a unit of capacity normally dedicated to one individual. For instance, at busy airports and train stations, where the supply of taxis is sometimes insufficient to meet demand, travelers going in the same direction may be given the option of sharing a ride at a reduced rate.
    - **Cross-train employees:** If employees can be cross-trained to perform a variety of tasks, they can be shifted to bottleneck points as needed, thereby increasing total

system capacity. In supermarkets, for instance, the manager may call on the stockers to operate cash registers when lines become too long. Likewise, during the slow periods, the cashiers may be asked to help stock shelves.

- o **Invite customers to perform self-service:** If the number of employees is limited, capacity can be increased by involving customers in co-production of certain tasks. One way to do this is by adding self-service technologies such as electronic kiosks at the airport for airline ticketing and check-in or automated check-out stations at supermarkets.
- o **Rent or share extra facilities and equipment:** To limit investment in fixed assets, a service business may be able to rent extra space or machines at peak times. Firms with complementary demand patterns may enter into formal sharing agreements.

Demand too High	Demand too Low
• Stretch time, labour, facilities and equipment. • Cross-train employees. • Part time employees can be hired. • Request overtime work from employees. • Rent or share facilities and equipments. • Subcontract or outsource activities.	• Perform maintenance, renovations. • Vacations to be scheduled • Employee training to be scheduled. • Lay-off employees.

Strategies for Match and Demand and Capacity

	High Demand / Risk Supply	Slack Demand / High Supply
Managing demand (Changing demand to fit capacity)	• Educate customers to curtail usage during peak periods (through signages or advertising) • Offer incentives for usage during non-peak periods. • Charge full price-no discounts or premium pricing. • Take care of regular customers first.	• Modify service offerings. • Offer discounts, sales promotion schemes. • Modify hours of operation. • Bring service to the customers. • Use sales and advertising to increase business from current and new market segments.

contd. ...

Managing capacity (Changing capacity to match demand)	• Hire part-time employees. • Keep employees overtime. • Cross-train employees. • Outsource, rent facilities or equipments.	• Schedule training of employees. • Maintenance, repairs, renovation. • Schedule employee vacations. • Take on subcontract employees.

(B) Managing Demand

The optimum level of demand for its given capacity should be determined by organisation. When the optimum level is determined, the marketing mix elements of product, price, place and promotion should change the demand in respect to the capacity.

- **(a) Product:** The service offering to even the demand, can be altered by the service provider. The changes which can be seen in service offering can be seasonal or based on days of the week or time of the day depending on the nature of demand fluctuations. However, as marketers you must ensure that by offering different types of services the image or positioning of the service firm is not diluted or confused. Take for example a hotel which does not get too much business on the weekends from business executives, can offer family recreation packages etc.
- **(b) Pricing:** During the periods of low demand to increase the demand, many service providers reduce the price. A perfect example would be when airlines offer low fares during exam time or during late night flights.
- **(c) Place (Distribution):** As a strategy to match demand and capacity, many service firms modify their time and place of delivery. Example: finance companies use mobile vans for distribution and collection of forms.
- **(d) Promotion:** If the communication to the customers is done in a proper manner, the demand can be shifted. The customers should be made aware of the peak timings of the demand and also the benefits they can get in availing the service during non-peak timings. Customers should be informed about the any changes being made to the product, pricing or distribution. Service firms can also use sales promotion to manage demand. Many airlines offer free ticket for companion in the business class.

3.4.4 Waiting Lines

Often waiting in lines is uncomfortable, when people are senior citizens, or there are no places to sit or the weather is not suitable. However, sometimes one has to wait. Many organisations face the problem of waiting lines during their functioning. People are kept waiting on the phone, listening to recorded messages like "your call is important to us." etc.

"Queues" or Waiting lines occur whenever the number of arrivals at a facility exceeds the capacity of the system to process them. Queues basically are a symptom of unresolved capacity management problems.

Many services are offered online these days, where the customer can do a lot of things like paying bills, searching for information, making travel arrangements online. The drawback might a slow internet connection.

Managing Waiting Lines

By adding more space or more staff is not always the optimal solution in situations in which customer satisfaction must be balanced against cost considerations, by simply increasing capacity. These are the factors to be considered in this respect:

1. **Rethinking the design of the queuing system**
   - **A single line to multiple servers,** commonly known as "SNAKE". This type of waiting line solves the problem of the parallel lines to multiple servers moving at different speeds. This approach is encouraged frequently at post offices and airport check-ins.
   - **Parallel lines to multiple servers** offer more than one serving station, allowing customers to select one of several lines in which to wait. Banks and ticket windows are common examples. Fast food restaurants usually have several serving lines in operation at busy times of day, with each offering the full menu. A parallel system can have either a single stage or multiple stages.
   - **In single line,** sequential stages, customers proceed through several serving operations, as in a cafeteria. Bottlenecks may occur at any stage where the process takes longer to execute then at previous stages. Many cafeterias have lines at the cash register because the cashier takes longer to calculate how much you owe and to make change than the servers take to slap food on your plates
   - **Designated lines** involve assigning different lines to specific categories of customer. Examples include express lines and regular lines at supermarket check-outs, and different check-in stations for first class, business class and economy class airline passengers.
   - **Take a number** saves customers the need to stand in a queue, because they know they will be called in sequence. This procedure allows them to sit down and relax or to guess how long the wait will be and do something else in the meantime. Users of this approach include large travel agents, government offices, outpatient clinics in hospitals, and supermarket departments such as bakery.

- **Wait list.** Restaurants often have wait lists where people put their names down and wait until their name is announced. There are four common ways of wait listing:
    1. Party size sitting, where the number of people is matched to the size of the table.
    2. VIP seating, this involves giving special rights to favoured customers.
    3. Call-ahead seating, which allows people to telephone before arrival to hold a place on the wait list.
    4. Large party reservations.

2. **Queuing systems can be tailored to market segments**

   The basic queuing system is "first come first serve", not all queuing systems are organised on this basis. Market segmentation is sometimes used to design queuing strategies that set different priorities for different types of customers.
   - **Urgency of the job:** At many hospital emergency units, a triage nurse is assigned to greet incoming patients and decide which one requires priority medical treatment and which can safely be asked to register and then sit down while they wait their turn.
   - **Importance of the customer:** A special area may be reserved for members of frequent user clubs. Airlines often provide lounges, offering newspapers and free refreshments, where frequent flyers can wait for their flights in greater comfort.
   - **Payment of a premium prices:** Airlines usually offer separate check-in lines for first class and economy –class passengers, with a higher ratio of personnel to passengers in the first-class line, resulting in reduced waits for those who have paid more for their tickets. At some airports, premium passengers may also enjoy faster lanes for the security check.
   - **Duration of service transaction:** There are many "express lanes" these days offered by supermarkets, banks etc. for shorter less complicated tasks.

3. **Customer Perception of Waiting Time**

   People don't like wasting their time on unproductive activities any more than they like wasting money, and they often feel they have waited longer than they actually do. This can lead to strong emotions and anger too.

   These are the suggestions made by David Maister and includes other researches on how the psychology of waiting should work by making the wait less stressful and unpleasant:
   - **Unoccupied time feels longer than occupied time:** When you are sitting around with nothing to do, time seems to crawl. The challenge for service organisations is to give customers something to do or to distract them while waiting. For example, BMW car owners can wait in comfort in BMW service centers where waiting areas are furnished with designer furniture, plasma TVs, Wi-Fi hotspots, magazines, etc.

- **Solo waits feel longer than group waits:** Waiting with one or more people you know is reassuring. Conversation with friends can help to pass the time, but not everyone is comfortable talking to stranger.
- **Physically uncomfortable waits feel longer than comfortable waits:** "My feet are killing me!" is one of the most frequently heard comments when people are forced to stand in line for a long time. When they are seated and temperature is too hot or too cold it becomes burdensome. So the service organisations can provide seating arrangements with appropriate temperature and pleasant ambience.
- **Pre and post-process waits feel longer than in-process waits:** Waiting to buy ticket to enter a theme park is different from waiting to ride on a roller coaster once you're in the park.
- **Unfair waits are longer than equitable waits:** Perceptions about what is fair and unfair sometimes vary from one culture or country to another. For example, people expect everybody to wait their turn and are likely to get irritated if they see others jumping ahead or given priority for apparently no good reason. Therefore service organisations can take advantage of this and make waits feel better.
- **Unfamiliar waits seem longer than familiar ones:** Frequent users of a service know what to expect and are less likely to worry while waiting. New or occasional users often are nervous, wondering not only about the probable length of the wait but also about what happens next.
- **Uncertain waits are longer than known, finite waits:** Although any wait may be frustrating, we usually can adjust mentally to a wait of a known length. It's the unknown that keeps us on edge. Imagine waiting for a delayed flight and not being told how long the delay is going to be.
- **Anxiety makes waits seem longer:** Can you remember waiting for someone to show at a meeting and worrying about whether you had gotten the time or location correct? While waiting in familiar locations, especially outdoors and at night, people often worry about their personal safety.
- **The more valuable or important the service, the longer people will wait:** People will queue up overnight under uncomfortable conditions to get good seats to a major concert or sports event even expected to sell out fast.

3.5 Standardisation: Customer Defined Service Standards

3.5.1 Introduction

In general terms the word **standard** (often used interchangeably with quality) *implies a level of performance that customers will find at the very least acceptable.* Whilst the formation of customer expectations has aroused interest, the process by which standards are determined has not attracted much attention in the services literature. Marketers must resort to the view that standards should be set in accordance with customer requirements or expectations.

The standard is a time period for responding to enquiries or resolving complaints. The standard is expressed in terms of expectations for the customers. The standard set is an expression of the service provider's view as to how long the process of responding to enquiries or resolving complaints should take. Service performance is the time it actually takes. A customer service standard is the interaction between a business and its customers. Customer service standards are excellence, response time, accessibility, delivery time and commitment. The customer loses out in terms of performance not even meeting the standard and also in terms of failure to meet expectations..

Companies continuously strive to improve the level of service they deliver. Customer service standards must be constantly monitored and incorporated into the strategic planning of the company.

3.5.2 Factors Necessary for Appropriate Service Standards

1. **Standardisation of Service Behaviours and Actions:** Goal setting and important elements of service provision are structures by the technology and improved work processes. Remember that standarisation of service does not mean that the process is performed in a mechanical or rigid way. Converting customer expectations into service quality stands will depend on the degree to which behaviours and tasks can be standardised. Customisation is essential for providing high-quality service and services cannot be standardised as thought by some managers. Professionals provide customised and individualised services, in certain services such as in accounting, consulting, engineering, and dentistry etc.

2. **Customer – Not Company – Defined Standards:** Instead, a company must set customer-defined standards. Operational standards based on pivotal customer requirements that are visible to and measured by customers. These standards are deliberately chosen to match customer expectations and to be calibrated the way the customer views and expresses them. Virtually all companies possess service standards and measures that are company defined – they are established to reach internal company goals for productivity, efficiency, cost, or technical quality. To close gap 2, standards set by companies must be based on customer requirements and expectations rather than just on internal company goals.

3. **Formal Service Targets and Goals:** In service businesses, Several types of formal goal setting are relevant such as:
   - There are specific targets for individual behaviours or actions.
   - The overall department or company target, most frequently expressed as a percentage, across all executions of the behaviour or action.

Companies that have been successful in delivering consistently high service quality are noted for establishing formal standards to guide employees in providing service. These companies have an accurate sense of how well they are performing service that is critical to their customers – how long it takes to conduct transactions, how frequently service fails, how quickly they settle customer complaints – and strive to improve by defining goals that lead them to meet or exceed customer expectations.

3.5.3 Types of Service Standards: Hard and Soft Measures

Customer-defined standards and measures of service quality can be grouped into two broad categories:
- Soft.
- Hard.

Organisations that have an excellent reputation for their services use both the hard and soft measures. They have excellent relationship with their customers as well as their customer contact employees. The larger the organisation, the more important it is to create formalised feedback programmes using a variety of professionally designed and implemented research procedures.

(a) **Hard Measures of Service Quality:** Operational processes or outcomes and include such data as uptime, service response times, failure rates, and delivery costs are referred as Hard measures. Multiple measures of service quality will be recorded at many different points, in complex service operation. Where customers are not involved in the service delivery operations such as low contact services. Many operation measures apply to backstage activities that have only a second order on customers.

Hard standards and measures relate to those characteristics and activities that can be counted, timed, or measured through audits. Such measures may include how many telephone calls were abandoned while the customer was on hold, how many minutes customers had to wait in line at a particular stage in the service delivery, the time required to complete a specific task, the temperature of a particular food item, how many trains arrived late, how many bags were lost, how many patients made a complete recovery following a specific type of operation, and how many orders were filled correctly. Standards are often set with reference to the percentage of occasions on which a particular measure is achieved. The challenge for service marketers is to ensure that operational measures of service quality reflect customer input.

(b) **Soft Measures of Service Quality:** According to **Leonard Berry and A. Parasuraman**: *Companies need to establish ongoing listening systems using multiple methods among different customer groups. A single service quality study is a* *snapshot taken at a point in time and from a particular angle. Deeper insight and more informed decision making come from a continuing series of snapshots taken from various angles and through different lenses, which form the essence of systematic listening.*

Key customer centric service quality measures include total market surveys, annual surveys„ transactional surveys, service feedback cards, mystery shopping, analysis of unsolicited feedback, focus group discussions and service reviews. Other soft measures are:

- **Ongoing surveys** of account holders by telephone or mail, using scientific sampling procedures to determine customers' satisfaction in terms of broader relationship issues.
- **Customer advisory panels** to offer feedback and advice a service performance.
- **Employee surveys and panels** to determine perceptions of the quality of service delivered to customers on specific dimensions, barriers to better service and suggestions for improvement. Designing and implementing a large-scale customer survey to measure service across a wide array of attributes is no simple task. Line managers sometimes view the findings as threatening when direct comparisons are made of the performance of different departments or branches.

Soft standards are especially important for person-to-person interactions such as the selling process and the delivery process for professional services. To be effective, companies must provide feedback to employees about customer perceptions of their performance. Soft standards provide direction, guidance and feedback to employees in ways to achieve customer satisfaction and can be quantified by measuring customer perceptions and beliefs.

As noted by **Valarie Zeithaml and Mary Jo Bitner**, "*Soft standards provide direction, guidance and feedback to employees on ways to achieve customer satisfaction and can be quantified by measuring customer perceptions and beliefs.*"

3.6 Service Delivery

3.6.1 Introduction

The method of delivery of services and that of manufactured goods differs considerably. In manufactured goods, the production of goods is followed by delivery whereas in services the two cannot be separated i.e. the services usually cannot be separated from the service provider. Hence due to this characteristic, the channels for most services are short and simple. The place on distribution of services refers to the availability of a service, i.e., when and where it can be purchased.

Intangibility, inventory, inconsistency and inseparability have led to specific forms of distribution. When the service is simply rented or consumed and when there is no transfer of ownership, these are known as Service products. The service must be available before it's consumption, and hence an effective distribution system must be in place. *The **distribution system** may be defined as the channels or means used, by which the service provider gains access to potential buyer of the service product.*

If the delivery system does not work, then a clever operating strategy intended to provide a service aimed at a particular market segment is useless. Systems that deliver successfully consist of well-thought out jobs for people with the capabilities and attitudes necessary for their successful performance, equipment, facilities and layouts for effective customer and work flow and carefully developed procedures aimed at a common set of clearly defined objectives. To meet most commonly experienced levels of demand efficiently, they provide sufficient capacity. They can help reduce customers' perceptions of risk. Services perceived by customers are differentiated from the competition, and that barriers to competitive entry are build and the delivery systems themselves often help insure that standards for service quality are met are ensured by the delivery systems.

3.6.2 Designing Service Delivery System

Designing the service delivery system and service encounters is the work of design of services. Service delivery system design includes:

- facility location and layout,
- the service scape, service process and job design,
- technology,
- information support systems,
- organisational structure.

Incorporating the above elements is essential to design a service that provides value to customers and can also create a competitive advantage. The service system can be affected to a great extent, if a poor choice of any of the above components is chosen.

The following facts are to be considered when designing a service delivery system:

1. **Facility Location and Layout:** Location plays an important component in the service delivery system. It can affect the customer's travel time and often plays a competitive priority in a service business. The layout of a facility affects process flow, costs, and customer perception and satisfaction. Health clinics, rental car firms, post offices, health clubs, branch banks, libraries, hotels, emergency service facilities, retail stores, and many other types of service facilities depend on good location decisions.

2. **Servicescape:** Servicescape provides the behavioural setting where service encounters take place. It is basically the physical evidence that a customer can use to form an impression. Around the world, customers can easily identify McDonald restaurants. Why? This is due to the way McDonalds projects itself, whether it is their menu or their seating arrangements, the embelm, colours, playground, drive-through etc. These all help support McDonald's competitive priorities of speed, consistency, cleanliness, and customer service. The standardisation and integration of the servicescape and service processes enhance efficiency. McDonald's servicescape helps to establish its brand image.

3. **Service Process and Job Design:** The activity of developing an efficient sequence of activities to satisfy both internal and external customer requirements is known as the service process design. The service process designers should concentrate their efforts on developing actions to make sure that things are done at the first take and the interactions between the service providers and customers are quick and simple and no human mistake is made. Fast-food restaurants have carefully designed their processes for a high degree of accuracy and fast response time. New hands-free intercom systems, better microphones that reduce ambient kitchen noise, and screens that display a customer's order are all focused on these requirements.

   In many services, the customer and service provider co-produce the service, which makes service process and job design more uncertain and challenging. Therefore, managers need to anticipate potential service upsets and develop appropriate responses, such as providing extra capacity, training service providers on proper behaviour, and empowering them to deal with problems when they occur. Superior service management training is critical for excellent service process and job design.

4. **Technology and Information Support Systems:** Hard and soft technology is an important factor in designing services to ensure speed, accuracy, customisation, and flexibility. Nurses, airline flight attendants, bank tellers, police, insurance claims processors, dentists, auto mechanics and service counter personnel, engineers, hotel room maids, financial portfolio managers, purchasing buyers, and waiters are just a few examples of job designs that are highly dependent on accurate and timely information.

5. **Organisational Structure:** The way in which work is organised indirectly affects the performance of a service delivery system. A pure functional organisation generally requires more handoffs between work activities, resulting in increased opportunities for errors and slower processing times. This is because no one takes ownership of the processes and hence very little incentive is there to make them efficient and to improve cooperation among business functions.

3.6.3 Self Service Technologies

According to **Hewlett-Packard**, "*an e-service is an electronic service available via the net that completes tasks, solves problems, or conducts transactions. E-services can be used by people, businesses and other e-services and can be accessed via a wide range of information appliances.*"

ATMs, travel websites, banks, stock trading are the E-services that are available these days. This list is huge and we have just listed a handful.

Ideally, SSTs are purposely created to automate routine interactions between customers and providers with the goal of providing convenience and efficiency to both parties. With respect to airlines, customers can easily compare prices of alternative providers, book their own tickets, select their own seats, and preprint boarding passes to bypass check-in procedures. Ultimately, consumers often enjoy the convenience, speed and case of using self-service technologies as compared to traditional assisted services. Service industries that employ self-service technologies include: auto rental chains, banks, insurance companies, hotels, movie rental chains and theatres, and a variety of other retail operations.

A major source of customer dissatisfaction would be when customers are unable to navigate SST menus, self-service, technologies. Customers must also be computer saavy. Customers view advances into SSTs as a purposeful strategy for the company to distance itself from its customers. Keeping these factors in mind, service firms must consider the customer's overall experience. SSTs or e-service plays a critical role in the transformation of the customer's online experience that progresses over time from a functional experience to a more personalised experience. A self-service must provide the customer a benefit in order to be implemented successfully. A self-service technology that is implemented purely to decrease the operating cost of the firm will most likely not be well-received.

3.6.3.1 Types of Self Service Technologies

There are **four** primary types of SST.

1. **Telephone and Interactive Voice Response (IVR) Systems:** This form of SST is utilised for customer inquiries, orders, billing and surveys. The best known examples who have taken advantage of these are the pizza companies, credit card companies etc.

2. **Interactive Freestanding Kiosks:** Many malls and retail outlets offer these both inside and outside their stores as a way to help you determine availability of a product, as well as to where to locate it in their facility. Large discount chains use kiosks in each store to help you determine what size battery or windshield wiper to put on your car, for example. You will also find kiosks at airports and hotels that print airline tickets and allow for quick checkout, and at movie theaters and malls that print movie tickets.

3. **Internet Based or Other On-Line Connection Systems:** Two well known examples of online technologies are ATM's and pay-at-the-pump gas stations. Other examples include bill management services and internet banking and more recently package delivery services which allows you to track the package 24 hours a day example DHL.
4. **Video/DVD/CD Based Technologies:** This form of SST is used for educational purposes or for corporate to train their employees and to introduce new products to consumers. Of late Universities are also using this technology where they provide graduates, ungraduates education classes by video and CD formats.

3.6.3.2 Business Goals for SST

Firms are typically seeking to fulfil at least one of three primary business goals when they choose to enter the self service arena.

1. **Customer Service (Technology Delivered Customer Service):** The intent here is to provide the customer service without tying up the company's human resources. If done correctly, it can also save firm money.
2. **Enabling Direct Transactions:** Customers order, buy, and exchange resources with the firm without any direct interaction with the firm's employees. These sorts of SST include: on-line shopping, automated kiosks, on-line stocks/security trading, and on-line travel/ticket services.
3. **Educational:** This helps to allow customers to educate and train themselves – typical example include information web site, training videos/DVD/CD and satellite TV-based training.

Points to Remember

- The **seventh** "P" of the marketing mix of services is PROCESS. The manner, in which the services are delivered, including the steps, procedures and mechanisms, is referred by the Process.
- **Services are** experiences from the customer's point of view from the customer's perspective. Processes describe the method and sequence in which the service operating systems work and specify how they link together to create the value proposition promised to customers..
- The **following steps** need to be kept in mind while designing and **managing a service process**:
  1. Flowcharting
  2. Service Blueprinting
  3. Identify failure points
  4. Failure Proofing
  5. Setting service targets
  6. Service Process Redesign

- **Service** refers to an act, something that is done to or for a customer (client, patient, etc.). It is provided by a service delivery system, which includes the facilities, processes, and skills needed to provide the service
- Two **key issues** in **service design** are:
  1. the degree of variation in service requirements, and
  2. the degree of customer contact and customer involvement in the delivery system.
- A **service blueprint** is a picture or map that portrays the customer experience and the service system, so that the different people involved in providing the service can understand it objectively, regardless of their roles or their individual points of view.
- **The key components of service blueprints** are
  1. Customer actions,
  2. Onstage/visible contact employee actions,
  3. Backstage/invisible contact employee actions, and
  4. Support processes.
- **Process of Service Blueprint:**
  1. Identify the Service Process to be blueprinted
  2. Identify the Customer or Customer Segment Experiencing the Service
  3. Map the Service Process from the Customer's Point of View
  4. Map Contact Employee Actions and/or Technology Actions
  5. Link Contact Activities to Needed Support Functions.
  6. Add Evidence of Service at Each Customer Action Step
- **Quality Function Deployment (QFD)** is a structured approach to for defining customer needs or requirements and translating them into specific plans to produce products to meet those needs.
- There are four basic scenarios that may result from different combinations of supply and demand:
  1. **Excess demand:** Demand exceeds maximum capacity; some customers may be turned away.
  2. **Demand exceeds optimum capacity:** No one is turned away but service quality may suffer.
  3. **Demand and supply balanced at an optimum level of capacity:** Staff and facilities are utilised at the ideal level.
  4. **Excess capacity:** Demand is below optimum capacity, and productive resources are under utilised, resulting in low productivity.

- There are two types of approaches to the problem of fluctuating demand:
    1. Managing Capacity
    2. Managing Demand
- "Queues" or Waiting lines occur whenever the number of arrivals at a facility exceeds the capacity of the system to process them.
- **Customer-defined standards and measures** of service quality can be grouped into two broad categories:
    1. soft
    2. hard.
- The distribution system may be defined as the channels or means used, by which the service provider gains access to potential buyer of the service product.
- **Service delivery system design includes:**
    1. Facility location and layout,
    2. The service scape, service process and job design,
    3. Technology,
    4. Information support systems, and
    5. Organisational structure.
- **An e-service** is an electronic service available via the net that completes tasks, solves problems, or conducts transactions. E-services can be used by people, businesses and other e-services and can be accessed via a wide range of information appliances.

Questions for Discussion

1. Describe the designing service delivery process.
2. Explain the service design and the types of standards involved.
3. Describe the process of service blue print.
4. Write short notes on:
    (a) Services of hotel
    (b) Waiting lines
    (c) SST
    (d) Steps for managing service processes
5. What are the strategies involved in managing demand and capacity?
6. Identify the aspects of service delivery.

Multiple Choice Questions

1. _____ is one of the major strengths of service blueprinting:
   - (a) Stability
   - (b) Flexibility
   - (c) Maturity
   - (d) None of the above

2. SST stands for:
   - (a) Self Service Technologies
   - (b) Self Support Technologies
   - (c) Sole Service Technologies
   - (d) Sole Support Technologies

3. _____ consists of a graphically-presented overview of the service process and its activities.
   - (a) SST output
   - (b) Delivery output
   - (c) Blueprinting output
   - (d) Cash output

4. Operational processes or outcomes and include such data as uptime, service response times, failure rates, and delivery costs are referred as _____
   - (a) Hard
   - (b) Soft

5. _____ is a technique for displaying the nature and sequence of the different steps involved in delivering a service to customers, offers an easy way to understand the totality of the customer's service experience.
   - (a) SST
   - (b) Blueprinting
   - (c) Delivery
   - (d) Flowcharting

6. The key components of blue printing are:
   - (a) customer actions
   - (b) onstage/visible contact employee actions
   - (c) backstage/invisible contact employee actions
   - (d) all the above

7. In the process of service blueprint, does the step "Map contact employee actions and/or technology actions" come before "Map the process from the customer's point of view"?
   - (a) Yes
   - (b) No

8. The essential/core features of a service, such as tax preparation is known as:
   - (a) Explicit services
   - (b) Implicit services

9. _____ describe the method and sequence in which the service operating systems work and specify how they link together to create the value proposition promised to customers:
   - (a) Price
   - (b) Product
   - (c) Processes
   - (d) Place

10. This form of SST is utilised for customer inquiries, orders, billing and surveys. Name the form.
    (a) Telephone and IVR systems
    (b) Interactive Freestanding Kiosks
    (c) Internet Based or Other On-Line Connection Systems
    (d) Video/ DVD based technologies

Answers

| 1. (b) | 2. (a) | 3. (c) | 4. (a) | 5. (d) | 6. (d) | 7. (b) | 8. (a) | 9. (c) | 10. (a) |

Project Questions

1. Suppose you are the manger of a credit card issuing bank, you have reached saturation for the last few years. You want new accounts to grow at a healthy pace. Draw up a comprehensive plan to achieve this objective. State the assumptions made.

2. Island Air Services provide airline services for a group of islands in the Pacific Ocean. The organisation is severely restrained by fixed capacity and variable demand. Consider what might be the pattern of demand and ways in which Island Air might adapt their marketing to manage the pattern of demand. Make brief notes advising Island's marketing manager about the key issues their marketing mix needs to take into account.

Chapter 4...

Service People and Physical Evidence

Contents ...
4.1 Introduction
4.2 Service People
    4.2.1 Employee Role in Service Designing
    4.2.2 Service Culture
    4.2.3 Internal Marketing
    4.2.4 Service Profit Chain
    4.2.5 Emotional Labour
    4.2.6 Customer's Role in Service Delivery
        4.2.6.1 Types of Customers' Roles
        4.2.6.2 Strategies for Delivering Services through Customers
        4.2.6.3 Customer as a Co-producer
4.3 Service Physical Evidence
    4.3.1 Role of Evidence in Services Marketing
    4.3.2 Guidelines for Developing Physical Evidence Strategy
    4.3.3 Elements of Physical Evidence
    4.3.4 Servicescape
        4.3.4.1 Types of Servicescape
        4.3.4.2 Roles of Servicescape
        4.3.4.3 Experiencescapes
        4.3.4.4 Elements of Experiencescapes: Architectural Designs in Servicescape
        4.3.4.5 Virtual Servicescape
- Points to Remember
- Questions for Discussion
- Multiple Choice Questions
- Project Questions

Learning Objectives ...
- To understand the employees role in service delivery
- To explain the process of internal marketing and discuss service culture, service profit chain and emotional labour in detail
- To describe the customers role in service delivery and strategies to manage it
- To discuss the concept of physical evidence and to identify the elements of physical evidence
- To discuss the aspects of servicescape like experience servicescape and virtual servicescape

4.1 Introduction

People are considered an important driver of value in services. Action deeds and performance of people generate value. There are a series of encounters between the customer and the system in the value creation process. Service, we can safely say is a summation of these encounters. The people who handle the frontline and interact with customers shape up customer experience by two sides of their performances: the technical and the functional. What is delivered to customer is not the sole of determinant of customer satisfaction. The service outcomes are created and passed on to the customer makes the interpersonal dimension equally vital. The competencies required in the frontline and backroom employee differ.

The so-called frontline jobs are among the most demanding jobs in service businesses. Frontline employees are a key input for delivering service excellence and competitive advantage. Employees are expected to be fast and efficient at executing operational tasks, as well as courteous and helpful in dealing with customers. Behind most of today's successful service organisations stands a firm commitment to effective management of human resources (HR), including recruitment, selection, training, motivation and retention of employees. The organisations are characterised by a unique culture of service and role modelling by top management. It is difficult for competitors to duplicate human assets than any other corporate resources.

The variables, which individuals consider while making a purchase decision, vary from product to product, situation to situation and individual to individual.. Buyers can physically examine the product for quality assessment and suitability in the case of tangible goods. They may also opt for a trial to test the functioning of the product. After a thorough assessment of the product the purchase decision will be taken. Unfortunately this is not the case in services; as such a process is not possible. Services are intangible and also variable. Consumers have to depend upon the search quality and experience quality for the assessment of the service. Doubts and suspicions arise while taking purchase decisions related to services. Physical evidence plays a key role in creating confidence in the consumers of the service. Service companies should use physical evidence as a strategic weapon to convince the customer. In the service sales deal nothing is transferred physically and no ownership results.

4.2 Service People

People, the fifth P, refer to the participants at the service system. All the officials employed by the services firm at the front office and at the back offices are the participants. As per the customer's expectations, the participants are supposed to deliver quality service. The needs and expectations of the customers are to be understood which will then be communicated to the top management and the internal team of the firm. They have to create a positive awareness on the customers and they handle the interactive components of the services marketing mix. These front office participants are the contact personnel with the customers. **Judd** called these personnel, *who are deployed in the front offices, as 'people power'. This power he believed should be made part of the institution of service and should be managed as the fifth component of the services marketing mix.*

The place of service delivery is also known as *moment of truth* and is highly significant during the dealings that take place between the customer and the employee. This point will decide whether the customer will come back for the services again and again or will he go to the competitor. The employee behaviour needs to be groomed, channelised and directed towards the building of relationship marketing by the organisations. Organisations have been developing, elaborate training programmes, grooming sessions for the front line employees. The level of interaction that happens between its customers and the employees may not be the same for every customer. The organisations have to arrange the training, development programmes and orientation sessions for all its employees to make sure that customer at the moment of truth gets to deal with the best face of the organisation.

4.2.1 Employee Role in Service Designing

Services are often characterised by the inseparability of the service provider from the customer. The customer and the service provider must interact in order for the service to occur, in delivery of services such as hospitality, health care etc. Example: a patient cannot receive medical treatment without interacting with a doctor or nurse.

Often open to customer scrutiny, the behaviour and appearance of the service employees and hence the services should be given properly. As compared to services, manufactured goods do not face this dilemma as customers do not care about the behaviour of the workers who assemble the product parts together. In services, the service workers with whom customers interact are integral parts of the service and are significant to their evaluation of it. Customers often rely on service workers as quality cues, since the core of a service cannot be seen and the service outcome is sometimes indiscernible.

Employees who, interact directly with the customer typically have the greatest influence on perceptions of the service. Service performance are dependent on the labour, which is out of sight of the customer; example would be the airline baggage handler, the chef etc. The skill with which backstage personnel perform their tasks affects customers' assessment of service excellence, particularly if the staff fails to perform adequately.

Front stage employees represent the service in the customers' eyes . The flight attendant, teacher, nurse, bank teller, waiter and other frontline employees are the service to the customer. Service workers provide human evidence of service quality through both their technical and social skills. Technical skills are the proficiency with which service employees perform the tasks associated with their position. Social skills are the manner in which service employees interact with customer and fellow workers, for example the level of friendliness, caring and communication the hairstylist or clerk demonstrates.

Strategies for Delivering Service Quality through People

According to **Wilson et al**, *a complex combination of strategies is needed to ensure that service employees are willing and able to deliver quality services and that they stay motivated to perform in customer-oriented, service-minded ways.*

The human resource decisions and strategies in companies are aimed at motivating and enabling employees to deliver customer-oriented promises successfully, they will move towards delivering service quality through their people.

To build a customer-oriented, service-minded workforce, companies must:

(A) Hire the right people,
(B) Develop people to deliver service quality,
(C) Provide the needed support systems, and
(D) Retain the best people.

The strategies have a lot of sub strategies and are discussed below:

(A) Hire the Right People

Recruitment and retention of valued employees is the major concern of the HR department. Companies should pay more attention to recruiting and hiring suitable service employees, in order to deliver service quality effectively.

Compete for the Best People: A company has to identify the suitable people and compete with other companies in order to hire the best man. The firms act as marketers and use their marketing expertise in competing with other organisations to pursuing th**e best employees.**

1. **Hire for Service Competencies and Service Inclination:** Companies need to attract new employees who will contribute to the company through their abilities and values. Companies require their service employees to have two complementary capacities:

    - **Service competencies:** These are the skills and knowledge necessary to do the job. Job applicants validate competencies, such as attaining the particular degree and relevant professional qualifications can determine whether he or she has the necessary technical or professional competencies to perform well on the job. But sometimes, service competencies may be related to basic intelligence or physical requirements rather than relevant degree.

    - **Service inclination:** The service competencies are the skills and knowledge necessary to do the job.

2. **Be the Preferred Employer:** Preferred employers are those organisations that outperform their competition in effectively attracting, motivating, and retaining talented employees. One new approach to gain a competitive position to attract and retain the best human resources is to be the preferred employer in a particular industry or in a particular location. They achieve this reputation through innovative and compelling HR practices - *"extensive training, career and advancement opportunities, excellent internal support, attractive incentives"* that benefit both employees and their organisations. And if the company fail to fulfil the promise to the customers and fail to live up to its employer brand promises, its employees will also leave.

(B) Develop People to Deliver Service Quality

Just by hiring the right people in the right place is not enough to develop and maintain a consistent customer oriented and service minded workforce. Proper training programmes should be given. Promoting teamwork is an important part in the service delivery process.

1. **Training for Technical and Interactive Skills:** Training is one of the important aspects of human resource strategies in the company. Providing necessary technical skills and knowledge and interactive skills to deliver the quality service have to be kept in mind by the companies. Training the technical skills of a firm's personnel may be a means of simultaneously improving quality and productive. In many cases, companies may teach the technical skills through formal education. Technical skills are often taught through on-the-job training which can combine the theoretical foundation and real work. .

2. **Empower Employees:** Companies need to empower employees to make decisions and *"take action in a large number of potential problematic situations. Empowerment means giving employees the desire, skills, tools and authority to serve the customer"*, to reduce job-related stress, improve job satisfaction and truly accommodate the customer needs. *The importance of empowerment is that the employees know their responsibilities and are given authority to make decisions on the customer's behalf.* Just authority is not enough, employees need to have the knowledge and tools to be able to make the decisions and they need rewards that encourage them to make right decisions. Successful companies allow their employees to make the decision and they also provide the "training, guidelines and the tools needed for them to make such decisions".

3. **Promote Teamwork:** Teamwork as a source of job satisfaction will enhance customer satisfaction in a service organisation. Employees can feel more confident within a team, when they know that they have a team backing them up as well as they can ease some frustrations and stresses so that they will be able to maintain their

enthusiasm and be improved performance of quality service delivery. Teamwork helps companies to handle internal problems where they allow employees to study and solve the problems. Companies can improve productivity and create better adaptability and flexibility if the organisation can enhance the employee's interpersonal skills to deliver excellent service and the support from team can make employees' jobs easier and more pleasant.

(C) Provide Needed Support Systems

Proper conditions for delivering quality service do not exist, without customer-oriented internal support and systems. The company requires the employees to take responsibility for the customer but it should also provide internal support system to the employees as without this the employees feel frustrated and uncertain and can make bad decisions. It is nearly impossible for employees to deliver quality service no matter how much they want to without supportive systems. The following suggested strategies are aimed at ensuring customer-oriented internal support.

1. **Provide Supportive Technology and Equipment:** For delivery of service to be successful, companies need to invest adequate funding for the employees to have the needed tools including effective technology and technological support and equipment. It is possible for the contact employees to deliver good quality service when the support peoples and systems provide the effective customer information databases, effective internal support and other service required for handling situation. On the contrary, employees can be easily frustrated in their desire to deliver quality service without the needed technology and equipment.

2. **Measure Internal Service Quality:** The companies can more easily deliver quality customer-oriented service by ensuring the internal service quality. Measure and reward internal service is a key way to develop and support internal service relationship. Before companies begin to develop an internal service quality, they should measure customer perceptions of internal quality first by using the internal customer service audits. The internal organisation use internal customer service audits can identify their customers, determine their needs, measure how well they are doing and make improvements. In a word, measuring internal service quality would enable organisations to efficiently design the service delivery process.

3. **Develop Service-Oriented Internal Processes:** All sections of the company must interact with one another and are independent with one another. In other words, the poor quality of sub-processes will influence the final service quality delivery to customers. In many companies "internal processes are driven by bureaucratic rules, tradition, cost efficiencies or the needs of internal employees". However, in order to

best support front line employees in their service quality delivery and hence meet the customer' needs, companies' internal procedures should be based on the premise of customer value and customer satisfaction.

(D) Retain the Best People:

Just by hiring the right person for the job is not enough. Retaining them is a bigger part of the HR department. Success to a good HRM is to attract, develop and retain the best people. If the company hires the right people and provides training, they must also work towards always retaining the employee.

1. **Treat Employees as Customers:** The company can attract and retain the best employees if the company takes care of their employees. Suppose that employees who feel they are treated fairly by their companies will treat their customer better, ultimately achieving greater customer satisfaction. In other words, satisfied employees make for satisfied customers. The companies can assess the employee satisfaction and needs through conducting periodic internal marketing research. At the same time, companies should treat their employees as internal customer and meet their needs hence enhancing the employees' loyalty.

2. **Include Employees in the Company's Vision:** Motivating of employees in sticking with the organisation is a major objective, and the employees need to share an understanding of the organisation's vision. Employees will be motivated by their pay, reward and other benefits, but the best employees will focus on whether they are committed to the company's vision and its goals. The employees cannot be committed to the company's vision and will attract away to other opportunities when the vision is kept secret from them. In contrast, employees are more likely to remain in the company when the vision and direction are clear and motivating.

3. **Measure and Reward Strong Service Performers:** A manager uses money to influence employee behaviours and improve organisation performance, in addition to treating pay as an expense. The way people are paid affects the quality of their work; their attitude towards customers; their willingness to be flexible or learn new skills or suggest innovations; and even their interest in union or legal action against their employer. This potential to influence employees' behaviours, and subsequently the productivity and effectiveness of the organisation, is another reason, it is important to be clear about the meaning of compensation.

Reward does not simply compensate employees for their effort but also influence the recruitment and retention of strongest service performer. Companies must reward and promote their employees if they want talented employees to be retained.

More and more companies have turned to a variety of rewards because they recognise the development of new reward systems and structures should focus on customer satisfaction.

4.2.2 Service Culture

A service firm's culture reflects the shared values and beliefs that drive the organisation - the formally written, the unwritten and actual occurrences that help employees understand the norms for behaviour in the organisation. Organisational culture establishes the "do's and don'ts" of employee behaviour and provides the basis on which various employees behaviours can unite. Sometimes, people may compare the good and bad service and blame it on the culture of the company.

Example: A customer may show his or her disinclination to travel by a public sector airline because of the poor service culture and prefer a particular private airline for its customer-oriented culture. People sense culture both as customer and as an employee. It is based on the perception of how things happen around in an organisation. Organisations are distinguished by people in terms of the prevalent culture.

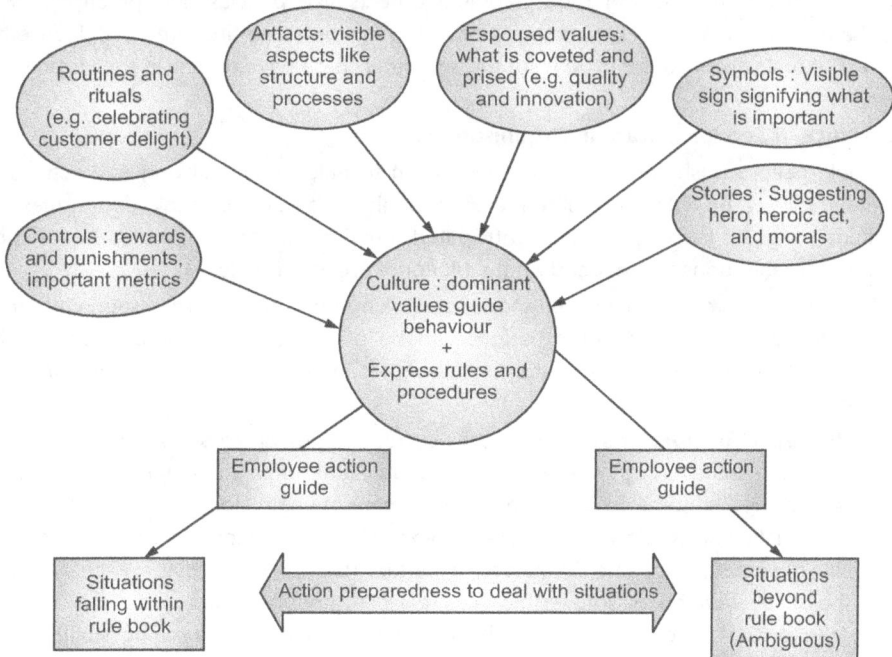

Fig. 4.1: Culture Provides Framework to Guide Action

Culture is important because of the influence it applies on the behaviour of people. It refers to the:
- values,
- norms,
- customers,
- traditions,
- rites,
- rituals,
- goals,
- beliefs
- artifacts that are present in an organisation.

The values and norms are highly intangible aspects which can only be sensed. Culture is like the hidden portion of the iceberg on which the visible portion rests. And it is these values and norms which manifest in more tangible aspects like policies and practices of the organisation. The goals and the methods of achieving the same are directly influenced by culture. Cultural values do not drop from the air, rather these have origins in the vision of the founders.

Importance of Service Culture in Organisation

People need a push and a guiding mechanism to guide their thinking and actions. All situations cannot be fully anticipated even though organisations bank upon rules and regulations to guide behaviour. Any unanticipated situation cannot be found in the rule book and those organisations that depend on the blueprint are very fragile

When variations occur, rule based model of working may put the organisation in a mess. In services, not all the kinds of situations can be anticipated and be provided, with a prescription to deal with the same. Culture is critical in service businesses for number of reasons:

(i) **Job Specification:** In services neither customers nor processes are uniform, unlike goods manufacturing where they are highly uniform. The inherent variability in services leaves some scope for the development of unanticipated service situations. It is virtually impossible to anticipate all types of service encounters and provide rules for governing the same. Therefore, a perfect rule book to govern each and every possible situation is impossible to create. Although service jobs are specified, possibility to go outside the specified legitimate domain is always a possibility.

(ii) **People are Important:** Services depend on people for their performance, unlike manufactured companies which have highly mechanised systems. In fact people's actions, deeds and performance make the service. The encounter is the point of interaction between provider and customer where the value is created. Excellence in services not only requires performance, rather these must be filled with passion.

Services are an *interaction-centric*. In the highly competitive services, when the basic core of the service product is commoditised, the organisations rely on culture to provide customer delight through sixth sense. The factors so created by developing a distinct service-oriented culture which manifests in unique organisational character becomes inimitable source of superiority. Inside the organisation, the top management must strive to build a distinct culture which is leveraged into cultivation of abstract superiority that defies articulation and measurement at the market end. A service culture can be said to exist in an organisation when a service orientation and an interest in customers are the most important norms within the organisation. Many companies have set the objective of being customer centric, but few seem to have really instilled the culture in the organisation so that it becomes the lifeblood of the organisation. A corporate culture is the set of common norms and values shared by people in the organisation. In common language, it can be described as the internal climate in the organisation. It is important to manage it because a service culture could be a basis for a sustainable competitive advantage.

4.2.3 Internal Marketing

Internal marketing (IM) *is a process that occurs within a company or organisation whereby the functional process aligns, motivates and empowers employees at all management levels to deliver a satisfying customer experience.* It has been integrated with employer branding, and employer brand management and it builds strong links between the employee brand experience and customer brand experience. According to **Burkitt and Zealley**, *"the challenge for internal marketing is not only to get the right messages across, but to embed them in such a way that they both change and reinforce employee behaviour"*.

From the basic understanding of marketing, comes internal marketing. The term **internal marketing** is defined as *viewing employees as internal customers, viewing jobs as internal products that satisfy the needs and wants of these internal customers while addressing the objectives of the firm.* Internal marketing is an ongoing process that occurs strictly within a company or organisation whereby the functional process is to align, motivate and empower employees at all management levels to consistently deliver a satisfying customer experience. It acts as marketing strategy where the employees themselves are customers and they are termed as internal customers. It is used as a philosophy for managing the firm's human resources based on a marketing perspective to build internal competencies for external success.

Internal marketing is critically important in a service industry.

Process of Internal Marketing

Employees are able and willing to deliver high-quality service and this is made sure by the marketers who develop techniques and procedures to do so. The internal marketing concept evolved as marketers formalised procedures for marketing to employees. Employees at all levels experience the business and understand its various activities and campaigns in an environment that supports customer consciousness. Internal marketing is the marketing aimed internally at the firm's employees. **The objective of internal marketing is to enable employees to deliver satisfying products to the guest**. As **Christian Gronroos** notes, "*The internal marketing concept states that the internal market of employees is best motivated for service-mindedness and customer-oriented performance by an active, marketing-like approach, where a variety of activities are used internally in an active, marketing-like and coordinated way.*" Internal marketing uses a marketing perspective to manage the firm's employees."

Internal marketing is a process that involves the following steps:
1. Establishment of a service culture.
2. Development of a marketing approach to human resource management.
3. Dissemination of marketing information to employees.
4. Implementation of a reward and recognition system.

1. Establishment of a Service Culture:

A service marketing programme is doomed to failure if its organisational culture does not support serving the customer.

Middle management is a big hurdle to most internal marketing programmes. Managers are always on the lookout for costs and increased profits. Their reward systems are usually based on **achieving certain cost levels**.

Turning the Organisational Structure Upside Down

The conventional organisational structure is a *triangular structure*. For example, in a hotel the CEO (chief executive officer) and COO (chief operating officer) are at the peak of the triangle. The general manager is on the next level, followed by department heads, supervisors, line employees, and the customers. **Ken Blanchard**, author of 'One Minute Manager', mentions that in this type of structure everyone works for the boss. The problem with this type of organisation is that everyone is concerned with satisfying people above them in the organisation, and very little attention is paid to the customer. .

The organisational chart is turned upside down, when a company has a service culture. Here, the corporate management is at the bottom of the structure and the customers are at the top. Everyone is working to serve the customer. Corporate management is helping their general managers to serve the customer, general managers are supporting their departments in serving the customer, department heads are developing systems that will allow their supervisors to better serve the customer and supervisors are helping line employees serve the customer.

2. Development of a Marketing Approach to Human Resources Management:

The development of a marketing approach to human resources management are as follows:

(a) Creating Jobs that Attract Good People: Managers must use the principles of marketing to attract and retain employees. They must research and develop an understanding of their employees' needs, just as they examine the needs of customers. Not all employees are the same. Some employees seek money to supplement their incomes; others are looking for work that will be their sole source of income. For employees, the marketing mix is the job, pay, benefits, location, transportation, parking, hours and intangible rewards, such as prestige and perceived advancement opportunities. Just as customers look for different attributes when they purchase a product, employees look for different benefits. Some may be attracted by flexible working hours, others are attracted by good health insurance benefits, and still others may be tempted by child-care facilities. Advertising should be developed with prospective employees in mind, building a positive image of the firm for present and future employees and customers.

(b) Continuous Training: Two principal characteristics have been identified in companies that lead their industries in customer service. They emphasize cross-training and they insist that everybody share certain training experiences. The development of a good training programme can start organisations on an upward spiral. Properly trained employees can deliver quality service, which helps the image of the firm, attracting more guests and employees to the organisation.

(c) Employee Involvement in Uniform Selection: The selection of uniforms is often left to designers and managers with little input from the service worker. Uniforms are important because employee dress contributes greatly to the guest's encounter with customer contact employees. Uniforms also become part of the atmosphere of a hospitality operation or travel operation; they have the ability to create aesthetic, stylish, and colorful impressions of the property. They distinguish employees from the general public, making employees accessible and easily identified. Clothing has been found to be a contributing factor in role-playing, acting as a vivid cue that can encourage employees to engage in the behaviours associated with the role of the employee. Putting on the costume can mean putting on a role and shedding other roles.

(d) Teamwork: Employees who are not customer oriented often try to pass the responsibility for serving employees to others. They are not team players. If one employee makes an error, other employees try to cover it before the guest notices. In these organisations, guests do not have to understand the hotel's organisation and business to ensure that their needs are met. The front desk handles most requests, relaying the guest's desire to the appropriate department. In restaurants that have used internal marketing to create a service culture, staff members cover for each other. Employees who see that a guest needs something will serve the guest, even though it may not be their table.

(e) **Initial Training:** To be effective, employees must receive information regularly about their company. The company's history, current businesses, and its mission statement and vision are important for employees to know. They must be encouraged to feel proud of their new employer.

(f) **Hiring Process:** Find employees who are good at creating a service experience is a vital goal and major hiring criterion of service organisations.

Selecting people for customer service roles is similar to casting people for roles in a movie. First, both require artful performances aligned with the audience expectations. Creating an interpersonal experience that customers remember as satisfactory, pleasant or dazzling is like an actor's mission of having audiences so caught up in the play or movie that they start believing the performer is the person portrayed. Second, both requirements need a casting choice based on personality.

An effective internal marketing programme demands close cooperation between marketing and human resources management. Hiring and training, traditionally the responsibility of human resources management, are key areas in any internal marketing programme. A marketing-like approach to human resources management starts with hiring the right employees. Selection methods that identify customer-oriented candidates are used as part of the hiring process.

(g) **Managing Emotional Labour:** The term emotional labour arises from the discrepancy between the way frontline staff feel inside and the emotions they are expected to portray in front of customers. Frontline staff are expected to be cheerful, genial, compassionate, sincere, or even self-effacing; emotions that can be conveyed through facial expressions, gestures and words. In the event that they do not reel such emotions, am required to quell their true feelings in order to conform to customer expectations.

3. **Dissemination of Marketing:**

Through customer-contact employees is the most effective way of communicating with customers. Employees often have opportunities to solve guest problem before these problems become irritants. To do this, they need information. Unfortunately, many companies leave customer-contact employees out of the communication cycle. The director of marketing may tell managers and supervisors about upcoming events, ad campaigns, and new promotions, but some managers may feel employees do not need to know this information.

Employees are looking up to the management for hints about the expected behaviour. Example if the CEO keeps the door open for a lady, other male employees can also follow that trend. A manager who talks about the importance of employees working together as a team can reinforce the desire for teamwork through personal actions.. Taking an interest in employees, work, lending a hand, knowing employees by name, and eating in the employee cafeteria are actions that will give credibility to the manager's words.

4. **Implementation of a Reward and Recognition System:**

Feedback must be given to employees so that they know how they are doing and how they can improve. An internal marketing programme includes service standards and methods of measuring how well the organisation is meeting these standards. The results of any service measurement should be communicated to employees.

Most reward systems in the hospitality and travel industry are based on meeting cost objectives such as achieving certain labour cost or food cost. They are also based on achieving sales objectives. Reward systems and bonuses based on customer satisfaction scores are one method of rewarding employees based on serving the customer.

Training programme and manuals can prepare employees to handle normal or routine transactions with customers. Internal marketing programmes will help than to deal with guests in a positive and friendly manner. But not all transactions are routine. *A non-routine transaction is a guess transaction that is unique and usually experienced for the first time by the employees.* One benefit of an internal marketing programme is that it provides employees with the right attitude, knowledge, communication skills, and authority to deal with non-routine transactions. The ability to handle non-routine transactions separates excellent hospitality companies from mediocre ones. The number of possible non-routine transactions is so great that they cannot be covered in a training manual.

Management should exhibit confidence in their ability to hire and train employees by trusting the employee's ability to make decisions.

The Internal Marketing Process

1. **Establishment of a Service Culture**
    (a) A service culture is an organisational culture that supports customer service through policies, procedures, reward systems, and actions.
    (b) An organisational culture is a pattern of shared values and beliefs that gives members of an organisation meaning, providing them with the miles for behaviour in the organisation.
    (c) Turning the organisational chart upside down. Service organisation should create an organisation that supports those employees who serve the customers.

2. **Development of a Marketing Approach to Human Resources**
   (a) Create positions that attract good employees.
   (b) Use, a hiring process that identifies and results in hiring service-oriented employees.
   (c) Provide initial employee training designed to share the company's vision with the employee and supply the employee with product knowledge.
   (d) Provide continuous employee training programmes.
   (e) Uniforms can affect an employee's attitude. Employees should be involved in the selection of uniforms.
   (f) Employees can be able to maintain a positive attitude. Managing emotional labour helps maintain a good attitude.

3. **Dissemination of Marketing Information to Employees**
   (a) Often, the most effective way of communicating with customers is through customer-contact employees.
   (b) Employees should hear about promotions and new products from management, not from advertisements meant for external customers.
   (c) Management at all levels must understand that employees are watching them for cues about expected behaviour.
   (d) Hospitality organisations should use printed publications as part of their internal communication.
   (e) Hotels can use technology and training to provide employees with product knowledge.
   (f) Employees should receive information on new products and product changes, marketing campaigns, and change in the service delivery process.

4. **Implementation of a Reward and Recognition System**
   (a) Employees must know how they are doing to perform effectively. Communication must be designed to give them feedback on their performance.
   (b) An internal marketing programme includes service standards and methods of measuring how well the organisation is meeting these standards.
   (c) If you want customer-oriented employees, seek out ways to catch them serving the customer and reward and recognise them for making the effort.

5. **Nonroutine Transactions**
   (a) A good internal marketing programme should result in employees who can handle non-routine transactions.
   (b) One benefit of an internal marketing programme is that it provides employees with the right attitude, communication skills, and authority to deal with non-routine transactions,

(c) A non-routine transaction is a guest transaction that is unique and usually experienced for the first time by the employees.
(d) Management must be willing to give employees the authority to make decisions that will solve guests problems.

4.2.4 Service Profit Chain

Heskett, Jones, Loveman, Sasser and Schesinger proposed the idea of *service profit chain*. It proposes that there *are direct and strong relationships between profitability, customer loyalty and employee satisfaction, employee loyalty and productivity*. The relationships proposed in the chain are self-reinforcing, as suggested in service businesses. To validate the links between elements of service profit chain, strong relationships were suggested between the profit and customer loyalty, employee loyalty and customer loyalty; and employee satisfaction and customer satisfaction.

The service profit chain proposes links between various elements:
(i) Profit and growth of a business are stimulated primarily by customer loyalty.
(ii) Customer loyalty is a direct result of customer satisfaction.
(iii) The customer satisfaction is largely influenced by the services provided by the firm to the customer.
(iv) Satisfied, loyal and productive employees create value.
(v) Employee satisfaction determined by the quality of support services and policies of the firm that enable them to deliver results to customers.

Internal service quality is the starting point in the service profit chain. Human resource issues like the workplace design, job design, employee selection and development, employee rewards and recognition and tools for serving customers influence the internal service quality. The human resource practices and procedures like recruitment, selection and training must be revamped. The employee compensation should be linked with the performance.

Internal Service Quality:	Employee Satisfaction:
Refers to the quality of internal environment where employees are expected to perform their jobs. Internal quality is influenced by factors like workplace and job design, reward and recognition systems, employee selection and development and tools provided to employees for performing services. It is reflected in employee attitude towards job, people and the firm.	Employee fulfillment response to the job. Satisfied employees tend to be productive and loyal.

In services it is only through the satisfied employees can a firm create satisfied customers. The employee satisfaction leads to employee retention and productivity. These two drive the natured value generated for customer. The value generated for the customer in turn affects customer satisfaction, further leading to the outcome, of customer loyalty. The service profit chain draws attention to internal quality. While most of the managers, focus their entire attention to external service quality, the internal quality never catches the attention. Internal quality is the starting point where investments must be made.

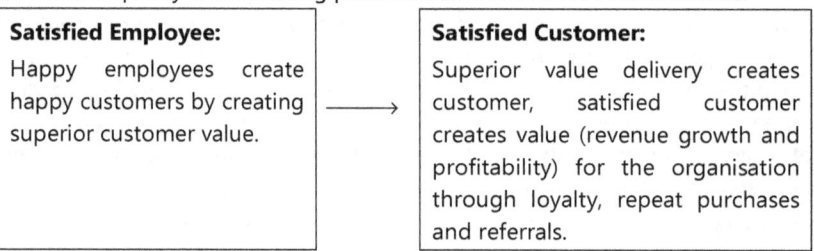

Internal quality in its entirety refers to the feelings the people in the firm have towards, their jobs, colleagues and the organisation. People link up in the system to form a chain in which one serves the other in order to finally create value for the external customer. The logic of customer satisfaction must pervade internally.

4.2.5 Emotional Labour

According **to Zeithaml and Bitner**, *friendliness, courtesy, empathy, and responsiveness directed toward customers; all require huge amounts of emotional labour from front-line employees who shoulder this responsibility.* The *term emotional labour* was first used by **Hochschild** and has been defined *as the necessary involvement of the service provider's emotions in the delivery of the service.* The display of emotions can strongly influence the customer's perception of service quality. Managers must hire employees who can cope with the stress caused by dealing with customers, to manage emotional labour. Some common techniques used to manage emotional labour include:

- Monitoring overtime,
- Avoiding double shifts,
- Encouraging work breaks,
- Support from fellow workers and managers, and
- Long hours.

If employees work long hours, they are emotionally and physically drained.

There are many service jobs which involve emotional labour, such as police officers, teachers, nursing staff etc. Emotional labour is exercise of control and management of emotions as a part of the job to promote achievement of organisational goals. The display of emotions which are consistent with organisational rules and realities irrespective of their mismatch with the internal feelings is at the core of the concept of emotional labour.

Many services are interaction oriented. Service jobs, because of this proximity with the customers, often tend to be emotion-sensitive for both the providers and the customer.

(i) Jobs that expect employees to produce some kind of emotional state in other person.

(ii) Jobs which have face-to-face or voice-to-voice contact with people

Strategies for Managing Emotional Labour

1. **Screening for Emotional Labour Abilities:** Many firms recruit and select the most suitable employees to meet the emotional labour requirements of the job, as mentioned by Wilson et al. To match the job's emotional labour requirements, companies put probable employees through a trial to find out how their values, experiences and personalities can be matched.

2. **Emotional Management Skills and Appropriate Behaviour:** Many firms recruit and select the most suitable employees to meet the emotional labour requirements of the job. Companies also may train employees in how to avoid absorbing a customer's bad mood. Customers on the other hand need not show courtesy or compassion and with this factor, the employee does not have the status equal to the customers who are the privileged lot. Employees face real challenges because they cannot express their true feelings.

3. **Carefully Constructing the Physical Work Environment:** To reduce the stress and pressure of the employees, the organisation can provide a comfortable environment such as having clean rest rooms, recreation area, good canteen etc. This can help the employee perform better in this work.

4. **Allowing Employees to Air Their Views:** Employees should be allowed to speak their mind so that whatever frustrations or troubles they have they can voice it out. Firms can provide emotional support and encouragement to employees where employees are allowed 'let off the steam'. They can feel their emotional contribution is recognised and can feel their company take much care about them.

4.2.6 Customer's Role in Service Delivery

The degree at which customers are involved and taking part in the service delivery process is known as Customer Participation. Services are actions or performances, typically produced and consumed simultaneously. In many situations employees, customers, and even others in the service environment interact to produce the ultimate service outcome. Customer participation at some level is inevitable in service delivery. Customers are indispensable to the production process of service organisations, and they can actually control or contribute to their own satisfaction.

Customer service delivery taps into business, marketing, and psychological research and practices to provide a wealth of knowledge about customer service. Customer service delivery also provides a framework for customer service as a process and an outcome, with contributions from some of the best-known industrial and organisational psychology experts in customer service. Customer service delivery explores human resource staffing practices and service delivery by including proven selection strategies for hiring top quality service workers, an analysis of the personality correlates of service performance, and a comprehensive review of assessment instruments that predict customer service performance.

Customers may understand their roles but unwillingly or unable to perform for some reason. If work schedule or illness keeps the members from living up to their part of the guidelines, the service will not be successful because of customer inaction. Since customers are not rewarded in any way for contributing their effort, customers may choose not to perform the roles defined for them.

Customer involvement in service development is natural, where person-to-person interaction between a customer and a service provider's employees is a constitutive element in the service. **Intensive business service** is that service, *where core value of the service is produced in personal interface between customer and service provider*. The importance of the customer to the service delivery process is huge:

1. It enhances two-way communication between companies and customers; thus, companies will have increased customer feedback.
2. It can help improve perceived service quality since customers are actively involved from the beginning of the service process.
3. It helps increase productivity as customers become partial employees of the firms.
4. It can be used as a criterion to segment customers leading to companies' greater capability of implementing service differentiation strategy.
5. It can enhance loyalty through Customer Participation Management (CPM) practice. CPM is considered a step beyond Customer Relationship Management.
6. It will lead to greater repurchase and referrals especially through the word-of-mouth channel.

4.2.6.1 Types of Customers' Roles

Customers can play a variety of roles. There are three major roles played by customers:
1. The customer as productive resource;
2. The customer as contributor to quality, satisfaction and value; and
3. The customer as competitor to the service organisation.

(A) Customers as Productive Resources: Customers are indentified as "partial" employees by organisations. This perception expands the boundaries of the service organisation to incorporate service recipients as temporary members or participants. Just like employees, customers contribute inputs which can have an impact on the organisation's productivity through the quantity and quality of the inputs and thereby the output is generated. The quality of the information patients provide can ultimately affect the quality of the outcome.

Since customers can influence both the quality and quantity of production, some experts believe that the delivery system should be isolated as much as possible from customer inputs in order to reduce the uncertainty, customers can bring into the production process. The greater the potential for the system to operate at peak efficiency, the less direct contact is between the customer and the service production system.

(B) Customers as Contributors to Quality, Satisfaction and Value: Customers also play the role of contributor to their own satisfaction. Customers may not care that they have increased the productivity of the organisation through their participation, but they probably do care a great deal about whether their needs are fulfilled. Effective customer participation can increase the likelihood that needs are met and the benefits the customer is seeking are actually attained. The same is true for an organisational customer purchasing management consulting services. Unless the organisation uses or implements the advice it has purchased, it cannot expect to get the full value of the service. To use the information they provide, many management consultants now get involved in teaching customers.

Some customers just like to enjoy participating in the service delivery; they find the act extremely attractive.

When things go wrong, customers often blame themselves, since they participate in the service delivery. When this happens they will be a little less dissatisfied with the service provider as compared to when they know that the service provider is at fault.

(C) Customers as Competitors: Many times, customers have the choice of purchasing services in the marketplace or producing the service themselves, either fully or in part. The decision whether to produce services for themselves (internal exchange) versus have someone provide the service for them (external exchange) is a common decision for consumers. Customers in a sense are competitors of the companies that supply the service.

Firms frequently choose to outsource service activities such as payroll, data processing, research, accounting, maintenance and facilities management. They find that it is advantageous to focus on their core businesses and leave these essential support services to others with greater expertise. Full participation, if he/she possesses the motivation and the needed skills, can be regarded as a prime candidate to engage in internal exchange and produce the service without the aid of a service provider. Similar internal versus external exchange decisions are made by organisations.

4.2.6.2 Strategies for Delivering Services through the Customers

Companies should always try to increase customer participation for betterment, such as:

1. **Hire Competent Staff:** Only skilled Customer Service Representatives (CSR) with proven experience in the given field should be recruited by the service businesses. They are motivated to obtain thorough training so as to harden their knowledge and interpersonal skills. Hiring competent customer service staff is crucial for any new business since they have experienced training and are the ones who will continually interact with and obtain feedback from consumers.

2. **Take Advantage of Innovation and Modern Technology:** New and effective ways to interact with the customers have sprung up recently such as live chats, and other programmes in their website which are user friendly to the customer. Rather than being put on hold on the telephone for an interminable period of time, customers are able to have an online chat with a live representative who can quickly address their concerns.

3. **Automated Sales Process:** Many companies enforce an automated sales process for customers who purchase items online. The customers are kept informed through emails and SMS about their purchase order and when the product will get shipped. Apart from this, they also have the ability to track the delivery of their packages through a shipping confirmation number.

4. **Customer is Always Right:** One of the major objectives of the company is to believe in the fact that the customer is always right. Customer appreciation is one of the leading reasons why loyal customers repeatedly do business with a company. Regardless of situation, it is always good practice to satisfy a customer's needs.

5. **Community Involvement:** Another advantageous strategy is through support forums and instant feedback on company websites. Through the use of similar online tools, businesses can easily find out the likes and dislikes of their buyers according to customer ratings. Customers, on the other hand, can publicly post their ideas about different products and make recommendations.

6. **Company Employee Retention Strategy:** Customer service jobs have a very high turnover rate. Sometimes it can be difficult to motivate an employee, especially if his job encompasses the same routine duties on a daily basis. In order to boost employee morale and commitment, many companies have made the ambitious move

to offer many different career incentives, including sponsoring higher education degrees. Customer service representatives are also given competitive salaries, internships, stock options, etc. By offering these different benefits to their employees, many customer service representatives will become more goal-oriented, attain job satisfaction, and take pride in their work. Employee turnover rate is more likely to be reduced through this retention strategy, and most importantly, service representatives will be able to provide superior customer service support.

7. **Choose the Right Customers:** Before the company begins the process of educating and socialising customers for their roles, it must attract the right customers to fill those roles. The organisation should seek to attract customers who will be comfortable with the roles. To do this, it should clearly communicate the expected roles and responsibilities in advertising, personal selling, and other company messages. By previewing their roles and what is required of them in the service process, customers can self-select into (or out of) the relationship. Self-selection should result in enhanced perceptions of service quality from the customer's point of view and reduced uncertainty for the organisation.

8. **Get Referrals/Leads from Existing Customers:** When existing customers are satisfied with a company's products and the quality of customer service, they are more likely to tell others of their positive experiences. Most often, these "referred" customers are also likely to do business with a company their friends have spoken highly about. It is crucial for every new business to effectively network in this manner and to treat their existing customers exceptionally well in order to gain credibility and increase both repeat and future customers.

9. **Reward Customers for their Contributions:** Customers must be motivated and rewarded for the roles they play, which will make them perform effectively and participate actively. Rewards are likely to come in the form of increased control over the delivery process, time savings, monetary savings, and psychological or physical benefits.

4.2.6.3 Customer as a Co-producer

Co-production is often defined with reference to customer participation. In the context of service-dominant logic, co-production is defined as *"participation in the creation of the core offering itself"*. Co-production encompasses all cooperation formats between consumers and production partners.

- **Etgar** describes co-production *as "the various activities involve intellectual work of initiating and designing, resource aggregating and processing activities which lead to creation of outputs that serve as platforms for delivery of values used/consumed later*

on, up till ensuring delivery and executing use (consumption). Co-production implies that consumers participate in the performance of the various activities performed in one or more of these stages".
- **Wikström** defines co-production as *"buyer-seller social interaction and adaptability with a view to attaining further value."*
- Customer participation is defined by **Dabholkar** as *"the degree to which the customer is involved in producing and delivering the service".*

When consumers are involved in the various value creating activities through which products and services are made, it is known as co-production.

These activities include:
- *The production and distribution processes which are usually performed in the course of manufacturing a product or creating a service for a given target group of consumers.*

The development of digital technologies which allow consumers to have instant access to stored information and to create and disseminate text, pictures and voice messages at minimal cost, has contributed significantly to this trend. Co-production reflects a conscious strategic decision by consumers to become involved in production-like activities.

Consumers are involved in activities such as:
(i) The production of their own individually designed and planned music compilations, movies and videos;
(ii) Assembling and self delivering their own furniture bought from @Home;
(iii) Designing their own travel packages;
(iv) Planning their own unique well-being and health maintenance services.

For each co-production situation, one can also find consumers who do not engage in any co-productive activity. In order to understand how to engage consumers in co-production activities, we must understand the mechanisms which lead them to participate.

Factors of Customer Co-production

Participation in co-production to create value can occur in varying degrees. It can be where the company does all the work to extensive co-production activities by the customer where customers actively co-produce a service.

The maximum possible form of customer co-production is "***self-service***"; customers perform activities entirely by themselves using own assets, or tools, facilities, and systems provided by a firm. Self-service is often carried out using self-service technologies (SSTs) that can be defined as *"technological interfaces that enable customers to produce a service independent of direct service employee involvement."*

Examples of self service are: Automated teller machines (ATMs), automated hotel checkout, banking by telephone, and services over the Internet etc.

The factors influence how much customers actually participate and the amount of value-in-use that can be created:

1. **Customer Role Clarity:** Customer role clarity, also referred to as ("motivational direction") is defined as "understanding how to perform a role". Role clarity determines knowledge and hence influences ability to coproduce. Customer's own experiences with a particular setting or a similar one may lead to role clarity. A customer entirely new to a particular service context may gain role clarity by relying on experience with related contexts and/or by using other customers' behaviour for guidance.

2. **Customer Ability to Co-produce:** Customer ability refers to customer's possession of the required operant resources to participate. A customer's ability to co-produce is determined by his or her pertinent resources such as appliances, knowledge, skills, experience, energy, effort, money, or time. Withdrawing cash from an automated teller machine is an example. The customer needs some skills to operate the automated teller machine, following a predetermined set of standard procedures. Furthermore, a plastic card is required. Additionally, a belief of self-efficacy is necessary. When a person believes that he or she is incapable of performing a particular task, he or she will not engage in the behaviour, even if he or she acknowledges that it is a better alternative. Changes in a customer's resource mix may change his or her ability to co-produce.

3. **Customer Willingness to Co-produce:** Co-production requires customer willingness to co-produce. Willingness to perform has been shown to be dependent on motivational levels. Notwithstanding, it should not be neglected that customers are typically not directly paid by the firm for the input they contribute. The input however may cause costs associated with the use of operant resources. Those costs can be evaluated objectively through market prices. This phenomenon is particularly fostered by:
   (i) Ubiquitous connectivity that enables customers to be well informed and networked,
   (ii) Convergence of technologies,
   (iii) Globalisation of information.

Customers look at the advantages they expect to gather from co-production. Benefits of co-production for customers may include
   (a) Efficiency in the process,
   (b) Efficacy of the outcome,
   (c) Hedonic/emotional benefits.

These motivating benefits are not mutually exclusive; different customers may carry out the same actions while seeking different benefits.

4.3 Service Physical Evidence

Physical evidence is the element of the service mix which allows the customer to make judgements on the organisation. Consumers will make perceptions based on their sight of the service provision which will have an impact on the organisations perceptual plan of the service. For e.g. If one moves into a restaurant his expectations are of a clean, friendly environment, besides high quality food which is the core service of the restaurant.

Everything that a company physically shows to the customer is physical evidence.

It includes the physical environment of:

- The service outlet,
- The exterior, the interior,
- All tangibles such as machinery, furniture, vehicles, stationery, signboards, communication materials, certificates, receipts, service personnel and so on.

It is a fact that service consumers cannot see a service but they can visualise various tangibles associated with the service. "*Physical evidence is often referred to as the environment that facilitates the performance and the communication of the service.*"

These tangibles serve as clues for the service that is invisible and help the consumers to grasp various aspects of the service. Particularly, tangible cues help in assessing the quality of the service provided.

4.3.1 Role of Evidence in Services Marketing

By exposing them to the critical objects of the servicescape, physical evidence plays a definitive role in influencing, the perceptions of customers and employees, in services marketing. **A. Parasuraman and L. L. Berry** identified six specific roles of evidence are:

1. **Shaping First Impressions:** Consumers form initial impressions once they are exposed to the exterior and interior of a service outlet. The first flash quickly creates an impression on the service provider. Such first impressions condition the mind and influence perception of the situations that follow in the service process. The service provider, thus, finds an opportunity to shape the first impressions of the consumers through the physical settings of the service outlet.

2. **Managing Trust:** Physical environment and the tangibles used in service processes stand as dues to consumers. The positive dues will clarify the doubts and suspicions of the consumers and build trust. The consistency in quality of the physical settings will help in managing the consumer trust,

3. **Facilitating Quality of Service:** A good servicescape facilitates employee-customer participation in the service production, delivery and consumption process. It makes sure all kinds of support facilities are present in the order and function as desired. The ambience itself has the capacity to stimulate positive moods and emotions to people engaged in service process.

4. **Changing the Image:** A change in the physical environment has the potential to change the image of the service outlet and the service provider. The up-scaling of facilities and structures like conversion of non-A/C to A/C, additional moving space to customers, new decors, new lighting systems, new dress code to contact employees, new way of reception, new machines, etc., contributes for the change of the image of the service provider.

5. **Providing Sensory Stimuli:** The aesthetics of the service environment has the potential to stimulate the senses. Such stimulations help the customer in participation of service production and in quality perceptions.

6. **Socialising Employees:** Many services need employee-employee cooperation and coordination in creating quality experiences to the customers. Servicescape facilitates employee interactions formally and informally and helps in developing social bondage among them.

4.3.2 Guidelines for Developing Physical Evidence Strategy

The following are the guidelines for developing physical evidence strategy:

1. **Identify the Strategic Requirement of Physical Evidence:** The evidence strategy must be linked clearly with the organisation's overall goals and mission. The goals of the organisation should be clearly understood so as to determine the kind of support that can be built through evidence strategy. The vision of the firm provides an understanding of the future. Most of the evidence decisions arc costly and have long-term standing. Therefore, the vision of the organisation should be kept in mind.

2. **Decide the Kind of Physical Evidence Required:** It is necessary to decide what kind of physical evidence is required and what is its role in services marketing. Accordingly it is possible to design service scape. Service blueprinting should be carried out to have absolute clarity over organisational service process, placement of equipment, furniture and other support material, people and other environmental features. Clarify roles of employees and customers in the service scape. The identification and definition of the roles to be played by employees and customers, machines and other elements in the service scape will aid in identifying opportunities and deciding who needs to be consulted in making decisions.

3. **Identify and Assess Physical Evidence Opportunities:** All service firms need to look for possibilities of introducing changes and improvements in the forms of evidence and the roles of the servicescape. What are the perceptions of the customers and employees on the physical evidence? What are missed opportunities? What are the defects in the present evidence strategy? Such questions are to be answered periodically. The answers to such questions will certainly bring to the fore the opportunities that can be exploited.
4. **Update and Modernise Evidence:** Some aspects of evidence require frequent or periodic updating and modernising. Service firms should be prepared to introduce changes as per the requirements of the market. The orientation to change makes the service firm innovative and capable of influencing the perceptions of the customers much better than its competitors.

4.3.3 Elements of Physical Evidence

The elements of physical evidence can be broadly referred to as the physical environment of the service unit and other tangibles. Service consumption is an experiential phenomenon since services are predominantly intangible processes. The environmental conditions of the service location facilitate consumption experience to service consumers. The environmental design needs to be neutral enough to please everybody as the service outlet is meant to serve a wide variety of people. The spatial dimensions of a physical setting are capable of creating moods and influencing behavioural intentions. The internal layout of the physical space, for example, may either ease or restrict the movement of the consumers. It may evoke a sense of either crowding when the space is conservatively designed or spacious when it is liberally designed. The conservatively designed space layout often creates confined conditions and makes customers feel uncomfortable. *The physical environment of a service unit is popularly called **servicescape**.*

Table 4.1: Elements of Physical Evidence

Servicescape	Other tangibles
Facility Exterior	Business cards
Exterior Design	Stationery
Signage	Billing statements
Parking	Reports
Landscape	Employee dress
Surrounding environment	Uniforms, Brochures
Facility Interior	
Interior design	
Equipment	
Signage	
Layout	
Air quality/temperature	

4.3.4 Servicescape

The concept of servicescape had been developed by **Booms and Bitner** *to emphasise the impact of the physical environment in which a service process takes place.*

Servicescape is defined as, *'the environment in which the service is assembled and in which the seller and customer interact, combined with tangible commodities that facilitate performance or communication of the service'.* (**Booms and Bitner**).

Servicescape is used for the services delivery point where the customers could visit to get all the experiences. Only after he absorbs the servicescape along with the service, the customer will be able to find the difference between a good and a bad service. Servicescape is the atmosphere and the ambience, the mood generating impression that the customer experiences before he actually savours the service.

4.3.4.1 Types of Servicescapes

Table 4.2 below is a framework for ategorizing service organisations on two dimensions that capture some of the key differences that will impact the management of the servicescape. Some of the types of servicescapes are:

1. **Servicescape Use:** First, organisations differ in terms of who actually comes into the service facility and thus is potentially influenced by its design. The first column of table suggests three types of service organisations that differ on this dimension:

    (i) **Self-service:** In a self-service environment, very few employees are involved and the customer performs most of the activities. If the service firm is focusing on a self-service environment, it has to attract the right market segment and offer easy-to-use facilities. ATMs, fast-food centres and movie theatres are examples of self-service environments.

    (ii) **Interpersonal Services:** Both employees and customers will be given adequate importance in interpersonal services. The servicescape should contribute to social interactions between and among customers and employees. In the case of hospitals, educational institutions and banks, the servicescape must be planned to attract, satisfy and facilitate both employees and customers simultaneously.

    (iii) **Remote Service:** The customer's physical involvement in the servicescape may be very little or even absent. In such service scape designs, only employees' needs and preferences will be considered. The goal of the service scape is to keep employees motivated and to facilitate productivity, team work and operational efficiency.

Table 4.2: Typology of Service Organisations based on Variations in Form and Use of the Servicescape

Servicescape Usage	Complexity of the Servicescape	
	Elaborate Environment	**Lean Environment**
Self-Service (Customer only)	Golf Land	ATM
	Surf' and Splash	Shopping mall information kiosk
		Post office kiosk
		Internet services
		Express mail drop-off
Interpersonal Services (both Customer and Employee)	Hotel	Dry cleaner
	Restaurant	Hot dog stand
	Health clinic	Hair salon
	Hospital	
	Bank	
	Airline	
	School	
Remote Service (Employee only)	Telephone company	Telephone mail-order desk
	Insurance company	Automated voice messaging
	Utility	Services
	Many professional services	

2. **Complexity of the Servicescape:** Another factor that will influence servicescape management is shown in the horizontal dimension. Some service environments are very simple, with few elements, few spaces and few pieces of equipment. Such environments are termed lean. Design decisions are relatively straightforward, especially in self-service or remote service situations in which there is no interaction among employees and customers. Shopping mall information kiosks and FedEx drop-off facilities would be considered lean environments because both provide service from one simple structure.

4.3.4.2 Roles of Servicescape

A servicescape has four roles and an evaluation of these roles will show how important it is to design a proper servicescape:

1. **Socialiser:** Design of servicescapes aids in socialisation of both the customers and employees, conveying expected roles, behaviour and relationship.
2. **Differentiator:** Clearly the design of the servicescape differentiates one provider from its competitors, and hints at the segment the services are targeted at. Companies adapt servicescape to reposition the services or identify new customer segments.
3. **Facilitator:** Assist both the customers as well as the service employees to make most of the opportunity by making the service consumption convenient for the consumer.
4. **Package:** Servicescapes 'package' the service offer and communicate an image to the customers of what they are going to get. Appropriate servicescaping is a sure shot way to create an image that the service provider is seeking to put up. It also helps moderate customer expectation and reinforces his experience and reminiscences. Servicescape is an outward appearance of organisation and thus can be critical in forming initial impressions or setting up customer expectation.

4.3.4.3 Experiencescapes

According to **O'Dell**,' *experiencescapes are not only organised by producers (from place marketers and city planners to local private enterprises) but are also actively sought after by consumers. They are spaces of pleasure, enjoyment and entertainment ...'*.

The servicescapes of different firms within a specific location are connected through experiencescapes. They are one of the means by which place is transformed into a destination product by virtue that experiencescapes have been consciously packaged through public-private partnerships. The design and packaging of a place in order to produce a desired set of experiences is a logical expression of what it is referred to as 'the experience economy' in which 'experiences drive the economy and therefore generate much of the base demand for goods and services'. Example: themed waterfronts etc. The thematic development of parts of a city for tourism and leisure purposes is an extremely common urban tourism strategy. Many cities, for example, have Chinatowns or other ethnic districts such as a 'Little Italy' or 'Little India' even though the social, political and economic processes that originally led to the creation of such ethnically distinct locations has long since past. Indeed, a major challenge in packaging destinations is not to damage the characteristics that differentiate it from surrounding places. For example, Chang's study of Singapore's Little

India Historic District suggested that its redevelopment had led to the taming of at least three dimensions of what had made the area distinctive:
1. A decline in traditional Indian-owned retail outlets and services (change in activities).
2. The transformation from a place of permanent residence into a retail attraction (change in community).
3. A dimming of its Indian cultural identity (changes in identity).

Such issues raise questions about how people experience place and this leads us to our third meaning of place.

4.3.4.4 Elements of Experiencescapes: Architectural Designs in Servicescape

Researchers have explored many dimensions of servicescape especially in stores or malls context which together affect the customer behavioural intentions.

1. **Aesthetic Factor:** Aesthetics refers to a function of architectural style, along with interior décor, colour scheme, pictures/paintings, plants/flowers, ceiling/wall decorations all of which customers can see and use to evaluate the aesthetic quality of the servicescape. Aesthetic factors are important because they influence ambience. Other aesthetic factors include the surrounding external environment, the parking and visibility of the facility. Architectural design and interior décor positively affects desire to stay and higher levels of spending. Store colour is said to influence the trust and store choice. Blue ambient colour generates more trust in subjects than green ambient colour which in turn significantly affects store choice. Also consumers reacted more favorably to a blue environment in retail settings, where in "blue stores" had higher simulated purchase rates. Colours also influenced emotional pleasure.

2. **Aroma:** Pleasant ambient odour has significant effects on consumer perceived value and the amount of time spent in the store. Pleasant scents increased the amount of time a consumer spent in the store. Also shoppers in the scented condition perceived that they had spent less time in the store than shoppers in the no-scent condition. Further in-store aroma influences consumer emotions of pleasure and arousal.

3. **Music:** Atmospheric music (tempo, volume and preference) is known to have tremendous impact on consumer responses. Customers have specific preferences towards music and its evaluation can influence the overall satisfaction. Under slow music people tend to move slowly, explore more, stay for long and end up paying more in a supermarket. Also customers selected more expensive merchandise when classical music was played in the background. Moreover shopping time and expenditures were observed to increase with the level of preference for the background music.

4. **Temperature:** The tactile factors such as temperature and air quality may help in creating a holistic atmosphere in a retail store. These cues signal store's merchandise quality, clientele, comfort, and have significant and positive impact on store image. Store temperature (air conditioning) potentially increases customers' value due to personal comfort and aesthetic values. Moreover stores or shopping malls that are too hot make the buyer dissatisfied. These factors increase customers' exploratory tendencies and sensation seeking behaviour and can potentially alter emotional experiences.

5. **Ambient Factor:** Ambient factors include background variables such as lighting, aroma, noise, music, air quality and temperature which affect the non-visual senses. Though these variables are not part of the primary service but their absence may make customers feel uncomfortable.

6. **Lighting:** Right lighting has been proven to influence the shopping behaviour of customers positively. Brighter lighting influenced shoppers to examine and handle more products. Further customers engaged in general communication in bright environments, whereas more intimate conversation occurred in softer light. Lighting makes a significant contribution on how a customer experiences a space.

7. **Cleanliness:** Cleanliness has been found to exert a strong influence on consumers' perceptions of retail stores and services. Cleanliness is important especially in those situations in which customers must spend several hours in the service setting and many consumers implicitly associate cleanliness with the quality of the servicescape. Cleanliness significantly affected the servicescape satisfaction of a slot floor in casino. Further the cleanliness issues were most reported problems in servicescape failures in food service industry.

8. **Variety:** Shopping mall or stores that offers variety in tenant occupancy and product variety both in individual store and across competing stores is likely to attract more shoppers because of the excitement it generates. Tenant mix is said to influence mall selection, frequency of shopping and shopping centre image. Further mall variety measured on food service, stores and entertainment options has the strongest influence on customer excitement and desire to stay in the mall. Variety of products has a significant influence on shoppers' satisfaction.

9. **Layout:** Spatial layout and functionality refers to the way in which machinery, equipment, and furnishings, seats, aisles, hallways and walkways, restrooms, and the entrance and exits are designed and arranged in service settings. These factors are important in many services (e.g., theatres, retail stores, concerts, upscale restaurants)

because these can affect the comfort of the customer. Layout that makes people feel constricted may have a direct effect on customer quality perceptions, excitement levels, and indirectly on their desire to return.

10. **Social Factor:** Social elements are the employees and customers in the service setting. These cues include physical appearance, number, gender and attire of employees and of other customers. Presence of more social cues in store environment may lead to higher levels of arousal. Bitner found that environment when a service failure occurred. Further, more number of sales personnel with professional attire, and greeting customers at the entrance of the store made customers perceive higher service quality. Additionally in an open service encounter sites (e.g., banks, restaurants) where consumers could observe service delivery to other consumers, the way services were delivered influenced not only the opinions of the consumers who received the service, but also the opinions of other consumers who observed service delivery.

11. **Sign, Symbols, and Artifacts:** Signs, symbols, and artifacts include signage and décor used to communicate and enhance a certain image or mood, or to direct customers to desired destinations. It was found that signs, symbols and artifacts were positively associated with customer patronage. Indeed, a service setting with legible (clear signage) arrangements may result in positive consumer moods, thus impacting on the relative spend during lunch.

4.3.4.5 Virtual Servicescape

The *offline service environment* is termed as servicescape, in which a service experience is organised and delivered by service providers and experienced by a customer, the **Internet service environment** may be termed as **e-servicescape**, **virtual servicescape or cyberscape**. While dimensions of servicescape versus e-servicescape overlap at some degrees, they apparently differ from each other at various aspects, due to the characteristics of the e-commerce service environment, where customers do not encounter services provided by service employees physically. The e-servicescape is critical for the service providers via the Internet, just as the servicescape is crucial for the service organisations.

When sales or service encounters occur through the Website, the e-servicescape may become particularly critical because it is the key factor representing the organisation to customers. The Internet allows customers a convenient way to explore a broader range of products and product attributes, and provides customers with chances to compare features of a product/service and prices on multiple websites. A study of virtual servicescape was conducted to examine the impacts of aesthetics and professionalism on customer feelings of pleasantness, satisfaction, and approach toward service interaction of a service organisation.

It was found that aesthetics aspects were influential on customers' feelings of pleasantness, satisfaction, and approach toward service interactions, as well as professionalism which influences customer satisfaction.

Points to Remember

- **People** is the fifth P.
- **To build a customer-oriented, service-minded workforce, companies must**
    1. Hire the right people,
    2. Develop people to deliver service quality,
    3. Provide the needed support systems, and
    4. Retain the best people.
- One benefit of an internal marketing programme is that it provides employees with the right attitude, knowledge, communication skills, and authority to deal with non-routine transactions. The ability to handle non-routine transactions separates excellent hospitality companies from mediocre ones.
- **The Internal Marketing Process**
    1. Establishment of a service culture
    2. Development of a marketing approach to human resources
    3. Dissemination of Marketing Information to Employees
    4. Implementation of a Reward and Recognition System
    5. Non routine transactions
- **Service Profit chain:** are direct and strong relationships between profitability, customer loyalty and employee satisfaction, employee loyalty and productivity and the links between these elements.
- Emotional labour is exercise of control and management of emotions as a part of the job to promote achievement of organisational goals
- There are three major roles played by customers. Through a review of literature which has contributed to our understanding of customer participation, we have identified three of these:
    1. The customer as productive resource;
    2. The customer as contributor to quality, satisfaction and value; and
    3. The customer as competitor to the service organisation
- **Strategies for delivering service through the customers:**
    1. Hire competent staff
    2. Take Advantage of Innovation and Modern Technology

3. Automated Sales Process
4. Customer is Always Right
5. Community involvement
6. Get Referrals/Leads from Existing Customers
7. Company Employee Retention Strategy
8. Choose the Right Customers
9. Reward Customers for their Contributions

- **Factors of Customer Co-production**
    1. Customer Ability to Co-produce
    2. Customer Role Clarity
    3. Customer Willingness to co-produce

- **Six specific roles of evidences are:**
    1. Shaping first impressions
    2. Managing trust
    3. Facilitating quality of service
    4. Changing the image
    5. Providing sensory stimuli
    6. Socialising employees

- **Guidelines for developing physical evidence strategy are:**
    1. Identify the Strategic Requirement of Physical Evidence
    2. Decide the Kind of Physical Evidence Required
    3. Identify and Assess Physical Evidence Opportunities
    4. Update and Modernise Evidence

- **Servicescape** is the atmosphere and the ambience, the mood generating impression that the customer experiences before he actually savours the service.

- **The types of servicescapes are:**
    1. Servicescape Use
        (a) self service
        (b) interpersonal services
        (c) remote service
    2. Complexity of the servicescape

- **Roles of Servicescape:**
  (a) Package
  (a) Facilitator
  (a) Socialiser
  (a) Differentiator
- **Elements of Experiencescapes:**
  1. Aesthetic Factor
  2. Aroma
  3. Music
  4. Temperature
  5. Ambient factor
  6. Lighting
  7. Cleaniness
  8. Variety
  9. Layout
  10. Social factor
  11. Sign, Symbols
- The Internet service environment may be termed as e-servicescape, virtual servicescape or cyberscape.

Questions for Discussion

1. Discuss the strategies involved in service delivery through employees.
2. What is internal marketing? Explain its relevance in service business.
3. Not all service situations can be anticipated. What role service culture can play in equipping the service people to negotiate these situations?
4. Explain service profit chain and emotional labour in detail.
5. Describe the customer's role in service delivery and strategies to manage it.
6. Discuss the concept of physical evidence and identify the elements of physical evidence.
7. Explain the aspects of servicescape like experience servicescape and virtual servicescape.

Multiple Choice Questions

1. Airline baggage handler is an example of:
   (a) frontstage employee
   (b) backstage employee
2. Waiter is an example of:
   (a) frontstage employee
   (b) backstage employee
3. In services inputs and processes are highly uniform:
   (a) True
   (b) False
4. _____ is a process that occurs within a company or organisation whereby the functional process aligns, motivates and empowers employees at all management levels to deliver a satisfying customer experience
   (a) Service management
   (b) Service process
   (c) Internal Marketing
   (d) External Marketing
5. When the core value of the service is produced in personal interface between customer and service provider, it is known as:
   (a) Intensive business system
   (b) Customer participation
   (c) Intensive business service
   (d) Customer service
6. Participation in the creation of the core offering itself is known as:
   (a) Co production
   (b) Co-producer
   (c) Intensive business service
   (d) Service management
7. Everything that a company physically shows to the customer is:
   (a) Customer role clarity
   (b) Physical evidence
   (c) Service management
   (d) External evidence
8. _____ cues help in assessing the quality of the service provided
   (a) Tangible
   (b) Intangible
9. The environment in which the service is assembled and in which the seller and customer interact, combined with tangible commodities that facilitate performance or communication of the service is known as:
   (a) Physical evidence
   (b) Co-producer
   (c) Tangible service
   (d) Servicescape
10. Which is a role of servicescape?
    (a) Socialiser
    (b) Package
    (c) Differentiator
    (d) All the above

Answers

1. (b)	2. (a)	3. (b)	4. (c)	5. (c)	6. (a)	7. (b)	8. (a)	9. (d)	10. (d)

Project Questions

1. Analyse the level of service orientation in your firm, or in any given firm, and determine the need for internal marketing. Also, discuss which internal marketing processes and activities might function well for your firm.
2. Describe and give an example of how servicescapes play each of the following strategic roles' package, facilitator, socialiser, and differentiator.

Chapter 5...

Applications of Service Marketing

Contents ...

- 5.1 Marketing in Tourism
  - 5.1.1 Introduction
  - 5.1.2 Characteristics of Tourism Marketing
  - 5.1.3 Marketing Mix of Tourism Services
- 5.2 Marketing in Hospitality
  - 5.2.1 Introduction
  - 5.2.2 Characteristics of Hospitality Marketing
  - 5.2.3 Marketing Mix of Hospitality Marketing
- 5.3 Marketing in Airline
  - 5.3.1 Introduction
  - 5.3.2 Characteristics of Airline Marketing
  - 5.3.3 Marketing Mix of Airline Marketing
- 5.4 Marketing in Telecom
  - 5.4.1 Introduction
  - 5.4.2 Characteristics of Telecom Services Market in India
  - 5.4.3 Marketing Mix of Telecom Marketing
- 5.5 Marketing in Information technology (IT) and Information Technology Enabled Services (ITeS)
  - 5.5.1 Introduction
  - 5.5.2 Characteristics of IT and ITES Services
  - 5.5.3 Marketing Mix of IT and ITES Services
- 5.6 Marketing in Sports and Entertainment
  - 5.6.1 Introduction
  - 5.6.2 Sports Marketing
    - 5.6.2.1 Characteristics of Sports Market
    - 5.6.2.2 Marketing Mix of Sports marketing
  - 5.6.3 Entertainment Marketing
    - 5.6.3.1 Characteristics of Entertainment Services
    - 5.6.3.2 Marketing Mix of Entertainment Services
- 5.7 Marketing in Logistics
  - 5.7.1 Introduction
  - 5.7.2 Characteristics of Logistics Market in India
  - 5.7.3 Marketing Mix of Logistics Services

5.8 Marketing in Healthcare Sectors
    5.8.1 Introduction
    5.8.2 Characteristics of Health Care Sectors
    5.8.3 Marketing Mix of Health Care Sectors
- Points to Remember
- Questions for Discussion
- Multiple Choice Questions
- Project Questions

Learning Objectives ...

- To understand more about marketing in tourism.
- To study marketing mix of tourism services.
- To learn about marketing in hospitality, airline, telecom, IT, sports and entertainment.
- To study about entertainment marketing and marketing in logistics.
- To learn about marketing in healthcare sectors.

5.1 Marketing in Tourism

5.1.1 Introduction

With its vast cultures and religious roles, India has immense scope of growth in the world tourism scene. India should have been a top tourism destination, as India is blessed with lovely scenic places such as beaches, mountains, forests, hills, religious, destinations, etc., which cater to the taste and preferences of tourists of all ages and economic background. Tourism is often referred as the world's largest business or industry.

The principal products provided by tourism businesses are experiences and hospitality and hence tourism is a service based industry. Services are intangible products which as we have learnt are more difficult to market than tangible products. Since services are intangible, quality control is difficult but also important. It also makes it more difficult for potential customers to evaluate and compare service offerings. But as long as the inherent sense of curiosity and adventure dwell in the hearts of human beings, the desire to travel and experience new things under different environments will grow. The customer has to move towards the product and not the product coming to the customer in this area.

5.1.2 Characteristics of Tourism Marketing

Different types of services marketing strategies in order to stay ahead of competition are employed by the firms in the tourism industry. The strategies vary from one firm to another, and depend on the customer segment that the firm is targeting. The firm has to account for the following factors of a tourism industry:

1. **Intangibility:** Services cannot be verified by any of the human senses. Customers can gather information about the quality of the service from people, price, communication, internet, reviews, etc. In case of the tourism industry for example, a customer would have a different outlook about the quality of services served in a 5 star hotel as compared to that in a 3 star hotel, and hence in this case the hotel will target the appropriate segment of the market by control.

2. **Inseparability:** Services have to be produced and consumed at the same time. The tourist and the service providers interact continuously, right front the tourist's arrival in the country till the completion of the entire tourism process. The service providers in such cases can continuously gauge the level of satisfaction of the tourists.

3. **Variability:** Services vary from one place to another. It is extremely difficult to maintain the same standard of service delivery. The service found in a beach resort would be different from a hill station resort. Each type of hotel has its own value proposition and intends to offer a different type of service to the tourists, and hence, the quality of service would invariably vary. In both cases, they have to ensure that they meet the consumer's expectations.

4. **Perishability:** Services cannot be stored. This implies that during the peak season as well as during unfavourable seasons, a potential mismatch may occur between the demand for tourism services and the supply, which is often the case with hotels in hill stations during summers. To rein in huge variances in demand and supply of tourism services, firms may adopt either demand-side strategies or supply-side strategies, or a combination of both.

Particular Characteristics of Travel and Tourism Services: Associated with the basic or generic characteristics common to all services, there are at least three further features that are particularly relevant to marketing travel and tourism services. These are:

- Seasonality and other major variations in the pattern of demand.
- The high fixed costs of operations, allied to fixed capacity at any point in time.
- The interdependence of tourism products.

5. **Seasonality: Peaks and Troughs in Demand:** The tourism market fluctuates from the different seasons of the year. In the United States, the summer months are between May to August and that is when they decide to take their main holidays as in the winter months it is too cold to travel and the daylight is less. In India, May is the peak season as all schools are closed and children have holidays. Many tourism businesses dealing with holiday markets fluctuate form peaks of 90 to 100% capacity utilisation of 16 weeks in a year, to troughs of 30% or less - and sometimes seasonal closure - for 20 or more weeks in the year.

   Daily flights or trains run are occupied in full capacity in the mornings but by afternoon it have only half the occupancy.

6. **High Fixed Cost of Service Operations:** It is generally the case that they reveal relatively high fixed cost of operating the available (fixed) level of capacity and relatively low variable costs, when the profit and loss accounts of service businesses in the travel and tourism industry are analysed. *A fixed cost is one that has to be paid of in advance in order for a business to be open to receive customers, a variable cost is one that is incurred in relation to the number of customers received at any given time.* The facts of high fixed costs of operation are combination with seasonality fluctuations focus all service operators' attention on the need to generate extra demand. The need focuses especially on additional or marginal sales of which a very high proportion represents 'pure' revenue gain with little or at no extra cost. In case of airlines, the main costs incurred could be:
   - Fleet costs and premises (capital costs, delay repayment, leasing costs, rates and annual maintenance charges). Airport landing charges and crew costs if overnights are involved.
   - Other equipment costs such as website and online services provision, other computer systems (including repairs, renewals and servicing).
   - Fuel charges and other heating and lighting costs.
   - Insurances.
   - Wages and salaries and social provision for full time employees.
   - Management overheads and administrative costs.
   - The bulk of marketing costs.

7. **Interdependence of Tourism Products: Collaborative Marketing:** Several products in the consumer's travel decisions are combined and not just one. Example - A person travelling on a business trip needs transport, accommodation, food and beverage and maybe car rental and conference facilities. Accommodation suppliers at a destination are therefore partly influenced by the marketing decisions of tour

operators and travel agents, attractions, transport interests and tourist boards, which together or separately promote the destination and its activities and facilities. Often overlooked is the vital interdependence between commercial sector interests in tourism and the local government bodies that determine much of the quality of public spaces or public realm within which most of the important experiences associated with destination visits take place. Internationally this is a common characteristic of tourism. Apart from public realm, commercial developers and operators of tourism facilities and events mostly need planning and other regulatory permissions in order to operate. Airlines need permission to use airports, hotels and permission to build and explain a visitor attracts are also closely regulated in their development plans and operations. Their commercial decisions have impacts on residents of destinations that have to be recognised under all democratic systems. Interdependence, if not natural synergy is, therefore, an inevitable process at destinations.

5.1.3 Marketing Mix of Tourism Services

There are 7 P's of tourism marketing mix:

1. **Product Mix:** The product covers the shape or form of what is offered to the prospective customers. The characteristics of the product as designed by strategic management decisions in responses to marketing manager's knowledge of consumer wants, needs and benefits sought. For tourism, product components include:
   - Basic design of all the components that are put together as an offer to customers, for example, a short-break package marketed by a hotel group.
   - Style and ambience of the offer. For service products dealing with customers on the premises where products are delivered, this is mainly a function of design decisions creating the physical environment, and ambience (also known as `physical evidence'), judged appropriate to the product's image and price.
   - The service element, including numbers, training, attitudes and appearance of all staff engaged in the processes that 'deliver' the product to the consumer-especially front of house staff.
   - Branding, the focus for communications, which identifies particular products with a particular set of values, a unique name, image and expectation of the experience to be delivered.

   To match the needs and expectations of target consumers and their ability to pay, products in travel and tourism are designed for and continuously adapted. Most organisations produce and market several products to match the identified requirements of several segments.

2. **Price Mix:** Price denotes the published or negotiated terms of the exchange transaction for a product between a producer aiming to achieve predetermined sales volume and revenue objectives, and prospective customers seeking to maximise their percept ions of value for money in the choices they make between alternative products. Almost invariably in tourism there is a published/regular price for a product and one or more discounted or promotional prices. Promotional prices respond to the requirements of particular market segments or the need to manipulate demand to counter the effects of seasonality or competition resulting from overcapacity.

3. **Place Mix:** Place is the location of all the points of sale that provide prospective customers. For example, 'place' for the Sydney opera house in Australia include numerous travel agents all across the globe who sell and plan out vacations to Sydney and which includes the opera house. Convenience of place for a self-catering operator, for example, includes direct mail to the homes of prospective buyers, using free-phone numbers and easy access to products via computerised reservation/booking systems. Over the past decade, for most travel and tourism businesses, the Internet and broadband access have revolutionised and globalised the concept of convenient access by bringing it directly into the homes of millions of prospective buyer.

4. **Promotion Mix:** Promotion includes advertising, direct mailing, sales promotion, merchandising, sales-force activities, brochure production, Internet communications and PR activity and is the most visible of the P's. Awareness of the product, stimulate demand and provide an incentive to buy are methods of promotion used by the promotional techniques. A broader view of communication by producer also includes supportive 'relationship' information provided to reinforce awareness and build a positive attitude to products that helps customer, especially repeat purchasers, make their purchasing decisions.

5. **People:** Front-line personnel are referred as the 'public face' of the service firm. Their physical appearance, behaviour, knowledge and attitude, have a powerful impact on the customer's perception of the organisation they represent. Employee satisfaction is a prerequisite for obtaining long-term and consistent customer satisfaction. If employees are kept happy, they give better performance which in turn triggers a happy customer. The mantra often used by firms is to keep the staff satisfied before the customer.

6. **Process:** It is the way of undertaking transaction supplying information and providing services on a way, which is acceptable to the consumer and effective to the organisation. Now to make this definition of process true, it is necessary for the tourism organisation which provides services to recognise the critical moments in the

entire process which makes the service acceptable or not acceptable to the customer depending on the zone of tolerance and effective or not effective to the organisation. Further to realise what the critical moments in the considered process, a concept of blue printing is introduced.

7. **Physical Evidence:** It is an important feature in travel and tourism in two distinct ways:

   (i) **As the Environment in which the Sales Takes Place:** Customer is often unsure whether he wants to enjoy the product or not and during this decision making process his expectations and emotions are influenced by factors like layout of the room, the furniture, noise level, temperature, lights, and other factors like the brochure of the company. In case of customers, whose purchase takes place electronically, the appearance of the website is the physical evidence.

   (ii) **Environment where the Product is Consumed:** In the travel industry where the product is being experienced is particularly important in securing repeat business, thus extensive facilities that prove to be physical evidence are provided to leave and win the customer. The tangibles include flat leads in business class, Wi-Fi connection in hotels, customized meals on board, telechecking of hours booking hotels, hotels providing laptops on request, internet access are complimentary for the corporate packages.

5.2 Marketing in Hospitality

5.2.1 Introduction

Marketing strategies and tactics in hospitality and tourism are principally concerned with adjusting each of these elements to provide a competitive offer to customers. The same concepts apply, therefore, to marketing to hotel and restaurant customers, as those apply to, marketing to laundry or financial service customers.

The word "hospitality" is derived from the Latin hospes, which is formed from hostis, which originally meant a "stranger".

Hospitality frequently refers to the hospitality industry jobs in hotels, restaurants, casinos, catering, resorts, clubs and any other service position that deals with tourists. *Hospitality refers to the reception and entertainment of guests, visitors, or strangers, with liberality and goodwill.*

Hospitality services is also known as "*accommodation sharing*", "*hospitality exchange*" and "*home stay networks*", *refers to centrally organised social networks of individuals who trade accommodation without monetary exchange.*

"A total system designed to plan, price, promote and make available to selected markets, hospitality products and services in the form of benefits and experiences that create satisfied guests and achieve organisational objectives".

The hospitality goals, objectives, principles, policies and actions are to be modified, keeping in mind the wants, needs and expectations of the guests. A lot of changes have taken place in the hotel marketing sector. Earlier it was focused on products but today it has moved from the product centered arena to the market centered arena. Hospitality marketing was oriented towards the past experiences of the guests but now it looks at the future needs and wants of the customer.

Rather than negotiation, hospitality marketer concentrates on competition. Hospitality marketing was concerned with the resource accommodation earlier but today they look at each opportunity as a learning experience. Hospitality marketing now believes in a relationship-based information system than a transaction-based information system. As compared to the traditional markets, it looks at benefit-based markets. It believes in network membership to face the future challenges rather than being a self-contained business.

The hospitality business is gaining its momentum as it is increasingly becoming important to the economic well-being of the society. The hospitality industry gains its importance as it brings in foreign exchange earnings to the country by processing its natural resources and destinations. Hospitality marketing encounters a wide range of activities related to travel. The development in the field of hospitality business ushers changes in technology, socio-economic environments, life styles and rising guest expectations.

Hospitality marketing deals with both tangible (bed, furniture etc) and also intangible product, therefore it is unique in nature. Hospitality marketing is very critical in the success of any hospitality and tourism product, organisation and tourist destination. Proper marketing effort promotes a product or service that fills the needs and wants of the consumers and at the same time, bring profits to the organisation or country that features it.

5.2.2 Characteristics of Hospitality Marketing

The special characteristics faced by services marketers are:

(A) Seasonality and Demand Fluctuation: Seasonality refers to the fluctuations and demand in any given period. In hospitality operations, seasonality can occur at:
1. Different seasons of the year
2. Different months of the year
3. Different times of the week
4. Different times of the day.

The demand for business people is during the weekdays whereas the weekends are quiet. The demand can be high during vacation periods like diwali, independence day, etc. Restaurants are usually seen busy on Friday nights and Saturday evenings.

Sudden unexpected increases in customers can lead to production problems, unacceptable waiting times and dissatisfied customers. The profitability of hospitality companies suffers during low season periods, so one of the challenging roles for marketing is to increase demand in low season periods and to deflect over-demand from peak periods to other times.

(B) Intangibility: Services cannot be heard, seen, smelt, tasted or touched prior to being purchased. Marketing intangibles create difficulties for the service provider. Consumers cannot actually examine the hotel before staying in the place like they cannot stay in the room without paying for it.

Customers need to be provided with information to help them to choose an appropriate hospitality outlet to satisfy their particular needs and wants. The challenge for marketers is how to provide such information in a way that will encourage customers to choose their offer without raising customer expectations too high, and then failing to deliver customer satisfaction. The role of marketing communications in designing effective promotional material to generate appropriate bookings is crucial.

(C) Perishability: Services cannot be stored; unlike manufactured products, which can be stored. This is known as 'perishability'. With a fluctuating demand pattern, the hospitality company faces the difficulty of managing their capacity. Hospitality managers recognise that managing the inventory is a critical issue in optimising customer satisfaction, sales and profitability. The key marketing principle is to ensure that the price at peak demand times is set to deliver the maximum return to the company, providing it is compatible with customer satisfaction. In low season periods, the aim is to generate additional sales by developing attractive promotions. Managing the booking process to ensure that the business achieves this balance is essential.

(D) Inseparability: The simultaneous production and consumption of services means that hospitality employees are an important part of the hospitality product. Customers sometimes too play an important part by bad mouthing the product or by praising the product to other customers. These factors mean that customer interaction with hospitality staff and other hospitality guests provides a variety of opportunities to influence customer satisfaction positively or negatively.

Ways to manage the problems of inseparability include:
1. Ensuring that customer segments are compatible.
2. Ensuring that the operations system is suitable for the projected market demand.
3. Adopting appropriate booking policies.
4. Organising effective queuing systems.
5. Training staff effectively.

(E) Variability: Hospitality operations suffer from considerable fluctuations in the standards of delivery of the service. This is called variability, and is influenced by human factors. Services comprise a high element of interaction between customers and staff. Human interaction cannot be standardised, and consequently it is impossible for service companies to deliver a totally non-variable experience.

Some customers may be highly knowledgeable about food and wine. These 'expert' customers, with their different understanding of service and quality, may be highly critical of the meal experience compared to less knowledgeable customers, who may have really enjoyed the occasion. Companies respond to this problem of variability by trying to standardise their operations and training their staff to perform according to the company's standard operating procedures, but with varying degrees of success.

(F) Interdependence: Tourists make a variety of travel purchase decisions in one trip, and their overall satisfaction with a visit is based upon a complex set of evaluations of different elements – including the travel arrangements, accommodation, attractions and facilities of a destination.

The choice of hospitality products is only one element on which the consumer needs to decide. Hotel accommodation sales in particular are influenced by the consumer's choice of other tourism products. First and foremost is the tourist's choice of destination. Visitors may base their decision to travel to a particular destination on the range of attractions, the ease and accessibility of transport to and from the area, the image of the destination, the price, and 'word of mouth' comments made by family, friends and the media. Destination marketing organisations work closely together with local government and tourism authorities to promote demand for tourism in their own particular area.

(G) Supply exceeds demand: The hospitality industry is frequently described as a fragmented industry with low barriers to entry. It is relatively easy to obtain finance and buy or build a hospitality company.

The last ten years have witnessed a dynamic building period, with massive investment in new resorts, hotels, restaurants, cruise ships, leisure facilities and casino operations culminating in excess capacity in most sectors of the industry and in many parts of the world. Despite record numbers of people traveling for business and leisure purposes, the growth in hospitality capacity has not always been matched by a sufficient growth in demand. When supply exceeds demand the competitive environment becomes more intense, and price competition can affect all firms' profitability.

(H) High fixed costs: The cost structure of hospitality firms influences marketing activity. Hospitality businesses are capital, labour and energy intensive. Typical hospitality firms have high property costs and also employ large numbers of staff, many of whom are fulltime, permanent employees. These costs do not change; they are 'fixed' regardless of the number of customers using the premises. During periods of low demand, high fixed costs erode the profitability of the business. Companies need to generate sales to help make a contribution towards the fixed costs. The marketing response to seasonality and high fixed costs is to design attractively priced promotions to stimulate sales in the low season.

5.2.3 Marketing Mix of Hospitality Marketing

The marketing mix is a core concept in marketing. *The term marketing mix is used to describe the tools that the marketer uses to influence demand.* The hospitality marketing mix is based on the eight marketing activities:

(A) Product/service offer: Hospitality products and services are primarily designed to satisfy the needs and wants of business and leisure travelers. Examples include:
1. **Accommodation:** A bed, bedroom, cabin or suite, in a hotel, inn, chalet, apartment, time-share, cruise ship, hospital.
2. **Food and beverage:** A drink, sandwich, fast food, family meal, gourmet dinner, in a café, cafeteria, restaurant, bar or pub, aeroplane, motorway service station or ship, at an attraction or leisure center.
3. **Business services:** A meeting, conference, communication bureau in a hotel or conference center.
4. **Leisure:** A short break, domestic holiday or international holiday, in a hotel, resort, self-catering accommodation, camping and caravan site, or a cruise.

Marketing, working with operations, should play a role in developing the product and service offers to ensure that the needs of customers are the focus of planning and product development.

(B) Location: The choice of location is the first and crucial marketing decision for hospitality companies, this text includes location as one of the main elements of the marketing mix. Location decisions are incorporated with distribution under the heading 'Place' in the generic marketing mix. Location decisions focus on where the hospitality business should build, buy, franchise or rent the site(s) from which it operates. Due to

(C) Price: The pricing decisions a hospitality organisation may include:
1. Setting the tariff, or rack rates
2. Agreeing the level of discounts for key accounts
3. Pricing all-inclusive packages (conferences, functions and leisure breaks)
4. Developing special priced promotions to increase sales during low season periods.

Pricing decisions influence demand, are crucial in driving profitability, and play an important role in presenting the 'image' the hospitality firms wants to project to customers and stakeholders.

(D) Distribution: How a company can make it timely and convenient for a potential customer to book hospitality products directly from the hospitality company or through intermediaries is the main concern of distribution in hospitality. The internet has changed the way distribution channels work and is changing relationships between hospitality providers and travel agents, tour operators, conference placement houses and incentive houses.

(E) Marketing communications: Marketing communication known as 'marcom' and earlier described as 'promotion', covers all the tools that hospitality firms can use to communicate with customers, employees and other stakeholders. This is the function of most marketing and sales departments. The key elements of marketing communications in hospitality are:
1. Brand/corporate identity
2. Personal selling (the sales team)
3. Print and publicity material (e.g. brochures)
4. Advertising
5. Direct mail (often part of a broader database marketing or direct marketing effort)
6. Sales promotion
7. Public relations
8. Merchandising
9. Sponsorship
10. Website design.

(F) Physical Environment: The physical environment consists of the external and internal appearance of the firm and these are the tangible factors. Intangible factors are intimately linked to physical evidence – the ambience or atmosphere – and clearly the success of a hospitality product is dependent upon the appeal of the physical environment to the customers.

(G) Process: Since the product is produced and consumed at the same time, the processes by which the consumers buy and consume the products are crucial to the marketers. Important processes include booking, checking in and checking out, queuing systems and service operations. Marketers need to ensure that the organisation's service delivery processes are efficient, customer friendly and competitive.

(H) People: When we refer to people we refer to both customers and employees. Managing the customer mix and ensuring that target markets are compatible plays a key role in delivering customer satisfaction.

Hospitality is a service where the interaction between customers and employees is also a critical element of the customer experience. *Marketing therefore needs to have an input into human resources aspects of the operation, and this is called* **internal marketing**.

5.3 Marketing in Airline

5.3.1 Introduction

Over the years, the airline industry has grown. Earlier only the rich could afford this luxurious form of travel but over the years it has now become the most preferred method of travel. Earlier the airlines were owned by the government but over the years private firms have taken over and hence the service quality and marketing has also changed.

An airline which is to apply the principles of marketing successfully needs a thorough knowledge of the current and potential markets for its services. Markets must be segmented and customers should be easily distinguished from consumers. Finally, and most importantly, they must examine their markets in a dynamic rather than a static sense and anticipate future changes in customer needs.

Table: Characteristics of a service and implications of airport marketing

Service characteristic	Implications for airport marketing
Inseparable The airport product is generally produced and consumed simultaneously, often through interaction between the airport, other service providers and the end-user.	Important for airports to develop and maintain close relationships because interaction determines the service outcome.
No transfer of ownership Airport customers do not generally gain personal or unlimited access to the products and services they pay for.	Important for airports to reinforce brand identity and encourage loyalty.
Intangible Airport products and services generally, have no substance; they cannot be seen, tasted or touched.	Important for airports to develop tangible cues that provide evidence of the benefits available (e.g. levels of service quality).
Heterogeneous The quality of airport products and services generally varies depending on when, where and how they are provided, and by whom.	Important for airports to invest in quality control (e.g. staff training and management systems).
Perishable Airport products and services generally cannot be stored for later sale or use.	Important for airports to anticipate and plan for future demand and use elements of their marketing mix to influence and respond to changes in supply and demand.

5.3.2 Characteristics of Airline Marketing

Airlines are also part of the service industry and are intangible in nature. The main goal for the consumer is to reach the destination quickly and with the least amount of inconvenience.

According to "**A Case Study on Classic Airlines: Practical Marketing Solutions,**" **published in** *The Journal of Business Studies Quarterly*, there are four unique elements of services.

These elements include:

1. **Intangibility:** Services can't be held, touched, or seen before the purchase decision. When you step onto an airplane, you expect certain qualities like comfort, a smooth flight, and prompt service from flight attendants. These qualities, while important to flyers, are typically impossible to gauge until after purchasing a plane ticket.

2. **Inconsistency:** Pricing and promotion of services changes rapidly. The airline industry is constantly changing and adjusting to meet economic concerns and consumer demand. For example, plane tickets quickly rise in price as the date of departure nears, and some airlines adjust policies such as baggage fees without prior notice.

3. **Inseparability:** The brand of the service provider and the service cannot be separated. Airlines are known primarily for the service they provide – flying. Airlines must distinguish the qualities of their service from each other to succeed.

4. **Inventory:** Companies must manage the goods and products associated with their services. Airlines are responsible for managing the quality of their aircraft, the in-flight food they provide, and other amenities associated with a satisfying flying experience.

5.3.3 Marketing Mix of Airline Marketing

1. **Product:** One might wonder what is the product in an airline industry. The product is intangible here but it is capable of providing customer satisfaction.

2. **Price:** Price is one of the major factors in the marketing mix of airlines. It is because of price and maintaining costs that the airlines have received so much success. To gain competitive advantage when travelers are comparing prices, this makes it one of the most sought airline services in India because of its quality services as well. With decrease in prices and increase in the number of passengers every day, airlines faces a tough competition.

3. **Place:** Customers who want to book their tickets can do so online or through various agencies throughout the country. The airline try to reduce the headache that one has

to go through to get a ticket and that is why it has availed the facility of online tickets. The airline's destinations can be found throughout the major cities of the country. The core strategies include keeping the airline the most affordable airline in India and keeping flying a pleasant experience. Further, the strategy is to provide more capacity on fewer routes than thinly spread itself over many destinations. This is advantageous as it helps contain costs because new destinations will require infrastructure costs and help in creating more customers because they will be viewed as reliable in the few destinations they operate.

4. **Promotion:** The airline relies on its cost and availability to promote its brand across the market. The airline adopts a strategy of connecting flights to other destinations from one destination such that customers will not have to book another airline to arrive to their destination. For instance, it has connected four flights from Ranchi to Delhi, Mumbai, Patna and Bangalore and plans are underway for it to add Kolkata and Raipur. The investments in advertisements are low because it affects the cost.

5. **People:** Unlike products that are promoted and sold on the basis of their own quality and physical attributes the quality of services is highly dependant on the people who sell and deliver them. It is for this reason that many customer-focused (and award-winning) service firms focus on hiring the right staff and providing comprehensive customer service training. Some even take on the slogan "our people are our product" as testimony to the importance of people as an ingredient of their success.

6. **Process:** The process is also considered by some companies by which their services are made available or supported as being important enough to give them a competitive edge.

7. **Physical Possession:** *Physical Evidence is the element of the service mix which allows the consumer again to make judgements on the organisation.* Physical evidence is an essential ingredient of the service mix, consumers will make perceptions based on their sight of the service provision which will have an impact on the organisations perceptual plan of the service. On an aircraft if you travel first class you expect enough room to be able to lie down.

5.4 Marketing in Telecom

5.4.1 Introduction

The Indian Telecommunications industry is one of the fastest growing in the world. In the last two decades, the Indian Telecom Sector and mobile telephony in particular has caught the imagination of India by revolutionising the way we communicate, share information and through its staggering growth helped millions stay connected. This growth, however, continues to be at the cost of the Climate, powered by an unsustainable and inefficient model of energy generation and usage. Simultaneously, this growth has also come at significant and growing loss to the state exchequer, raising fundamental questions on the future business and operation model of the Telecom sector. Government policies and regulatory framework implemented by Telecom Regulatory Authority of India (TRAI) have provided a conducive environment for service providers. This has made the sector more competitive, while enhancing the accessibility of telecommunication services at affordable tariffs to the consumers.

5.4.2 Characteristics of Telecom Services Market in India

The competitive situation of the telecom industry of India can be described by way of the following features specific to the industry:

1. **Predominantly Buyers Market:** The customer profile of a telecom service market is quite gigantic and diverse. The market consists of the individual customer, urban customer, rural customer, corporate customers, and government and public sector customers. Each segment has its own diverse needs and priorities and the Indian telecom companies have been successfully meeting these needs with very high standards of professionalism. This is so because the telecom industry has moved from the monopoly of state to the position of perfect competition. It is an open telecom industry and each player fights for a fraction of a market share by announcing special value added services for their segments; price benefits are always in the favour of the customers. But the largest benefit can be counted in terms of the infrastructure development being provided by these companies. The telecom service companies understand that their customers are highly educated about their demands and needs of telecommunication. The companies that fail to match these expectations end up losing their customer base to the competition.

2. **High Entry and Exit Barriers:** The telecom rules and regulations are decided by the government and so are the investment avenues, regions and areas of work operations, tariffs, and other competitive conditions. Telecom Regulatory Authority of India still rules in spite of the fact that the industry has been deregulated to a large extent. Besides the investment levels in the industry are very high with further need to invest large capital in building the infrastructure. The intense competition and also the governmental conditions have made the industry a very low yield industry in the country. Such competitive conditions can put lots of dampers on the investment plans of the newcomers in the industry. Hence, the exit barriers too are equally high in the industry.

3. **Higher Acceptance for Wireless Services:** Mobile technology is being adopted in India in a big way (An average of four million subscribers is being added every month for the past six months itself). The Indian customers prefer wireless services compared to wire-line services.
4. **Intense Competition:** The competition level is very high in the Indian telecom industry. The telecom services like any other service are intangible, inseparable, and more of personal experiences hence it is very difficult to establish a perception different from the existing service companies who have already developed a strong brand for themselves in the minds of their customers. The telecom companies, thus, try to establish differentiation by way of offering improved physical evidence in terms of setting up better infrastructure. The differentiation is also achieved by way of providing extra value added services, process, and people interaction.

5.4.3 Marketing Mix of Telecom Marketing

It is obvious that the telecom services marketing will have to adopt such strategies that could differentiate their services distinctly from amongst the long list of service providers that dot the scene of the Indian telecom industry. The companies need to strategise the marketing mix in the following fashion by focusing on all the seven Ps of marketing but more so, on the additional three P's that relate to the physical evidence, process and people. We will have a detailed discussion on the marketing strategies in case of each P as under:

1. **Telecom Service Products:** The service companies can establish differentiation in their services by way of creating the physical evidence by providing newer and better products, even though service companies offer almost similar products, 18 per cent of the mobile users are open to buy new handsets every year. It is up to the service providers to offer such newer models with more features, to attract new customers.

   The operators of landline and wire-based services have only limited options to generate additional revenues through valued-added services. As against this, the mobile operators have large options of generating non-voice revenues from their customers.

2. **Telecom Service Place:** The telecom service providers like MTNL, BSNL, Department of Telecom, had enjoyed the governmental protected monopoly and hence they would always prefer the customers to come to the service delivery points, and insist upon the services being dispensed to the users from the government telephone exchanges and the telegraph offices. Things have changed ever since the private sector has been allowed in the service sector.

   The place has come to play a very large role in the success or failure of the service and its acceptance by the users. The telecom services companies like Reliance

Telecom. Bharti Airtel, and Idea have set up not only franchisee offices, distribution points, but have also been establishing customer relation or customer service centres all over the country. This has made even the government owned companies like BSNL, MTNL to provide multiple service points through post offices, banks, and even privately set up franchisees. The places have been done up keeping in view two basic needs of the service customers:

   (i) the convenience of approach,

   (ii) the need of physical evidence and ambience

3. **Telecom Service Pricing:** The strategy to greatly fight the competition by way of pricing is the latest phenomenon in India as otherwise the same industry has been very protective about its pricing policies and strategies. There have been many hidden costs and charges that the industry has been recovering from the customers without educating the customers on the cost components. Even though the governmental control had been there on its pricing systems and transparency, the industry manages to push prices higher by way of introducing new service offers. This kind of pricing based on competition is followed by every service provider in the country. The intensity of competition is likely to increase further as new players enter the field and exercise pressures on call rates. The industry is highly price sensitive and the service provider has to be very careful in pricing its services products. The industry has been using the strategies such as cost plus pricing, target profit pricing, break even analysis system of pricing and currently it is focusing more on prevailing value pricing. The telecom services companies however have to get into continuous innovation and up gradation of technology, services value addition packages, and differentiating strategies to remain ahead of the competition in realising better price than the next competitors.

4. **Telecom Services Promotions:** The telecom services are being promoted by way of direct marketing, press advertising, outdoor advertising ,event organising by the services marketing companies and through the electronic media.

5. **Telecom Services People:** People play a very important role in telecom services marketing, in establishing an understanding of the customer expectations and the effects of having delivered as per the expectations established and understood by the telecom service organisation. Most of the companies in telecom services marketing realise this and they, have set up two different kinds of people set ups in dealing with the customer. Telecom service companies are strong believers of

arranging training schedules and developing programs for their people in the front offices and the people in the back offices. The people in the front offices of the franchisees too are often sponsored for such intensive training in customer handling, customer sensitivity, etc., in order to make sure that the process of services marketing internally is managed very well. The competition in telecom services being very intense, each company ensures their people are able to recover any kind of service loss immediately as otherwise it is quite difficult not only to retain an existing customer but it is still more difficult to enlist a new customer. Hence, each company has a very strong people development policy and strategy.

6. **Telecom Services Physical Evidence:** The tangibility for the service experiences of telecom services are provided by the companies by way of attaching physical products to the service offers. The inseparability and the intangibility makes it difficult for a customer to build a distinct perception by the use of service alone, hence companies take the help of mobile telephone sets, ambience of the service administering outlets, events, and extending invitation and participation of their customers in such events. The physical evidence is also obtained by way of providing value adding service, such as dial tones, voice mails, internet facilities, ring tones, and free short messaging services of social value to the customers.

7. **Telecom Services Process:** The process in telecom industry has been the major shortcoming during the days of state monopoly. However, the current competition and quality service expectation of the demanding and discerning customers have exercised enough pressures on all service providers to provide essential infrastructure to run an efficient and trouble free continuous telecom services. The process issues that these telecom companies need to attend to on priority relate to:

    (i) **Ensuring availability of new connectivity immediately:** This issue has largely been solved. All companies are in a position to issues new connections instantly.

    (ii) **Ensuring network availability at all times and in all places falling under the jurisdiction of the telecom company:** This issue has still not been solved satisfactorily. There are companies whose network gets blocked during peak hour. The connectivity also drops frequently as the person travels away from main towns.

    (iii) **Ensuring transparency in billing systems and the definition of prices or charges being recovered from the customers:** There is still a need to open up further and it is expected that the increasing competition will bring in not only transparency but business ethics too, as the franchisees have yet to evolve the standardised ethical practices.

5.5 Marketing in Information technology (IT) and Information Technology Enabled Services (ITeS)

5.5.1 Introduction

The information technology (IT) and information technology enabled services (ITeS) industry has been one of the key driving forces fuelling India's economic growth.

The IT industry has pumped the economic growth as well as India's image on the world front. IT has also encouraged the higher education sector in the engineering and computer science fields and many Indians have been employed due to this sector which has contributed to the social transformation in the country.

To make their business process efficient and streamlined, Indian firms largely depend on the IT & ITeS services. The Indian manufacturing sector has the highest IT spending followed by automotive, chemicals and consumer products industries.

In the current economic environment, the Indian organisations are depending on IT to help them expand in their business. It is seen as a change and a source of business value.

In the domestic as well as the foreign market, the business process outsourcing sector (BPO) has seen amazing results of activity both onshore as well as offshore. The companies continue to move up the value-chain to offer higher end research and analytics services to their clients.

The key IT enabled services are:
- Call Centers
- Electronic Publishing
- Medical Transcription
- Data Centers
- GIS Mapping
- Portals
- ERP(Enterprise Resource Planning)
- Knowledge Management & Archiving.

5.5.2 Characteristics of IT and ITES Services

1. **High Economies of Scale:** The marginal cost of each unit of additional software or hardware is insignificant compared to the value addition that results from it. Economies of scale for the information technology services are high.
2. **Knowledge-Based:** It's services are all knowledge based unlike some other industries.

3. **Skilled Labour Forces:** As it is knowledge based industry, the workforce is also skilled and efficient use of this skilled labour can help in the economic growth.
4. **Helps in Growth:** The IT industry helps many other sectors in the growth process of the economy including the services and manufacturing sectors.
5. **Acts as the Business Processes:** Information Technology services act as the business processes and the different services performed or provided from a location different from that of their users or the beneficiaries and are then delivered with the help of the information technology over the telecom networks.
6. **Inherently Ubiquitous:** Information technology services are inherently present everywhere. The use of service is independent of time and space. Thus, production and consumption of service can be described as spatiotemporally separated, especially in terms of human labour involved
7. **Coping with Unexpected Inputs:** Whereas humans can flexibly cope with unexpected inputs from the customer and still co-create value, IT services are inherently limited to dealing within the range of inputs and requests it was designed to do. The design of an IT enabled service is therefore very important.
8. **Eliminate Human Labour:** IT enabled services eliminate human labour from direct co-creation of value. This has a two-faceted effect. On one hand, customers receive predictable, reliable, and consistent outcomes from the service. On the other hand, the supplier organisation has no direct, active way to co-create value with the customer.

5.5.3 Marketing Mix of IT and ITES Services

(A) Product: The various categories in which IT marketing can be done are given below:
   (i) **Professional Services:** Professional services relates to offering a variety of skills, specific to an individual which can be utilised on projects. These services can be offered in country as well as overseas. The way such services are sold is unique. Regularly updated computer databases of individual skills are maintained. Predominantly this type of services is export oriented. The user often assesses the skills of the provider. Business is done by matching this demand with available skills at the appropriate price. Major projects are generally given to companies with groups of professionals who can undertake segments of large Information Technology projects and implement them at competitive costs in different parts of the globe.
   (ii) **Application Software:** Specific sector segments such as banking, financial services, mining, power, steel, transportation and ports are merged with information technology application. In this segment specialist used the expertise of the concerned sector specialist to design systems to meet the objectives of the organisation.

(iii) **Maintenance Services:** This service relates providing services for maintaining existing system. Maintenance services ensure the availability of maximum hardware time. The strategy of Annual Maintenance Contract (AMC) is being extensively followed in these types of services.

(iv) **Technology Oriented Applications:** The technology explosion in different fields makes it impossible for any vendor to keep track of and invent in all technologies. This has resulted in companies taking on an approach of focusing on a few technologies they feel comfortable with and discarding the rest.

(v) **Education and Training:** Training upgrades skills requiring either familiarity with a particular hardware, a particular operating system or maybe an application. Training institutions to provide training to upgrade the skills of the man power. The training institutes having reservoir of manpower integrate forward into professional services and system integrators.

(vi) **Systems Integration:** It is specialised segment of the industry which comprises integrating systems. There are multiple hardware vendors, multiple data base choices and multiple application software available for different industry segments. The user is not competent to make a decision. He has to rely on experts to make the correct choice while selecting hardware for a particular job and looking at all facets of available vendors and solutions before final implementation. It is "one shop stop" approach. It needs a marketing capability and marketing profile which is vendor independent. The user is, thus, assured such services are not identified with or biased towards any specific hardware vendor.

(vii) **Segment Packages:** The marketing techniques are similar to those of consumer products and it is a competitive and dynamic segment. The software packages are probably the most well known to most users and cater to that end of the market which is most familiar. It requires developing a package, often very broad based software that take on a range of applications that can be written on it and yet must be simple enough to be used by an initiated user.

(B) Price: There are many models that are used to determine prices of software services.
- The line of code model is the most used model, where the price depends upon the number of lines written in a program.
- Function Point model where price is based on the number of inputs and outputs.

These methods only determine the basic/primary cost of the service but apart from this travel and conveyance, taxes, documentation, legal charges, consultancy fees, professional charges, royalties, etc., are also taken into consideration to determine the final price. Annual maintenance services are charged on a different basis depending on the annual maintenance contract.

(C) Place: IT does not suffer from the constraints of place unlike other services. Delivery can be onsite or off site. The software packages can be developed or produced anywhere in the world and can be delivered in real time to the client. However, in case of off-site development of software, the customer is required to have the necessary infrastructure in terms of hardware and software back-up to avail of the services at his workplace.

(D) Promotion: Promotion should arouse demand by moving the product and services towards customers. The means of promotion most commonly adopted by the IT industry is media based advertising. Advertising through hoardings displayed at public places has also become popular, especially in commercial cities and business centers. Web-based promotion is also quite common in the IT industry. Other forms of advertising used are seminars and workshops for training people in the latest technology, word of mouth holding, IT expos, News items and press releases etc.

(E) People: The IT industry we know is knowledge based industry and it is formed on the intellectual presence of the people – employees need to have a strong base Technical knowledge and skills and the managerial abilities. The industry however is populated with very talented and young people and retaining them poses to be the major problem. Hence across the world, companies are offering several incentives to the employees such as stock options, maternity leave etc.

(F) Process: The process of manufacture and delivery of quality service at the lowest possible cost is very important in the IT industry. In fact, it is true for any service industry. The production process involves understanding the nature of the project, assessing and capturing customer requirements, preparing a project plan, developing the software to meet the objectives, testing it and delivering it to the customer. Delivery of services can be either on-site or off-site depending on the project. Models like Capability Maturity Model (CMM) are developed to test the efficacy of the process in an organisation. Such models help detect problem areas and take measures to correct them to ensure the quality of the product. Other certifications like ISO also help to assure the quality of the manufacture and delivery of services.

(G) Physical Evidence: Excellent infrastructure and state-of-the-art technology can be used as means of providing physical evidence, but they cannot be true indicators of the proficiency or capability of the service provider. It is not very easy to provide physical evidence to customers in the IT industry. Certifications like CMM and ISO can be used alongwith certificates from clients. Websites of most IT companies display the appreciative comments of some of their prominent clients.

5.6 Marketing in Sports and Entertainment

5.6.1 Introduction

Sports and entertainment offers a lot of services and products. Marketers of sports and entertainment products and services must assess consumer demand, the competition, and the financial valuation of the goods and services they offer, as individuals have limited time and financial resources and they choose the sports and entertainment events most carefully. Marketers must consider the marketing mix and the core standards of marketing.

Product offerings for sports and entertainment must be constantly evaluated and updated. Individuals have many entertainment options for their limited discretionary income. Discretionary income is the amount of money individuals have in hand after spending for essentials such as housing and car payments. Choosing the right products to meet the needs and wants of the market is essential to the marketing mix. In addition, marketers must consider the quantities of the products. Too much of a product could result in price markdowns. Price influences the purchasing decisions made by consumers. A business must, offer its customers products and services they need and want at prices they are able and willing to pay, while at the same time covering the costs of the business and making a profit. Prices charged for sports and entertainment events must be sensitive to consumer demand and the state of the economy. Championship teams will increase consumer demand and ticket prices. However, when the economy becomes questionable, consumers are likely to spend less money on sports and entertainment events.

Distribution, involves transporting or delivering goods to final customers. Distribution of an event involves planning the location where the event will take place.

Promotion is essential to inform prospective customers about sports and entertainment events and products. Promotion requires creativity to keep the attention of prospective customers. Promotion costs large sums of money, making it important to select effective promotion plans that can reach the largest audiences at the most reasonable price.

5.6.2 Sports Marketing

Finding out a group of spectators' interests and planning a product or service that the spectators will buy is the main function of sports marketing. Sports marketing is using sports to market products. Sports marketing capitalises on the popularity of sports.

Marketers research the demographics and spending habits of fans in order to maximise profits on the items that fans may purchase in association with the event. The price that fans are ready to pay depends on the importance of the event, popularity, and interests of the market. They usually are willing to pay for their favourite team or a celebrity endorsed clothing. The goal of sports marketing is to use the right marketing mix to meet customer needs while generating a profit.

5.6.2.1 Characteristics of Sports Market

Following are some special features of the sports market:

1. Product salience and strong personal identification lead many sport consumers to consider themselves experts. The "expert mentality" was clearly revealed two decades ago in a famous national survey.

2. Demand tends to fluctuate widely. Athletic club members crowd facilities during winter 'Prime-time" hours and then trade their indoor sports for something else in the summer, when they crowd public tennis courts or golf courses. Each sport form tends to have an annual life cycle, and spectator sport fans are especially prone to quick changes in interest. Season openers bring high hopes and high demand; but midseason slumps, injuries, or weak competition may kill ticket sales.

3. Many sport organisations simultaneously compete and cooperate. Few sport organisations can exist in isolation. Professional, Intercollegiate, and interscholastic sports require other franchises and schools in order to have meaningful competition. The same is true for private and amateur sport clubs.

4. Sport has an almost universal appeal and pervades all elements of life. Although there is clearly a "Western" tradition in most of the world's most popular sports, there is also clearly a wide world of sport.

5. **Eating and drinking:** From the bournvita box to the Pepsi advertisment, sport images are part of the consumption experience.

5.6.2.2 Marketing Mix of Sports Marketing

In sports marketing the seven Ps are:

1. **The Sport Product:** A product can be described generally as "any bundle or combination of qualities, processes, and capabilities (goods, services, and/or ideas) that a buyer expects will deliver want satisfaction." A peculiar bundling distinguishes the sport product, including at least the following elements:
   - Playful competition, typically in some game form
   - A separation from "normal" space and time
   - Regulation by special rules
   - Physical process and physical training
   - Special facilities and special equipment

2. **Pricing:** It is important not only to match people's needs with appropriate products but also to do so at prices they are willing to pay. Price is an important signal to both consumers and producers in the market system. For many products demand is more price sensitive, particularly in markets where there is strong competition between

alternative providers, or for market segments which suffer from socio-economic disadvantage, such as older people without private pensions, the disabled and the unemployed.

3. **Place:** A critically important decision for facilities is where the location should be, in relation to their anticipated markets Place, or distribution, is the final contact with the customer, after other marketing decisions such as product, price and promotion have been taken. In sport and leisure services the product is often centred on particular types of facility, which means that instead of the distribution of goods to customers, as in manufactured goods, the customer very often has to attend a facility. Distribution decisions should be based on the market research about customers, their home and work locations, transportation and other accessibility factors.

4. **Promotion:** Promotion's purpose is twofold: creating awareness of the opportunities provided by the supplier; and seeking to attract and persuade customers to purchase the particular service or product. Promotional activity can be defined as an exercise in communications. There are many factors affecting demand, some of which consumers may not be conscious of. Restricted impressions or preconceptions, for example, can determine consumer responses.

5. **People:** People are an essential part of the marketing mix. Face-to-face interaction between the supplying organisation and the customer is inevitable and the success of a service is very dependent on this people relationship. Avoiding this relationship is not a solution – a commercial fitness centre once tried to dispense with its line staff to reduce costs, by making everything card swipe controlled, including entry and use of all facilities. Sport and leisure marketers must therefore be concerned not only with what motivates people to take part in sport and leisure, but also what demotivates them.

6. **Physical Evidence:** Another defining characteristic of services is that they are intangible, yet ironically it is often the physical circumstances or 'tangibles' of a service that are most important to customers. Out of twenty service attributes certain tangibles are among the most important to customers, i.e. water quality for swimmers, and cleanliness of changing areas and activity spaces. These tangibles relate to the core or actual product. Other tangibles which are part of the augmented product are less important to customers, e.g. quality of food and drink, quality of car parking. The setting of a sport experience and the design of a facility are further important ingredients of the physical evidence. They can reinforce the image of a service when they excite, when they give a sense of occasion. Alternatively there may be a danger of Skills and techniques deterring the customer if these 'atmospherics' are missing and the setting/facility is dull and uninspiring.

7. **Process:** Due to the inseparability of consumption and production in services, the process of service delivery is under the spotlight throughout. This process runs from finding out about opportunities, through booking an activity, finding the facility, parking, entering the facility, finding the way round the facility, engaging in the activity, possibly buying food and drink, to leaving the facility. The whole process of service delivery determines the relationships between the organisation and its customers.

5.6.3 Entertainment Marketing

Entertainment is wherever people are willing to spend their money and spare time viewing rather than participating in. It includes sports and art that can be viewed in person or broadcasted in recorded form.

For entertainment purposes, sponsors of the event want to gather as much marketing information as possible about the audience. This information helps them to design the product promotions for the audience and they must understand the needs of their customers.

Definition provided by **Sayre** for entertainment marketing is *'techniques and strategies developed to sell tickets for activities that amuse and involve us'*.

Entertainment marketing can be defined as: *strategic activities designed to develop and manage mutually satisfying value-based relationships with audiences, visitors and customers in order to entertain them and achieve organisational goals.*

An entertainer must get an audience's full attention to elicit positive responses, such as applause, good reviews and word of mouth, and, ultimately, the motivation to purchase more tickets.

To obtain audiences' attention, marketers must deal with the following characteristics talked in the next section.

5.6.3.1 Characteristics of Entertainment Services

1. **Rapid Changes:** Businesses periodically fail and new ones replace them in this industry. The speed with which companies break up and new ones re-form is rapid, as companies depend on the one big hit to mask their lack of resources in this capital intensive industry. Solid business planning and business management often falls by the wayside in efforts to pursue trends, to pursue the latest project, and to pursue the shifting trends in the marketplace.

2. **Volatility:** The entertainment business, including movies, television and music, is characterised by substantial volatility.

3. **Short-Term Approach:** The entertainment industry is growing and the mix of its components is constantly changing. The entertainment industry itself is made up of a rapidly changing mix not only of aspiring entrants but of existing and aspiring businesses. Some are low-tech, some are high-tech and all are interweaving with each other in ever new combinations to enable one project after another. Hence, in much of the business there is no long-term, just a series of short-terms. Traditional business planning is often pushed by the wayside. Too many producers consider success a matter of simply having a film produced and distributed without a thought for the cash flow consequences.

4. **Adaptation to New Technology:** The entertainment services has been always interested in the adaptation to new technology for production and management practices, for both product development and cost control, and to keep tabs on the race among developers and service providers to serve that trend.

5. **Unknown Demand:** The demand for entertainment is discovered by the consumers after the product has been consumed.

6. **Horizontally Differentiated Services:** Entertainment services are horizontally differentiated products. Each product is unique and must be experienced before demand is known.

5.6.3.2 Marketing Mix of Entertainment Services

A sound marketing mix is necessary for the entertainment organisations to provide quality services to the users. The marketing mix consists of:

1. **Product:** Entertainment service providers can try to differentiate themselves from other service providers in terms of product by offering a package that is much better than that of competitors, in terms of quality of entertainment. The product in entertainment services is in the form of music, movie, a television program, or an animation film.

2. **Price:** Pricing of music is an issue for marketers of the service. In India it depends on the purchase price of the music title and the singers involved in producing the music. Marketers of music follow a differential pricing policy in India with the prices being determined by demand and timing of the year. The marketer keeps in mind that any increase in the price would make the audience download pirated music albums.

3. **Place:** Service providers in the entertainment industry can try to tap new channels of distributing their product. For example, music has traditionally been distributed through audio cassettes and CDs. Music companies can use new channels of distribution such as the windowing approach.

4. **Promotion:** Advertising in print, radio, and television, and through publicity, and trailers are methods by which a movie is promoted. Film-makers can adopt new forms of promotion such as cross-promotions, product placements, and film-based merchandising to increase their revenues.. Merchandises of the film such as the characters, costumes, clothes can be sold which will result in additional revenue

   Product placement is a marketing strategy adopted to showcase brands through the medium of entertainment. Placing prominent brands of products at crucial junctures of the entertainment makes the viewer take notice of the brand, which may result in its purchase.

5. **People:** The industry is a creativity based industry like advertising and hence people form an important element in the marketing mix, such as the actors, singers, directors, cameraman etc, apart from the audience.

6. **Process:** The process in entertainment services begins right from idea development stage to production, distribution, promotion, and marketing of the product. Developing the right storyline, picking up the right star cast, director, music director and other technicians, choosing an appropriate location/setting, making the movie, editing it, planning the distribution and releasing it, all constitute the process. Technological advances have improved the various elements involved in creating and distributing an entertainment product.

7. **Physical Evidence:** The physical evidence in entertainment services plays a significant role in its marketing. By making the labels and online catalogues more attractive, music companies can attract more number of consumers to purchase the music and in the movie industry, it can be in the form of posters, hoardings, advertisements etc.

5.7 Marketing in Logistics

5.7.1 Introduction

Logistics can be broadly defined as the time-related positioning of resources, ensuring that materials, people, operational capacity, and information are in the right place at the right time in the right quantity and at the right quality and cost.

To move the goods around the world cost efficiently and quickly, logistics is a vital component for the economic growth. There are some circumstances such as transport delays, poor communication, lack of packing that can go wrong in logistics. *Professional logistics management is in essence the application of skills which ensure that every part of the above definition is successfully accomplished.*

Logistics consists of the customs, distribution, warehousing and international distribution. It basically covers the whole supply chain from manufacturers to the consumers. Better job of communicating, or marketing logistics will have to be done by the logistics leaders. To move materials into and out of a company is done by the logistics service, which involves packaging, security, transportation and warehousing.

While logistics services have become a significant source of competitive differentiation between firms, significant challenges exist relative to developing logistics service offerings for global business customers. Diverse regulations across borders, longer lead times, and increased transportation costs all add to the difficulty of managing logistics services internationally.

5.7.2 Characteristics of Logistics Market in India

India's logistics market is huge but unexploited. With the increasing globalisation, logistics players in India have to face the challenges since worldwide sourcing and deliveries requires global logistics support.

Apart from providing the prime logistics service functions such as transportation, warehousing and distribution, and freight forwarding, the logistics players in India have also started to handle other activities like inventory management, order processing, collection of bills, sales and excise duty documentation, among others. The main characteristics of logistics market in India are:

1. **Transportation:** Transportation is the largest component in the logistic cost and an essential and a major sub-function of logistics that creates time and place utility in the supply chain management. In India, about 40% of the logistics cost is due to transportation alone.

2. **Distribution:** The large distances, inhospitable terrain, poor highway infrastructure, an over-stretched railway network and a myriad of state and central excise laws are among the challenges faced by logistics players in India in the distribution of goods within the country. As a result, the delivery process at times takes longer period and is expensive and can be unreliable too. However there have been efforts in this area with some logistics players trying to set up complex distribution models using multimodal means of transportation to achieve which achieve right balance between cost and, efficiency and reliability.

3. **Freight Forwarding:** The freight forwarders in India are typically described as an agent who arrange the transportation and prepare shipping documents. However, today their roles have changed and they are expanding their service portfolios by offering more services including port handling, chartering, custom broking, project management, packing and moving, road and rail transportation, through bill of lading and air freight import and export services. Due to their ability to manage international freight movement through air and sea freight, there are increasing chances for freight forwarders to become full-fledged logistics service and solution providers.

4. **Warehousing:** Warehouse management is one of the critical components of supply chain that ensures that products are properly handled, stored and delivered. In India, warehousing industry is mostly dominated by state warehousing corporations and public sector undertakings such as Central Warehousing Corporation (CWC), Punjab State Warehousing Corporations and others. Besides the warehousing corporations, most of the major ports of India also provide warehousing facilities through their own warehouses and also through privately-owned warehouses located within or outside the port area.

5. **Value added Services:** Besides the prime logistics functions above, logistics players in India are also providing value added services as a strategy to stay competitive in the logistics industry. Among the value added services provided by many players today includes kitting, packing, repacking into various sizes, labelling, light assembly, consolidation and cross-docking, and among the value added services provided in the overall supply chain processes are order processing, inventory management, payment collection, insurance, tax management, reverse logistics and information management. With the increasing trend of companies to outsource their logistics requirement such as the above, logistics market and the 3PL industry are also growing in the country.

5.7.3 Marketing Mix of Logistics Services

The marketing mix of logistics services are:

1. **Products:** Service is the logistics product. First the customer needs to be identified (whether internal or external and their needs are different too). The logistics needs of external customers are constantly growing and changing. The logistics executive must be sensitive to this, along with being aware of what is driving these changes. Logistics service offerings to these industrial customers must include not only the goals and requirements of the providing firm but also the goals of the receiving firm.

   These customer requirements will drive the service or product offerings from logistics.

2. **Price:** A direct impact on a product's price and profitability will impact the logistics service. The price of logistics investments will have an impact on the revenue and profitability of the firm. These cause changes in the cost of providing logistics service, thereby changing the price of logistics service to the firm. Customer profile, product profile, and order profile are examples of logistics price drivers. Changes in these are usually not under the control of the logistics executive but require some type of logistics reaction. If logistics price increases because of a change in a logistics price driver, the logistics executive must be able to explain and justify this increase to senior management.

3. **Place** Traditionally speaking place means logistics but in logistics marketing the transaction between the logistics organisation and its customers is the place. The 'hassle free' service has four dimensions:
   (i) The logistics organisation must make its backroom operations invisible to the customer. Customers do not care how things get done but what gets done. They are more concerned with the output than the process.
   (ii) Make information easily accessible to the customer. Successful logistics organisations manage three flows between themselves and their customers – product, information, and cash.
   (iii) Make it easy for the customer to find the store easily. It must be visible to its customers and it must be easy to contact. If the logistics company facilitates the transaction for its customer, its customer will continue to come back.
   (iv) It is inevitable that logistics service will periodically fail. Nothing is perfect. This does not mean that the logistics organisation should lower its service goals below 100 percent conformance. What it does mean is that the successful logistics organisation will identify where possible failures will occur and develop plans to recover from these failures. This concept is called "Service Recovery". The logistics organisation must make every effort to make logistics failures seem insignificant to customers. All attempts must be made to make customer satisfaction the focus of the logistics organisation.
4. **Promotion:** When things go wrong everyone complains and hence logistics executives avoid promoting or communicating. Successful logistics marketing programs must make customers aware of the strengths of logistics and its potential contributions to the bottom line.
5. **People:** Without effective people, the other four P's are meaningless and hence the most important marketing mix of logistics is People. The logistics executive has the responsibility to develop a culture for consistent performance from the individuals in the organisation, such as:
   (i) Help develop an enthusiasm for the business.
   (ii) Develop a commitment to bring ideas to fruition; delegate responsibility and authority to the people in the logistics organisation to make things happen.
   (iii) The logistics executive must develop a team environment within the organisation.
   (iv) The logistics executive must believe in the "pressure up" concept versus the "pressure down" concept. In other words, the logistics executive must provide the atmosphere for individuals to ask for help, to communicate their frustrations, to raise issues with management, and to have inputs to plans.
   (v) The logistics executive needs to be a leader.

6. **Process:** Process can be defined as set of activities in order to produce output. Following are the important elements in carrying out logistics marketing:
   (i) All the marketing activities carried on by logistic company help them in taking orders from different manufacturing companies.
   (ii) Prices are negotiated on the basis of pricing strategy.
   (iii) Orders are taken as per the requirement of customers.
   (iv) Committed delivery is provided to the customer with the help of technologies like TPS (Transaction Processing System), GPS (Goods Processing System), calling facility, etc.
   (v) Anywhere cheque deposition facility is provided to the customers.
7. **Physical Evidence:** This industry manages physical evidence carefully as it knows the profound impact on customer's impressions. The appearance of infrastructure such as buildings, landscaping, vehicles, interior furnishing, equipments, staff members, sign, printed materials, and other visible cues of Logistics Company provide tangible evidence of a firm's service quantity.

5.8 Marketing in Healthcare Sectors

5.8.1 Introduction

The management tasks of any service organisation, profit or nonprofit, are more complex than for a typical manufacturing enterprise. The "product" of most service enterprises is intangible. The product is intangible, it is difficult to measure productivity in the sense of definable, manageable relationship between input (labour and goods) and output (product). While it is inherently more difficult to manage service organisations for productivity, as will be seen later, it is eminently possible.

They tend to be oriented toward selling the product to a customer whose needs are, more often than not, defined in a self-serving way.

Health care is not a commodity; it is the most intimate personal service. Patients expect their physician to be reasonably accessible, and they expect to trust his or her medical judgment in managing their illnesses. They also have some concerns about the reasonableness of the fee, since they are likely to bear a greater portion of that cost than for other services.

5.8.2 Characteristics of Health Care Sectors

1. **Intangibility:** Health care services being highly intangible, to beat this intangibility the irony of modern marketing takes place such as use of more tangible features to make things real and believable.

2. **Inconsistency:** Quality of service offered differs from one extreme to another. This is because of total dependence on human interactivity or playing human nature, i.e. because human beings can never mechanise or replicate themselves.
3. **Inseparability:** Service transaction becomes unique because it mandates, during transaction, the physical presence of the provider and the consumer.
4. **Perishability:** Services are intangible, they cannot be packed and neither can be stored nor can they be inventoried. The implication is that the service has to be produced and consumed instantly; there is no scope of storage.

5.8.3 Marketing Mix of Health Care Sectors

The marketing mix for health care sectors are:
1. **Product:** The product here will be the correct diagnosis of the disease, methods of operation, and the cure of the disease, apart from the professional and medical credentials of the doctors and a support staff apart from the patients care and counselling. The tangibility within the intangibility will be created by the cleanliness in the services, promptness in attending to the patients, and the treatment to the people accompanying the patient.
2. **Price:** It is very difficult to give a common strategy to the pricing of hospital and healthcare services. The pricing of the services will form the cost of doctors attending and treating the patient to the actual cost incurred on running the establishment, be it the hospital or a pathological laboratory. But in hospital and healthcare services, the hospitals and facilities use a complete differential pricing policy for many products. The pricing of the hospital and healthcare services will depend upon the income level of the customer, length of the treatment, kinds of operations, kinds of pathological and diagnostic tests, the facilities provided by the hospital, the brand perception of the hospital corporate and the pricing policy of the service provider, Often the service provider operates with two kinds of pricing policy, the commercial pricing policy and the charitable pricing policy, The charitable pricing will be recovering the basic cost factors only and burden for charity causes could be loaded to the commercial pricing of the hospital.
3. **Place:** The hospital and healthcare services can ideally be delivered at the place of the services provider or the delivery point that has to be inspected, approved to be up to the original standard of the principal service provider. For example, often sample collection centres are spread all over the country by the major laboratories situated elsewhere and the franchisees collect and tranfser the samples to other places. In such cases, care is the same as that of the original services provider under whose brand umbrella the franchisee unit is functioning. Then there are joint clinics

where many doctors are employed or made partners to provide their services to the patients visiting the hospitals. Nowadays many doctors do not depend only on one chamber but circulate their services all over the town and also into many towns by associating themselves with many clinics on a sharing basis and or even on the retainership basis. This is done to share the specialists with many hospitals in different towns and now even countries so that the specialist skills reach many patients.

4. **People:** The hospital and healthcare industry is completely people intensive and people extensive. The services are rendered by the involvement of people at every stage of dealing with patients and his relatives. These dealings are done by people for outdoor services, indoor services, pre-operative counseling and analysis or dealing with the patient and his relatives at the time of operation. The dealing with the public also involves the administrative functioning of people within the labs, on the hospital receptions, in the hospital wards and lifts, corridors and offices. The services providers must organise and institute the internal marketing of these services to meet the expectations of the customers. The service providers are to ensure that the doctors, surgeon and the operative staff like, the para staff, helpers, nurses, clerks are all fully competent, experienced and skilled, technically and medically qualified. All the staff from the top to the front doorman must be trained into the art of people handling and providing comfort and succor wherever needed to build a positive, friendly, and caring perception of the service organisation.

5. **Promotion:** Promotion includes advertising, sales promotion, personal selling and publicity and customers need to be aware of these services. Hospitals generally do not undertake aggressive promotion. Different health services can be introduced so that they have a bigger client base apart from camps conducted in rural areas.

6. **Physical Evidence:** It does play an important role in health care services, as the core benefit a customer seeks is proper diagnosis and cure of the problem. Physical evidence can be in the form of smart buildings, logos, mascots etc. a smart building infrastructure indicates that the hospital can take care of all the needs of the patient. For a local small time dispensary or hospital physical evidence may not be of much help. In recent days some major super specialty hospitals are using physical evidence for distinguishing itself as something unique.

   Three aspects of physical evidence are:
   - **Ambient Factors:** Smell in the hospital, Effect of Colors used on walls.
   - **Design Factors:** Design of the rooms, plush interiors, ICU location, etc.
   - **Social Factors:** Type of Patients that come to the Hospital.

7. **Process:** It is the way of undertaking transactions, supplying information and providing services in a way that is acceptable to the consumers and effective to the organisations. Since service is inseparable, it is the process through which consumers get into interaction with the service provider. Process generally forms the different tasks that are performed by the hospital. The process factor is mainly dependent on the size of the hospital and kind of service it is offering.

Case Studies

Case Study 1: Tourist Experience - Trip to Vaishno Devi and Varanasi

Experiences: Good and Bad as Tourist

Many students from European countries come to India on student-exchange programmes. IMM Lucknow is one destination that has become very popular among them. During their stay, these students visit various tourist locations in India. One thing that has impressed them the most is the warm nature and hospitality of Indians. Here, we narrate some of the delightful experiences that these students had while travelling in India.

Trip to Vaishno Devi-Celebrating Diwali, the Festival of Lights

Nuria and Isobel, both from Spain, were studying at IIM Lucknow on the exchange programme and visited Vaishno Devi during their term break. In their words, 'It was a memorable experience.' For them, visiting Vaishno Devi temple after walking for hours and finally going through the tunnel was a very novel experience. But the best moment of their trip was celebrating Diwali, on their way to Jammu, with their driver's family. They were overwhelmed by the gesture and hospitality of the driver. Celebrating Diwali is one thing that has been entrenched in their memories forever. This experience of theirs epitomises Incredible India - Diwali celebration by Europeans in the house of a Muslim Indian.

"Older than history, older than tradition, older even than legend. And looks twice as old as all of them put together. - Mark Twain

Trip to Varanasi

The exchange students of IMM Lucknow set out on a journey to visit the ancient religious city of Varanasi. While the tradition and history of this ancient city beckoned them, there were some unpleasant experiences as well. The city and its religious embodiment are really captivating; a boat ride in the calm waters is one of the precious memories Nuria and her friends have office place. However, the swarm of humanity on the streets did not seem to be very accommodative to them. They were charged exorbitant rates during shopping. As said by Vivian, 'The rickshaw pullers and the locals were not very warm, instead they treated us with suspicion.' So, what could hove been a great journey left some bitter memories because of improper hospitality.

Question: Critically examine the case study and bring out the impact of customer experience on tourism industry.

Case Study 2: Service Quality at the Excelsior Hotel

Kristen Adams had recently transferred to the Excelsior Hotel to improve the level of customer service. She had been with the company for five years and had been quite successful in improving the level of customer satisfaction at the two pervious hotels to which she had been assigned. Kristen knew that the Excelsior was going to be a real challenge. The mix of business was 60 per cent individual transient guest and 40 per cent group business. Of this group business, about one-third was motor coach tour groups.

On the first day on the job, she witnessed quite a sight. There was a line of about 20 guests waiting to check in when motor coaches arrived and more than 80 additional guests and guides walked into the lobby to check in. Needless to say, the two front desk agents had a look of terror in the eyes as they worked diligently to process the registrations for those waiting to check in. Some 40 minutes later, everyone had been checked in, but The general manager said to Kristen, "I am glad that you are here, we need to work out at better system. Let us meet for lunch tomorrow to discuss your initial ideas". Kristen had just picked up a pen to start brainstorming ideas to present to the general manager when a guest approached her desk.

"Hello, my name is Bill Foster, and I stayed at your hotel last night with my family. We really did not have a good experience, and I want to tell you about. It went to make sure that this does not happen again, to me or any one else". Mr. Froster when proceeded to tell Kristen his account of events. "I was traveling with my wife and our son, who is four years old. Our connecting flight was delayed, so we did not arrive at our final destination until 10 p.m. The Excelsior had an advertised check-in facility at the airport, and I assumed that I would be able to secure my room while waiting for the luggage. When I approached the employee at the hotel's airport facility. I was told that check-in service was not available at that time of the day. I found this to be surprising, since this was the very type of situation in which an airport facility would be beneficial.

"Next, my family took a shuttle van from the airport to the hotel, where we were given directions to the front desk. Two front desk clerks were on duty when the passengers from the airport shuttle arrived a little before 11 p.m. However, one of the front desk clerk was apparently going off duty at 11 and she proceeded to close her drawer at that exact moment. This left a line of approximately 10 to 12 guests to be checked in by one clerk. Needless to say, it took sometime to process all of the guests, and we had to wait 20 or 30 minutes for our turn. We were assigned to a room, but at this point we had a few bags and my son was fast asleep and had to be carried. When I asked for assistance with our luggage, I was told that no one was available at that time of night. The hotel was large, having over 1,000 rooms and the rooms were spread out among several adjacent buildings. Our room was two building away from the lobby area. My wife and I struggled to carry the luggage and our son to the room. We arrived there about 11:30 and attempted to enter the room. The key unlocked the door, but the door would not open. After a couple of attempts, we heard a woman's voice in the room. Obviously, the room had been doubled-booked and the woman woken from her sleep. I used the house phone to call the front desk and explain the predicament. The front desk manager offered a quick apology and said that she would send someone with a key to a nearby room. About ten minutes later, a housekeeper happened to be going through the hallway, and she let my family into the room that I had been given over the phone. However, the housekeeper had no idea what was going on and took my word. After we had been in the room for ten minutes, the phone range and I spoke with the front desk manger, She acted as though she had sent the housekeeper to open the room, but she still needed to send someone with the room keys. She apologised one last time and told me to call the front desk if I had any other problems.

Questions:
1. What steps would Kristen recommend to the general manager?
2. What action steps and timetable should she recommend? How should decisions be made about which steps should be done initially?
3. Develop a service blueprints of the check-in process. How might this be used to improve the situation?
4. Discuss the gaps in the service quality process that Bill Foster experienced.
5. What kind of service failures occurred and what recovery strategies were employed?
6. How did the Excelsior Hotel fail to meet Mr. Foster's expectations?
7. What other actions could have been taken?

Case Study 3: Entry of Vodafone into the Indian Telecom Services Market

Background

Vodafone Group Plc is the one of leading mobile telecommunication company of the world that has a very significant presence in Europe, the Middle East, Africa, Asia Pacific and the United States of America, by way of direct investments, subsidiaries, joint ventures associated undertakings and strategic partners network agreement Vodafone is the brand name under which the mobile subsidiaries of the group operate. However in United States, the groups associate undertaking operates as Version Wireless. In the countries where the company does not have direct stakes it operating through the partner network agreements, where the group and the partner networks mutually promote the marketing of telecom services under dual brand logos. The group as on 30th June 2007 directly or indirectly serves about 232 millions mobile customers (paging customers not included) all around the world, which by now would have added many millions more to the fold.

Vision of Vodafone: The vision of Vodafone is to become a communication leader in an increasingly connected world.

Vodafone strategic goal:
1. Delight our customers
2. Build the best Vodafone team
3. Leverage global scope and scale
4. Expand market boundaries
5. Be a responsible business
6. Provide superior shareholders returns.

Key drivers of growth:

Vodafone: unique positioning	Focused approach
Strongly cash generated core business	Exploiting new revenue opportunities
Fast growing emerging market business	Aggressively reducing costs
An unrivalled customer footprint	Applying rigorous criteria to future acquisitions
Proximity to many adjacent revenue pools	Investing prudently in new business area
	Gearing upto increase returns to shareholders

International Business Strategy

Vodafone has a very strong presence in Europe, the Middle East, Africa, Asia, Pacific and the U.S.A. The company finds emerging and developing markets, as the right markets for driving its growth further. The company is continuously expanding its business in these markets. Vodafone has divided its market into two strategic business units:

(i) EMAPA: Consisting of Easter Europe, Middle East, Africa, Asia, Pacific and affiliates.
(ii) Europe region consisting of Italy, Germany, the UK, Spain, Greece, Netherlands and Portugal contributes 80 per cent of total revenues.

An Overview of Indian Alliance

Vodafone Pic (Vodafone) announced its major entry into the Indian telecom market by acquiring a 52 per cent stake in the Indian telecom company. Hutchison Essar Ltd. (Hutchison Essar), by entering a deal with the Hong Kong-based Hutchison Telecommunication International Ltd. (HTIL). The deal will serve and fulfill its strategy of expanding into emerging and high growth markets like India. India has emerged as the fastest growing telecom market in the world outpacing China with low penetration rates within many parts of the country. This kind of situation makes Indian telecom markets the most lucrative market for global telecom companies, HTIL decided to move out of India as the urban markets in the country arc facing saturation levels and do not offer much scope of further growth. Any international telecom firm looking for growth in India has to find future expansion only in the rural areas that can lead to falling average revenue per user (ARPU) and consequently lower returns on its investments.

On 11 February 2007, the Vodafone Group Plc (Vodafone), a UK-based telecom company, announced to the general public and its shareholders that it now owns the Indian share holding of the fourth largest Indian mobile operator; Hutchison Essar Ltd. (HEL). Vodafone managed to grab the Indian company against other three very strong competitors like Reliance Communications Ventures Ltd. (Reliance). Essar and the Hinduja group. The deal could be finalised after the Indian Government's decision in 2006 to raise the limit on Foreign Direct Investment (FDI) in the telecom sector from 49% to 74%. The government accepted that such allowances will infuse large FDI into the sector to meet the proposed targeted numbers of 500 million customers connected to telephone/mobile services by 2010.

HEL with a pan-Indian presence was the fourth biggest player in the Indian telecom sector with a subscriber base of 29.2 million in July 2007. HEL had a with a presence in 13 of the tota 28 circles in the country. HEL also had the second highest average revenue per user (ARPU) of ₹ 340.15, second only to the market leader Bhani India Ltd. (Bharti Airtel) that had an ARPU of ₹ 343.17.

The fast growth of the Indian mobile market coupled with a relatively low penetration level made it a very lucrative market for Vodafone. Before initiating the bidding process, Vodafone had to clear many regulatory issues. Bharti Airtel, in which Vodafone had a 10% stake, asked its partner to make it clear whether Vodafone wanted to continue its relation with it.

Following are the key highlights of this major deal of Indian telecom services marketing:

1. Acquisition of controlling interest in Hutch Essar thus gaining control of 67 per cent controlling shares.
2. Infrastructure sharing MOU with Bharti to materially reduce the cost of delivering telecom services to Indian customers.
3. Cover network coverage in rural India also quickly.
4. Will make an offer to buy Essar stake at the price at which HTTL had been bought.
5. India's foreign ownership rules will be adhered to by arrangements with existing local minority partners
6. Granted an option to Bharti one of the group companies to buy 5.6 percent listed interest

Strategic Benefits of this Deal

1. Vodafone gains controlling position in a leading mobile services operator in Indian telecom market.
2. Hutch Essar delivers a market brand, a respected team, and access to nationwide network and market.

3. Infrastructure sharing with Bharti results into saving huge expense on capital and infrastructure investments.
4. Vodafone gains access to high growth emerging market which is second only to China in the world.

Exercise Questions:
1. Explain how Vodafone Plc has strategised its growth into Indian telecom market by acquisition.
2. Why do you think it was necessary for Vodafone to enter into resource sharing MOU with Bharti?

Case Study 4: Indian 13P© Service Provider: Courtesy of Client Partner Manager Based in UK

The service provider is a BPO arm of a major IT outsourcing vendor based out of India. The parent company primarily engages in IT outsourcing, whilst its subsidiary focuses on the BPO sector. Within the UK tile firm offers Human Resource Outsourcing, Finance and Accounting Outsourcing and Data Management Outsourcing to a select number of industries; including the healthcare industry, the market research industry, the legal sector and to a lesser degree the manufacturing and engineering sector.

The firm provides what may be considered traditional non-core outsourcing services such as data entry, transcription services and rules based processes, however, it is increasingly trying to position itself to provide more core services to its clientele, adding longer term value to the client and moving into what is called knowledge process outsourcing services.

This is largely driven by the need to move away from a pure cost focus which the interviewee suggested tends to dominate the client's priorities when choosing to outsource peripheral activities. This is not say that cost : does not feature as a key requirement, but the aim, the interviewee; a client partner tells me, is to bring to bear additional drivers that are more important when activities which the less peripheral are outsourcing these drivers include efficiency, quality of end to end service and flexibility.

Another interesting development, especially given its parentage, is the development of converged services to the market, which combine and utilise.

IT to automate, streamline and deliver the firms BPO services. This is seen to be critical in a crowded vendor landscape where there are a few select vendors to dominate the corporate space offering a multitude of outsourcing services and a large range of niche vendors offering specialist service offerings to certain verticals or concentrating on certain processes.

Being stuck in the middle is increasingly seen as a real challenge. Converged IT and BPO services allows the firm to specialise and compete in an increasingly competitive market; this is also evidenced by the recent trend towards more single sourcing deals rather than multi-sourcing.

Clients it seems prefer sourcing a vendor that can deliver more than just a single outsourcing process. The company's response to this market trend, has been development of applications, one specifically for the travel and logistic, industry and another for the legal sector - these applications now enable the firm to establish a leadership position in the delivery of specific BPO services, driven by the applications that support these processes.

What is also in favour of the firm is the greater acceptance by its client and prospective clients towards offshoring. This aligns the vendor with the recent focus that clients place on cost reduction as their major outsourcing driver. This drive towards cost reduction also means that there is a greater appetite for outsourcing processes and functions that may have been 'off the table' a few years ago, e.g. Financial Planning and accounting is now becoming something that clients are looking, to outsource, whereas a few years back it was seen as central to the business and not something that should have been outsourced. In other words, the traditional boundaries and limits placed on offshoring are now changing.

From an offshoring perspective, the Asian countries, and in particular India remain at the forefront. China is still very much a destination for service providers looking to access cheaper resources, but not end user clients, who still see it as a major challenge given language and cultural differences. In terms of near-shoring, the interviewee sees this as something that appears to have been talked up by media than reality, it is still seen as an expensive choice given labour rates and euro currency. There are however many other destinations coming up that pose a greater threat (or opportunity), such as Egypt, Mauritius, Botswana, Kenya and Sri Lanka. These destinations not only offer labour arbitrage opportunities, but offer things that are unique, such as multi-lingual language skills, diversity of talent or just natural skills that may not be available in the traditional locations, such as India or Philippines.

The firm, as it moves to higher value service delivery, would like the decision making process within clients to also change. Today for peripheral activities most firms include a range of stakeholders in the decision making process, with the COO ultimately making the decision to outsource, procurement setting the boundary conditions for vendors and tile line of business driving the specific requirements. Other stakeholders are involved but usually only to contribute their opinions. What doesn't appear to happen, is client's willingly providing the vendor end, to end visibility of the operations.

The procurement function in some instances inhibit his process by imposing strict interfaces - this is not to say that procurement does not provide useful role within the process (at contract negotiation stage they provide useful structures and procedures that allow both parties to make objective decisions and check the health of the relationship), but that their role should diminish post contract to allow interfaces to be built between vendor and client at multiple points within the organisations.

The problem is attenuated, as clients tend to be reluctant to share deeper insights into their processes and internal performance measures for a number of possible reasons; from not having the data, to fear of losing control, to fear of the impact this may have on internal departments or teams that would face competitive scrutiny if performance data was shared with a vendor. From the interviewee's perspective, such dialogue is essential to create a partnership model for outsourcing.

From the vendor's perspective,, the contract and SLAs are important, but should be considered hygiene factors (albeit with flexibility - although this appears to be only through scope changes).

A partnership offers both parties points of reflection where each can judge the strengths and weaknesses as well as opportunities for the relationship over the course of.

The procurement function in some instances inhibit this process by imposing strict interfaces this is not to say that procurement doesn't provide a useful role within the process (at contract negotiation stage they provide useful structures and procedures that allow both parties to make objective decisions and check the health of the relationship), but that their role should diminish post contract to allow interfaces to be built between vendor and client at multiple points within the organisations.

The problem is attenuated, as clients tend to be reluctant to share deeper insights into their processes and internal performance measures for a number' of possible reasons, from not having the data, to fear of losing control, to fear of the impact this may have on internal departments or teams that would face competitive scrutiny if performance data was shared with a vendor. From the interviewee's perspective, such dialogue is essential to create a partnership model for outsourcing.

From the vendor's perspective, the contract and SLAs are important, but should be considered hygiene factors (albeit with flexibility - although this appears to be only through scope changes). What is ultimately important is to create a partnership between the client and the vendor. A partnership offers both parties points of reflection where each can judge the strengths and weaknesses as well its opportunities for the relationship over the course of the deal - such a relationship can help the client organisation meet their overall corporate objectives,

However, the, interviewee suggested steel these things take time; it would take a minimum of 3 years before you could say you have a partnership and 5 years before could judge the relative success of a partnership (this isn't including the pre-contract period, but post service delivery). This time is required to build the trust that is required at all levels within the organisations, to build a good understanding of the organisation's business and its customers and their buying behaviour and to have tested the quality of the partnership during limes of need.

But for a good partnership, it needs more than just time, it needs transparency, so the vendor has a good understanding of the end to end value chain of the client; and the involvement of the right people from the client and not necessarily the CxOs. Most organisations just assume because there is a good relationship at the CXO level, they have a good partnership: This is dangerous as the CxOs may be oblivious to what happens on the coal face of service delivery, The traditional approach with set interfaces and governance meetings that happen only at a peer level may hinder a partnership approach rather than help. What is required is interface and governance structures that involve the team as a whole, front the operational delivery team to the senior executives, one which paints a good and true picture of the relationship and one that harmonises perceptions and realities throughout the organisations.

The interviewee was keen to point out that a good partnership doesn't necessarily need to include a risk or equity contribution, because that positions the relationship more in terms of what value can be extracted from the other party and what control can be exerted to the other. In fact a risk or equity model assumes there is not the genuine level of trust in the partnership such that formal controls and incentive structures are required.

Points to Remember

- The principal products provided by tourism businesses are experiences and hospitality and hence tourism is a service based industry
- Characteristics of Tourisms Marketing
  1. Intangibility
  2. Inseparability
  3. Variability
  4. Perishability
  5. Seasonality: Peaks and Troughs in Demand
  6. High Fixed Cost of Service Operations
  7. Interdependence of tourism products
- A fixed cost is one that has to be paid of in advance in order for a business to be open to receive customers, a variable cost is one that is incurred in relation to the number of customers received at any given time
- The term marketing mix is used to describe the tools that the marketer uses to influence demand
- 7 Ps of marketing mix are:
  1. Product
  2. Price
  3. Place
  4. People
  5. Promotion
  6. Process
  7. Physical evidence

- Hospitality frequently refers to the hospitality industry jobs in hotels, restaurants, casinos, catering, resorts, clubs and any other service position that deals with tourists. Hospitality refers to the reception and entertainment of guests, visitors, or strangers, with liberality and goodwill.
- The IT industry has pumped the economic growth as well as India's image on the world front. IT has also encouraged the higher education sector in the engineering and computer science fields and many Indians have been employed due this sector which has contributed to the social transformation in the country
- Strategic activities designed to develop and manage mutually satisfying value-based relationships with audiences, visitors and customers in order to entertainment them and achieve organisational goals are known as entertainment marketing
- Logistics can be broadly defined as the time-related positioning of resources, ensuring that materials, people, operational capacity, and information are in the right place at the right time in the right quantity and at the right quality and cost.

Questions for Discussion

1. Explain why air travel now dominates long and middle distance travel.
2. Highlight the importance of BPO industry in maintaining client relationship.
3. What is ultimately important is to create a partnership between the client and the vendor.
4. Discuss the 7 P's of Sport Marketing.
5. What do you understand by logistics? What are the factors that can go wrong in logistics?
6. What are problems in service marketing due to intangibility characteristics?

Multiple Choice Questions

1. Strategic activities designed to develop and manage mutually satisfying value-based relationships with audiences, visitors and customers in order to entertainment them and achieve organisational goals is known as:
   (a) Entertainment marketing   (b) sports marketing
   (c) IT marketing   (d) airline marketing
2. The product in _____ is in the form of music, movie, a television program, or an animation film
   (a) airline industry   (b) IT services
   (c) entertainment services   (d) sports services

3. The time-related positioning of resources, ensuring that materials, people, operational capacity, and information are in the right place at the right time in the right quantity and at the right quality and cost is known as
   (a) Entertainment (b) Logistics
   (c) Service marketing (d) None of the above
4. When products are properly handled, stored and delivered, it is known as
   (a) Transportation (b) Logistics
   (c) distribution (d) warehousing
5. Which service does not use aggressive methods of promotion?
   (a) Airline (b) Entertainment
   (c) Healthcare (d) IT
6. Services be verified by any of the human senses.
   (a) True (b) False
7. A _____ is one that has to be paid of in advance in order for a business to be open to receive customers
   (a) Fixed cost (b) Variable cost
   (c) changing cost (d) none of the above
8. The reception and entertainment of guests, visitors, or strangers, with liberality and goodwill is known as:
   (a) Services (b) hospitality
   (c) Logistics (d) None of the above
9. Which is not a marketing mix?
   (a) Product (b) Price
   (c) Profit (d) Place
10. Which is the most important marketing mix?
    (a) Product (b) Price
    (c) Place (d) All the above

Answers

| 1. (a) | 2. (c) | 3. (b) | 4. (d) | 5. (c) | 6. (b) | 7. (a) | 8. (b) | 9. (c) | 10. (d) |

Project Questions

1. A restaurant has a great reputation as the result of providing consistent food for over ten years. The restaurant is full every weakened and has above-average business during the week. The manager claims that they do not practice marketing because they do not need marketing; that they have more than enough business now. Discuss the possibilities of not using marketing practices.
2. When people are new to a city, one of the first things they may do is consider where they go to get hospital care if needed. When you are thinking about hospitals, what things are most important to you?

Case Studies

Case 1: Tata Infotech Refocussed on the Corporate Segment

During the boom times, many firms providing computer education to students used to survive and thrive in the Indian market. But the boom did not last forever. The bust which followed took its tool on the educational IT services sector, with Aptect selling off its business to SSI and many other firms exiting from the business.

Tata Infotech also found its business squeezed and had to think of new segments that it could venture upon. The company refocussed attention on the corporate segment which also requires computer training for its employees and over a period, the percentage of business which came from the corporate segment changed from 20 per cent of its total to about 65 per cent of the total.

At the same time, its affiliate channels through whom a lot of its consumer (student) business was done, came down from about 200 to about 125 in number, signaling a decline in that segment.

What this case shows is that in bad times, it makes sense to take a re-look at your segmentation and target marketing strategy. Of course, this may involve repositioning yourself at times, inline with the requirements of the new segments being targeted. Also, it could involve changes in the 7 P's of marketing.

Question : Can you think of what changes Tata Infotech would need to make in its positioning and its 7 P's (the marketing plan) to successfully serve the corporate market?

Case 2: Bel Air Motel

Will Smith moved from Philadelphia, Pennsylvania, to take over as the general manager of the Bel Air Motel in California. Will had been the assistant general manager of a large chain hotel in the downtown area of Philadelphia. He encountered problems with some of the employees and felt it would be a good idea to move to a move related atmosphere. Will had worked for the chain for ten years, starting in the management training program and working his way upto his position as the assistant general manager.

The Bel Air Motel is one of the oldest properties in the area, but it has been renovated periodically over the years. The motel is owned by a group of independent investors and has 116 rooms with the basic amenities. There is no restaurant or pool, but there are some restaurants in the local area. The motel's room rate is at the low end for the market, which consists mainly of upscale properties.

Upon starting his new position as general manager, will realized that there were major differences between working for a large chain and working at a small, independent motel. The chain hotels had sophisticated computer systems for reservations motel. The chain hotels had sophisticated computer systems for reservations sales and catering and revenue management. In addition, customer information was gathered through surveys and comments cards. This provided managers with valuable information that could be used to make important decisions about rates and services. Unfortunately, the Bel Air Motel had a very simple reservations system and no additional information except for some historical figures on rate and occupancy. The average room rate was $ 125 and the occupancy rate was around 60 per cent before will took over.

Will understood the necessity of gathering more customer information and developed a comment card to be placed in every room. Customers were asked to complete the comment card and leave it in the room for housekeeping to collect. The purpose of the comment card was to determine how guests staying in the motel felt about the property and the services. Will wanted to make sure the guests were satisfied. At the end of the first year, he received a total of 169 completed comment cards. The first question he looked at was the one dealing with customer satisfaction.

Question : Which of the following best describes your experience at the Bel Air Motel?

The motel exceeded my expectations	19.9%
The motel met my expectations	55.9%
The motel failed to meet my expectations	24.3%

Case 3: Credit Cards in India : Defining Competition

Is the credit card market heading for clutter? Are credit cared companies struggling to differentiate their respective brands? Although industry experts claim that the market is growing at a rate of 25-30 per cent every year, with a customer base of seven million people, they feel that the usage of the card, and understanding of the card users are not high and that only 20 per cent of the card base actually generates revenue for the card issues.

Says T.R. Ramachandran, Director (Marketing - Cards), Citibank India, "Cash and cheque payments continue to be the biggest competitors for us. The percentage of card spends to overall PCE (personal consumption expenditure) for the industry as a whole, is less than one percent. As the date, there are only around 1.1 lakh card-accepting merchants in the country.

Question :
1. Which other categories of services in India are at a similar stage of evolution, where the category competes for attention for substitute products?
2. What are the reasons for the Indian consumer's obsession with cash or avoidance of a credit card even when they own one?

Case 4: Info Systems Ltd.

Info Systems is in the business of information technology. It does not sell any hardware, instead of offers something that in the IT vocabulary is called solutions. The end deliverables that get talked about with the company are productivity, efficiency, quality enhancement, responsiveness and enterprise solutions. And then there is something called verticals. These are referred to in order to signify the industry domains which are pitched by the company for IT solutions. For instance, Info System has a powerful solution for banking which integrates the banking sub-systems to seamlessly offer information to touch point. The other verticals for which Info Systems offer IT solutions include retail, airlines, transportation and insurance.

Marketing of IT solutions is a tough area. This is more so because the people who work on different projects, especially the software engineer are driven by a technical perspective.

They often lack domain knowledge. Their liability to view the reality from the client's perspective often acts as a barrier in developing solutions that clients usually look for. Gaurav, like many others, has joined the company with a software engineering background. His expertise lies in software development but his knowledge falls short when his brief includes work on a specific company belonging to a sector. The lack of sector-specific knowledge imposes a great handicap. The handicap does not work from this side only. The client whose business the company pitches for also often fails to appreciate what Gaurav can offer. The knowledge void with respect of each other's perspective on the one hand and over-flowing knowledge of their respective domains on the other, makes mind-matching a Herculean task.

There can be four types of customer situations involved in the marketing of information solutions. The first aspect relates with knowledge of problem on the side of client. The potential client may be in the know of the problem (unhappy customers, delayed response to customer queries, low productivity, messed distribution) or client may be unknowledgeable about the presence of a problem in his/her business (poor quality or low productivity but client is contented). The other dimension is related to the solution. Here there are two possibilities. The first possibility is when the client knows the solution of the problem and the second when he/she has no idea about the solution. In the marketing of IT products these four situations present four types of difficulty levels.

The customer knows the business problem and also knows the solutions thereof. The customer knows the business problem but does not know its solution. The solution is known but the problem is unknown. The customer knows neither the problem nor the solution.

In any of the above situations, the issue is absence of knowledge either about the problem or solution. The situation with Info System is relatively when the customer realises the presence of a problem. Here the customer is in the need-activated stage and the job, for people like Gaurav, is simply to suggest solutions. On the other hand, the job is much tough when the client is not in a state of activation or problem recognition. The marketing challenge here is now to get the potential client into appreciating the hidden deficiency and the demonstrating the means of getting rid of the same.

The managerial challenge for Gaurav is equally daunting. While the technical competence of IT experts allows them to easily work out a solution once the problem is shown to them by the client, when the problem has to be proactively found out, their skills run thin for the lack of domain knowledge.

The partial blindness both on the part of the solution provider and the client creates marketing of IT solutions difficult. The onus to be proactive lies with a company like Info Systems and people like Gaurav. It is their responsibility to convert prospects into customers. Gaurav is assigned to task of evolving guidelines to enhance the marketing of IT solutions. He believes guidelines cannot be developed by a person who although has technical expertise but grossly lacks both ability and skill to appreciate the client perspective. He wants somebody to help to him look at the field of IT solutions from the customer's perspective. Besides when a company market something like IT solutions, which comes in the from of a hypothesis - not as something tangible and concentrate what thoughts and feelings dominate their minds.

Question : How can the choices be made when nothing tangible expect for the promises are offered as a product?

Case 5: Bank Significantly Improves Service Quality by Using a Service Management Solution

Jordan Ahli Bank (JAB) needed to ensure that the Service Quality department was effectively monitoring and resolving incidents. Equally important was the speed in which these were fixed, as outlined in the service-level agreement. By using Microsoft System Center Service Manager 2010, the department's service quality dramatically improved. In some cases, incidents that previously took days to resolve were fixed within hours.

Business Needs

Established in 1955 and being the first bank in Jordan, Jordan Ahli Bank later grew and expanded its presence in other regions like Lebanon, Palestine and Cyprus. It is a provider of banking solutions and has approximately 1,400 employees.

The bank's Service Quality department is tasked with providing IT services, as well as ensuring that there is minimal disruption to its services and infrastructure. The department was struggling in responding effectively to incidents or change requests raised by its business units and employees. There was a big chance that these would not reach the department, as incidents and change requests were either submitted through phone calls, or filled up using paper forms and sent by fax or delivered personally. Furthermore, some requests required several signatures because of security procedures. It wasn't uncommon that the necessary approver was working in a different location. This made the approval process stressful and time-consuming.

"At the bank, all IT-oriented incidents were handled through phone calls or paper forms in a decentralized environment. Calls often got misdirected, by either reaching the wrong party or by not properly tracking the calls. We didn't have internal service management processes/workflows in place. For example, when someone needed internet access, we had the problem of not receiving the appropriate form because we don't have work flows in place with certain policies that everyone needs to follow. This was one of the biggest initiatives for us to move into a service management system, says Eng. Ghaith Alqasem – Special Projects Department Manager of Jordan Ahli Bank, who was the project manager for this engagement.

Furthermore, one of the department's challenges was that it didn't have an overview of all incidents that were being reported, its urgency, who was assigned to it and what efforts were made to fix it. This often placed the department in a fire-fighting mode, trying to cope with all the incidents and change requests that were being submitted every day. "Some of our colleagues would actually come over to our department and anxiously ask us to get their issues resolved without knowing the urgency, priority, and SLA time set for reported issues/incidents," says Mohannad Wahbeh, who works as a Service Quality Senior Analyst at the bank.

Question: How bank could significantly improve service quality by using a service management solution?

www.ingramcontent.com/pod-product-compliance
Lightning Source LLC
Chambersburg PA
CBHW080924180426
43192CB00040B/2706